MW00437368

The Trail is the Thing

A Year of Daily Reflections
based on
Pathways to Recovery:
A Strengths Recovery Self-Help Workbook

Lori Davidson
Suzette Mack, Lesa Weller
Julie Bayes

Illustrations by Jan Kobe

The University of Kansas School of Social Welfare
Office of Mental Health Research & Training

Initial Production Coordinator: Joanna McCloud
Illustrator: Jan Kobe
Cover Design: Joy Butterfield, Lori Davidson, Tonya Hinman, Jan Kobe, Suzette Mack & Joanna McCloud
Authors: Lori Davidson, Suzette Mack, Lesa Weller, Julie Bayes

---

Copyright © 2010 The University of Kansas School of Social Welfare
ISBN 10: 1475042132
ISBN 13: 978-1475042139
Price: $13.50
www.pathwaystorecoverybooks.com

All Rights Reserved. No part of the material may be reproduced in any form or by an means, electronic or mechanical, including photocopying, recording, or by any information storage and retrieval system, without written permission from the authors.

The authors of this book do not receive profit from sales of this workbook. Profits are designated for reprinting of the book, developing innovative consumer-based initiatives in Kansas, and providing scholarships for Kansas residents with the lived experience of mental illness or trauma to return to post-secondary education.

The Trail is the Thing: A Year of Daily Reflections based on Pathways to Recovery is supported through a contract with Kansas Department of Social & Rehabilitation Services, Division of Health Care Policy.

Published by The University of Kansas School of Social Welfare
1st Printing, November 2010
2nd Printing, June 2011
On demand printing via CreateSpace™ and Amazon™, June 2012

"The thing to remember when traveling is that the trail is the thing, not the end of the trail."

~ Louis L'Amour

May all who read the words gently shared throughout this book meet
courage, (re)discover hope & find strength along their journeys,
knowing that even when they feel the most alone,
they are surrounded each day by the courage,
hope & strength of those who truly care.

Once again...for Tom & Jerome and now, Lizzie Lou
I know you're there, laughing from above...
And to my dear brother, Rod
Your peace & gentle spirit have been a true delight!
Lori

To those...especially my mom and dad...who taught me
how to live strong in our faith, and to know deep in our hearts
that what we have are all blessings meant to be shared
every day with those we meet along our path.
Suzette

To all who have cared and those who have shared
in this journey of recovery, thank you.
To my husband and son, you are great travelling mates.
Lesa

To all who have loved me through thick and thin...
I dedicate this book to Sage, Ryan, Isaac, Parker and Marian
who helped me see the truth of youth
which gives me hope and joy daily.
Julie

"As we express our gratitude,
we must never forget that the highest appreciation
is not to utter words, but to live by them."
~ John F. Kennedy

No project can be completed without the help, support, wisdom and encouragement of many individuals. So it is with *The Trail is the Thing*. We send our most sincere gratitude to:

School of Social Welfare, Office of Mental Health Research & Training

Our thanks to the members of the mental health team at The University of Kansas under the direction of Charles A. Rapp, Mark C. Holter and Rick Goscha. Your willingness to support this project is greatly appreciated. We are especially thankful to the individuals who reside on the "garden level" of Twente Hall. Your ability to make laughter occur, even in the midst of deadlines and frustration, has been an invaluable gift! We also send a very heartfelt thanks to Joanna McCloud. Joanna is responsible for all our book sales and distribution, yet she gladly took time every week to send each of the authors an inspirational message to help us stay motivated. While we didn't always stay on track as planned, we always felt inspired!

Kansas Social & Rehabilitation Services

We continue to be extremely grateful to Kansas Social and Rehabilitation Services/Division of Health Care Policy for providing ongoing funding for *Pathways to Recovery: A Strengths Recovery Self-Help Workbook*. The ability to share free resources to individuals in Kansas is truly making a difference in their lives. Thank you!

Editors, Advisors &"Ghost Writers"

We are incredibly indebted to those individuals who gave freely of their time and talents to serve as editors, advisors and, in three or four instances, as "ghost writers." The merging of four writing styles was dependant on your grammatical skills and the feedback we received was vital in how we adjusted language, described experiences, shared examples and included activities. And when the authors were struggling, we enlisted the help of a few people—you know who you are—to share their thoughts when our words felt lacking. Many thanks to Juliana Alvey, Robert Anderson, Ronald Bitmann, Jennifer Bryan, Karen Cook, Don Dailey, Eliot Garcia, Rick Goscha, Jean Higbee, Lamar Hudson, Jeffrey Hunter, Joanna McCloud, Steve Moffitt, Tonya Hinman, Tonja Speer, Amecia Taylor, Sherrie Watkins-Alvey, Jack Weller, James Winston and Erin Wright.

"Just for Today" Contributors

It's one thing to have an inspirational writing each day; it's another to incorporate activities that encourage the inclusion of the writing into one's personal life. We are thankful for individuals who shared their ideas with us at the 10th Annual Kansas Recovery Conference and at the 2010 Alternatives Conference. Thank you for taking the time to share your tools, resources and suggestions with us. Your contributions served to move this book from mere words to action.

Our appreciation to the original authors of *Pathways to Recovery*— Priscilla Ridgway, Diane McDiarmid, Sarah Ratzlaff and Julie Bayes, along with several of the original contributors. We welcomed your support and trust we have remained true to the original vision of the book.

Finally, a special thanks to all the readers of *Pathways to Recovery*. We hear from you weekly with your stories of how the workbook has impacted and changed your lives in ways you never imagined. When things get wild and we have too many things to do in too little time, we pick up the phone or get an e-mail from you. We treasure these gifts and hope you will continue to share your words with us. We are honored and humbled.

Lori, Suzette, Lesa & Julie
June 2010

Introduction

"The dreamer and the dream are the same.
The powers personified in a dream
are those that move the world."

~ Joseph Campbell

The idea for this book came as one of those stray thoughts that occur when you're driving down the highway or taking a shower—one of those 'aha' moments that begins to pop into your head over and over and over again.

We've certainly been thrilled at the response we've seen to *Pathways to Recovery* in the years since it was first published. But there's always been a couple of questions that keep popping up. "Are you going to revise the book?" and "I've finished *Pathways*; now what class do I take?"

As we've talked with people across the globe about their experience using the *Pathways* workbook and other self-help recovery tools, what became evident was not more information or another class but rather a way of incorporating the material in these resources into one's daily life. While it's helpful to attend classes and complete these tools, if the material is not used to help "get a life"—our favorite definition of recovery—then all the tools in the world won't change anything. The questions, however, continued and it seemed clear there should be a next step in the journey.

The first step was to bring together some writers. Four wildly creative souls—each with their own passion for *Pathways* and a true connection to the healing power of self-help—said yes.

The first meeting was in a noisy coffee house in Kansas City. We carried in our big bags of all the daily reflection books that each of us owned, trying to decide what we thought we could do. We left that day, determined to bring our idea to life.

But as we started, it quickly became clear that this project was creating more questions than we were initially prepared to answer. How will we organize it? What should we include? How were we going to split up the writing assignments? Will anyone even think this is a good idea? We didn't know the answers to those questions but we moved forward, doing our best to stay excited and committed.

Each of the authors went home after that first meeting, mostly wondering how we were going to organize the book. Our first idea was to follow the twelve chapters of *Pathways*. "That's perfect," we thought! Perfect until we realized that September—Chapter Nine which focuses on the roadblocks to recovery—was not going to inspire a lot of positive thought and forward movement! What seemed so easy became our initial stumbling block.

With any book, it seems there's a lot of synchronicity and happenstance that occurs. Sitting on her deck during the summer evening, Lori was visited by her friend, Tonya. Tonya had served on the original advisory committee for *Pathways to Recovery*, so she was quite familiar with its contents.

As Lori shared the dilemma the authors had, she jokingly said, "Maybe we'll just cut up all the quotes in the book, throw them in a hat and randomly assign them." Tonya laughed, probably realizing this was exactly what needed to happen. "Well," she said, "recovery isn't a linear path!"

Of course! Since we knew people might get the book at any time during the year, this organization made sense. It really wouldn't matter where one started reading the daily passages. Recovery is about growth, but not in any particular way.

The next time we got together, we literally took a Pathways book, cut all the quotes out and put them in a hat. We selected each quote and randomly assigned it to a day of the year. And then we started writing.

Over the next year, we met several times in a high school classroom at a local church on Saturday mornings. We chose the weekend because we still weren't sure if anyone outside of ourselves would support us, much less allow us the time to work on the book.

As we began our random writing, we also realized that we were interpreting some of the quotations very differently than how they were originally used in *Pathways to Recovery*. So we decided to continue making our own interpretations—recovery does require some creativity! You will find the pages in *Pathways* listed on each reflection—but the topic chosen by the author may be a bit different than what you'll find in the original text. For those of you who do prefer a more linear style, our apologies...but we encourage you to keep reading!

Of course, life always steps in and the deadlines you anticipate have to be expanded...and expanded...and expanded again. New projects grabbed more priority. A marriage took place. We learned a new baby would be on the way. We lost loved ones and friends. But we never gave up on our vision, knowing that we would ultimately complete the book.

What you have before you is almost two years of work and something we trust our readers will find helpful throughout the year. As with any good self-help book—and even some bad ones—readers will find a variety of ways to use the material found within its pages. That's probably going to happen to you, too. But there is no right or wrong way to use this book. It's absolutely your choice!

However, if you need a little help, here are some ways you might choose to incorporate the different parts of each reflection:

- Use only the title as a positive affirmation or mantra, repeating it frequently throughout your day.

- Simply read the quotations each day and determine your own meaning.

- If you're only looking for activities or questions to help move your journey along, then you might just explore the "Just for Today" activities (these are suggested activities, questions or thoughts to think about for that day). You also might want to keep a journal of your thoughts and ideas.

- Read the entire passage. You still have the opportunity to choose what fits for you.

- Use the reflections for opening or closing a group session.

We know our readers will also find many creative ways to incorporate the material! And we hope you'll let us know how to use it.

We also know there will be passages in the book in which you may not agree. You might not like the language or how we've interpreted the many quotations. If that's true for you, then mark out those sections—a nice black marker works wonders! There's no reason to read those parts again next year if you don't want to.

We hope you won't feel pressured to read every day. If you miss a day, a week or even a month or more, just pick back up on the current day.

So many of us get the message very early on in our recovery that our illness, our symptoms or our struggles and challenges will always be with us. We're told this is the best it can be and that we will never have a time in our life without these experiences. But we don't have to believe that!

We think recovery—a true process of discovery—is all about creating the life you want. It's about finding the things in life that give us passion, purpose and meaning. It's about living where we want to, feeling safe and secure. It's about learning and growing and reclaiming only those parts of our past that we need to in order to move on. It's about taking each day as it comes, living and appreciating *this* moment, for we can't change the past and we sure can't predict the future.

By jumping on the pathway to recovery, we find ourselves creative, powerful and hope-*full*...especially when we realize that "the trail is the thing, not the end of the trail..."

January

"It is the memory that enables a person to gather roses in January."

~ *Unknown*

The Single Step

"A journey of a thousand miles must begin with a single step."
~ Chinese Proverb
Pathways to Recovery, p. iv

Sometimes we get caught up in feeling that our lives—as we once knew them to be—are over. This is when it's hardest to move in a new direction. If we don't take that first step out of who we were, into the beautiful person we have yet to become, we get stuck. We find ourselves going in circles.

Taking our first step is probably the most difficult—and at the same time—the most rewarding. Because when we begin that journey, there are no ends to the possibilities life holds.

Just for Today
Write a letter to yourself today, including all the things you hope to accomplish during the coming year. As you write, remember the possibilities and include your single steps. Make it the journey YOU want!

Opening Our Souls to the Sun

"A thankful person is thankful under all circumstances.
A complaining soul complains even if he lives in paradise."
~ Baha'u'llah
Pathways to Recovery, p. 349

We each have some sort of image about how life is supposed to look. As a child, we begin dreaming about what we'll be once we're all grown up.

Some of us dream of being rich and having a big house, a great car or traveling the world. Others want to have a home filled with children… and then grandchildren. Some of us want jobs that will lead to fame, while some of us want lots of time to enjoy hobbies.

Life usually doesn't turn out just the way we dreamed it would be. Disappointments, financial problems, family struggles and other challenges toss us around. The path can get rough and become uncertain.

A huge piece of recovery is about discovering the good things in our lives, things that make us amazing and unique. If we focus on what isn't working, we're giving our attention to the things we don't like. If we stop complaining and just start saying "thank you" for the gift of today—even when it feels so imperfect—it's like opening our souls to the sun, letting in the warmth and comfort of that day. When we do that, there just simply isn't room for the heavy, dark clouds.

Just for Today

Do you find yourself complaining about every little thing? Just for today, stop! Do your best to open up your soul and give thanks for your journey!

As Bricks Are Laid

"Just as bricks are laid, one on top of another, to build a house,
so do your thoughts build on each other, moment by moment. The
person you become, the things you accomplish, the joy and fulfillment
you find, all depend on the thoughts you use to build your life."
~ Ralph S. Marston, Jr.
Pathways to Recovery, p. 276

A woman was told by her doctor she was very sick and needed to quit her job to spend quiet time at home. She thought, "What a gift! I will finally have time to learn to paint and have friends over for coffee." And she went home and did just that.

A man planned a fishing weekend for months, only to awaken to a three-day rainstorm. He thought, "What a gift this rain is to the earth! I will plant a lovely garden when it stops. And he spent the weekend shopping for seeds and sketching out a magnificent garden design.

A woman had trouble sleeping because she kept thinking about all the "bad" things in her life. She felt anxious and sad. One night she picked up a notebook and wrote down things that were causing her sorrow. Then she wrote about the good things in her life. She began to see her life as a gift. She lay down and slept a wonderful sleep.

Our thoughts and reactions to life have a huge impact on how we feel inside. Life will toss storms our way—but we can choose to think about them positively, laying down bricks of happiness along the journey.

Just for Today

Imagine your life at 70 or 80 years of age. What will you look back on with pride, something that made you happy? Once you identify these things, see if your ideas change the decisions you make during the day.

Laughing at Oneself

"One loses many laughs by not laughing at oneself."
~ Sara Jeanette Duncan
Pathways to Recovery, p. 365

We all experience times in our lives when we need to gather all our inner resources to focus on the serious things in our lives. We search diligently to discover, value and develop our strengths so we can draw on them during the difficult times of our lives. But often, in our intense focus on the serious parts of our lives, we overlook one of our most important gifts: humor and the ability to laugh at ourselves

Learning to laugh at ourselves gives us the opportunity to be free, even if momentarily, from the burdens of the serious. How many of us have searched frantically for our glasses only to find them resting on the top of our head? How about spending an hour trying on clothes for a special occasion then to realize our socks don't match when we get to the party? Being able to laugh at ourselves in these moments—especially when we try to judge ourselves because of our mistakes—opens our spirits and sets us free.

Our laughter and sense of humor can change the way we look at the world. Laughter *is* infectious! It's difficult not to laugh when we hear it, no matter where it comes from! Humor can be an important part of our recovery process, especially when we realize how healing it feels to just laugh!

Just for Today

Have a deep and long belly laugh — the kind that forces all the air into your lungs and out again. It's even better if you can laugh at some funny or silly thing that you did!

Somewhere There's Someone

*"Somewhere there's someone who dreams of your smile, and finds
in your presence that life is worthwhile. So when you're lonely,
remember it's true: somebody somewhere is thinking of you."*
~ Unknown
Pathways to Recovery, p. 220

We matter. Our lives are special. We have special talents and gifts that make a difference to others. We have abilities that make us unique.

We make others smile. We make others feel loved. We make others know they're special. We help others, even when they don't ask for help.

We have a sense of humor. We can make it through the toughest things in life and still find a way to smile.

We are smart. We are courageous. We are survivors.

We know where to turn when we need support. We know, too, how to be a good friend.

We are loved and we are cared for. We are special. The world is a better place because of us.

Just for Today

Who's thinking of you today? Is it someone you haven't talked to in a while? Why not pick up the phone and give them a call!

Participating In Life

*"Even if you are on the right track,
you will get run over if you just sit there."*
~ Will Rogers
Pathways to Recovery, p. 271

Have you ever watched runners at a race? Remember the shrill sound of the whistle that marked the beginning…ready, set—*the whistle blows*—GO? The runners were off! Down the track, striving to reach their goals of being champions. Making it to the end.

In life, it doesn't matter if we're the best, if we win prizes or if we're number one. Life isn't about comparing ourselves to the achievements of others. It's about being active participants in our own lives, living each day as fully as we can—filling our time with what's meaningful to us. It's a little like a race because we have to get "out there" every day.

But sometimes, we can spend too much time as a spectator in our own life and not enough as a participant. There may be things getting in our way that keep us from being a star performer. Maybe it's a poor diet, the need for a coach or mentor, getting more rest or finding some motivation. Whatever it may be, we can take action to improve our life!

Just for Today
What can you do to become a better participant in your life? Ask yourself these questions: What are you in training for? What do you want to be doing? How will you get up and move so you don't get run over?

All Your Heart

"Wherever you go, go with all your heart."
~ Confucius
Pathways to Recovery, p. 73

No one knows where life will lead. We only know we have the control to react to life with all our hearts, and in that reaction, we truly live. It takes a lot of energy to keep ourselves objective about what we're experiencing.

If we let experiences affect us, we find we have choices in our responses.

Like the little baby who tests everything and experiences all that surrounds him, so we too can take on life and actually live it. We can touch and feel, look and see, walk and notice our footsteps one-by-one.

In doing this, we more fully create a presence wherever we go. We're experiencing the moment, a moment that is much more fulfilling as we go down the path of discovery. We are open to what comes. We are being renewed and refreshed. We are living with all our hearts!

Just for Today

It's pretty easy to lose sight of your passions and instead, give in to the pressures all around. Just today, take 5 minutes and do something you absolutely love. Give it your all and be open to how you feel. Try to live with all your heart!

Getting Stronger

*"I think the recovery process is good because it helps me think of how far
I have come as a person. I am realizing that as I continue on the path
to recovery, I am getting stronger and more determined every day."*
~ Sue Bennet
Pathways to Recovery, p. 128

Survival of our life challenges is an admirable goal, but to genuinely thrive is remarkable. It's *getting there* that's the journey — the steps we take along the path that will get us to our goals.

Thriving in life is possible. It takes a lot of work and there are many obstacles to overcome, but it *is* worth it. To come out on the other side, to see how far we have traveled, and to delight in that passage are our greatest rewards.

In knowing that we've taken the long journey — the small steps and the huge ones — we can let go of the past to see it for what it really is — a pathway to satisfaction with who we were, who we are and who we are going to be.

Just for Today
*Take a few minutes to make a list of the sorrows you have
experienced. Don't be too hard on yourself, just write them
down without judgment. Then list the joys in life that you've
experienced. Can you feel how each list is different?*

Breaking Rules, Making Mistakes

"Creativity is inventing, experimenting, growing,
taking risks, breaking rules, making mistakes and having fun."
~ Mary Lou Cook
Pathways to Recovery, p. 343

So many people think they aren't creative; they reserve that for the artists, the great thinkers, the people who always seem to have new and fresh ideas. But if you're breathing, you're creative!

It's so important for us to include creativity in our recovery journey. Without it, we stay right where we are, sometimes so stuck that we become immobilized. But when we can change course and actively look for new things or try new activities, when we step out and take risks—even if we fail or make mistakes—and yes, even when we can break a few rules, we become more alive than we would ever have imagined!

Just for Today

Take a few minutes today to create a personal symbol — from any material of your choice — that expresses what your creative spirit holds. Use this symbol as a reminder of your commitment to expand your own creativity...whatever form that might take!

A Circle of Support

"Nobody, but nobody, can make it out here alone."
~ Maya Angelou
Pathways, p. 224

Many of us encounter times when we feel lonely. We can go through days at a time, not feeling connected to anyone. We can be out in public, or among family or friends, and still feel alone. Perhaps dark thoughts begin to cloud our path. We may feel abandoned, upset with ourselves that we don't have more friends, certain our loneliness is somehow our fault, maybe even worried that things will never get better.

Being alone is not necessarily bad. It gives us time to be still and reflect on our inner journeys, and to rest and relax. When we feel lonely around others, sometimes it's a signal that we just need to let go and let things *be* without thinking about it so much. That loneliness can be a signal that we're around someone who isn't positive or supportive.

Sometimes it takes a little more effort to feel engaged in the situation. In time, we get better at figuring out who we trust on our journey, and the way we experience loneliness will shift. We can give ourselves permission to learn these lessons, to have some lonely times without panicking and feeling as if something is wrong with us. We can learn to respond to loneliness by reaching inside our own souls, and knowing we are loved.

Just for Today

For those times when you're feeling lonely, try making a self-care calendar. Identify something you can "do" that you find soothing; add that activity to each day of your calendar. When you start to feel you need a little perk to get you through the day – perhaps when you're feeling lonely – turn to your calendar for a little well-deserved self care!

For the Good of the Whole

*"We are members of one great body, planted by nature
in a mutual love, and fitted for a social life. We must consider
that we were born for the good of the whole."*
~ Seneca
Pathways to Recovery, p. 85

Many of us have experienced mistreatment, rejection and outright discrimination when trying to access things in the community. This is *stigma* and it can have long-lasting effects that lead to feelings of hurt, anger, distrust of others and feeling a lack of power over one's life.

Involvement in the community is key to recovery. It means each one of us is a person who has the same rights as everyone else does. It means each of us has the right to do things others do. It means our lives can be filled with activities and opportunities to do fun things and meet new people. It means we can go to school and have jobs. It means we can volunteer to help others, drive a car, own a per, spend the day playing in a park or doing whatever else we want that makes us feel like we're living our lives with purpose.

Community participation means reaching out beyond our mental health support systems—a little at a time—to meet new people and explore other opportunities to make our lives fuller. We do this because we're part of a larger whole, and because we have much to contribute. It might not be until we start participating more and more in our community that we start seeing how strong and confident we really are. That's when the bonds of stigma can only be broken.

Just for Today
Choose to do one thing today that might help someone in your community. It doesn't have to be difficult or even big. Simple acts are often the most meaningful.

We Are in Ourselves Unique

"What works for you is not necessarily going to work
for me since we are within ourselves unique."
~ Chris Shore
Pathways to Recovery, p. 108

No two people are exactly alike. Our personalities differ. We look different. We do things in different ways. But, we are often lumped together in groups and labeled with just a few similar features. When that happens, we lose our individuality; we each ask ourselves, "Who am I?"

A newly divorced woman found she had to reinvent herself, her lifestyle and her surroundings. She had been in a relationship for so long that she didn't know herself as an individual. She ached to find out who she truly was…to find her own uniqueness. She decided to get curious and figure this out.

The woman engaged in activities to discover herself. To find her likes and dislikes, she created personalized paintings and collages. She would write the pros and cons of each question she faced in order to make a good decision. She tried volunteering at a theater to find out who she truly was.

As she searched, she found her uniqueness. She could say who she was, and she grew inside. Life became easier as she claimed her individuality and her strengths shined. She felt whole when she found her self.

Just for Today

Let go of your own insecurities. The fear of what others might think is a key reason for people to confirm. Trust in your uniqueness!

Round The Corner

"Still round the corner there may wait,
a new road or a secret gate."
~ J.R.R. Tolkien
Pathways to Recovery, p. 119

Making goals for ourselves, and working to get there, is often like having a two-headed animal tap on our door. We're afraid to turn the corner to see what might be there, for we may find something we didn't expect or want, something so exotic to us that we can't wrap our minds around it.

In reality, what awaits us is our destiny and a slew of possibilities we never knew were there. When we make goals for our future, we find that things are not as overwhelming as we once thought.

How many times have we missed the new road or the secret gate? How many times have we turned the corner in the past to find ourselves able to cope with what was there? Doesn't it make sense to just turn the corner?

Just for Today
The first step in setting goals is for you to decide what your wants, desires and aspirations are, writing them down so they don't get lost amidst all the things you're doing. As you become more comfortable with what you want in life, you may find yourself needing to dream even bigger!

Dare To Be Unique

"Let's dare to be ourselves, for we do that better than anyone else can."
~ Shirley Briggs
Pathways to Recovery, p. 69

It can be easy to stay detached from our surroundings and the people around us. In fact, some of us learned at an early age to do this in order to survive.

But as we grow, we learn there are healthier ways to deal with what's going on around us. We learn to be present in the moment, to allow life to touch us and give us opportunities to respond in freedom.

To learn to be present in each experience, we need to realize that a threat is not necessarily there. We are older now and more in control of our lives. Things in our environment don't need to affect us as they once did. Instead, we can take a step back from our reactions, taking a few moments to think clearly to find responses that are more fitting. In being able to do this, we're able to be more ourselves in different situations.

In being ourselves, we find out who we really are—and others are given a glimpse too. Although this might be scary, it's more than worth the effort. Staying present in the moment allows us to be the unique individuals that we really are. We already know what's behind us—now we can look forward to what's ahead!

Just for Today

Find a few minutes today to do a little people-watching; any place with a few people will do. See if you can pick out one individual who you find interesting and who appears to be living their 'real' self. What about this person is interesting to you? Try to recreate for yourself what you see in them!

One Positive Thought

*"It takes but one positive thought when given a chance to
survive and thrive to overpower an entire army of negative thoughts."*
~ Robert Shuller
Pathways to Recovery, p. 359

Ever stood in front of one of those circus mirrors that make us look
short or tall, thin or fat? They're usually a lot of fun because we know
their real purpose is to twist and distort how we look.

Yet all too often, we can get stuck with the same kind of twisted
image about ourselves. It doesn't matter how well we do at a task
or how much others encourage us, we still see our reflection in the
circus mirror. Each unrealistic message we send ourselves twists and
distorts the view we have of ourselves—only this time—it's not so
fun.

Negative thinking makes every part of our world more difficult.
Learning to stop our negative thoughts is not only helpful, but necessary
if we are to embark on a recovery journey that moves us forward.
Recognizing negative self-talk—which are often just distortions—is
the first step toward overcoming it. And once we turn our thoughts
around, thinking more rationally, our mood will follow.

Just for Today

*Create a set of affirmation cards that you can use each day.
Create your own affirmations like "I love myself," or "I am
willing to let goodness into my life." Focus on a specific area of
your life that you'd like to change, especially as negative thoughts
come up.*

Reaching Goals

"The tragedy of life doesn't lie in not reaching your goal.
The tragedy lies in having no goal to reach."
~ Benjamin Mays
Pathways to Recovery, p. 267

How often do we sit back and wonder what we're reaching for in life? Are we just moving through each day or do we have real goals that we're trying to achieve?

When we wake up in the morning, what's the first thing we think about? Do we find ourselves excited about what the day might bring or do we just go through the motions, finding few things that motivate us for change?

When we're resting at night—getting ready to drift off into sleep—what are we thinking about? Are we ready to face a new day ahead, clearly focused on the things that bring our lives joy? Or do we let the distraction in life get in our way?

We've got to challenge ourselves—today, next week, next month and next year—to find goals that excite us and push us forward, goals that are more fulfilling. Moving toward a goal is so much better than letting ourselves go through each day without them.

Just for Today

Take the 100 Minute Goal Challenge – turn off the distractions (TV, negative thoughts, computer, etc.) for 10 minutes a day for the next 10 days. Spend the time focusing on your goals. You'll be investing 100 minutes of effort towards reaching your goals!

Dreams of Possibilities

"We see the possibilities in others,
but do we ever dream of the possibilities in ourselves?"
~ Sandy Hyde
Pathways to Recovery, p. 74

It's easy for us to see strengths in other people. It seems as though everyone else has something going for them: they make friends easily; they have some kind of natural talent; they realize their dreams by living them.

It's not so easy to see strengths within ourselves. We struggle to see our own talents, skills and dreams. It could be that we never learned to look within ourselves to see the wonderful possibilities within each of us holds.

We *are* our dreams, our reflections, our hopes and desires. We each have strengths, though often we don't even realize such truth. Once we recognize in ourselves the many things that make us beautiful and one-of-a-kind, we can open our minds to what every human being has—potential. Unleashing that potential—dreaming of the possibilities—is our gift to ourselves; it becomes our gift to the world.

Just for Today

What are your greatest dreams — the ones of possibility — that you're holding today. Consider putting together a dream board. Look through magazines for pictures or words — or create your own picture — of how you visualize your dream. Being able to 'see' your dream will help you actually achieve it!

Just Lie Down

"Stress is basically a disconnection from the earth,
a forgetting of the breath. It believes everything is an emergency.
Nothing is that important. Just lie down."
~ Natalie Goldberg
Pathways to Recovery, p. 317

Ever heard of the "Five Principle"?

Basically, you can apply anything you do to these "fivers"—five minutes from now, five days from now, five weeks from now, five years from now...Who's going to know and who's going to care that you did or didn't do_____?

Although a true perfectionist will almost always answer, "I will," do any of the stressful things that happen each and every day really matter enough that in five year's time, we will remember that we did or didn't do something? Probably not.

Stress seems to be one of the common denominators found in our journey of recovery. It can be good stress; it can be bad stress. It really doesn't matter. While we can't always keep stress out of our lives, we do have the power to decide how we will work to handle its impact.

Using the "Five Principle" is just a start.

Just for Today
What's one thing in your life that you can apply the "Five Principle" to that will help reduce your stress? Go ahead; you can do it!

Each New Step

"Each new step becomes a little surer, and each new grasp
a little firmer."
~ Sarah Bon Breathnach
Pathways to Recovery, p. 136

Some of our steps have not been easy, especially when others have told us we can't do this or that.

Being told we *can't* puts us in a position of doing the things others tell us to do—or expect us to do. When we're told we can't, a piece of our soul can feel weary and discouraged, and we might start doing less than that which we're really capable.

Our challenges might really mean there are some things we can't do—or that there are some things we find are more difficult to do than they used to be. There are always new things to learn. There are always new things to do. But if we want to, we can learn new ways to do what we did before.

As we discover what we can do, we give less energy to how we respond to the things we "can't" do. Our confidence increases and our journeys grow even bigger.

Just for Today
It's often easier to think about all the things you can't do. So today, start something different. Keep a list handy and try to write down everything you do. At the end of the day, you'll have a long list of strengths, skills and abilities!

When True Recovery Began

"I struggled for years — angry, denying my illness. Finally, I searched for answers to gain a better understanding to make peace with my illness. That is when my true journey of recovery began."
~ Kathy Shinn
Pathways to Recovery, p. 87

When we're first diagnosed, we can find it quite confusing and discouraging. We think our lives will never be the same. We are human beings on a winding road, often unable to see what is coming ahead.

We can't believe what we're being told.

Anger and fear come at us like tornados on a Kansas prairie — fast and strong and turning us around in circles. Which way is up? Which way is down? How do we find our feet again?

Understanding and peace come with knowledge — knowledge that can come through visits with our peers, discovering something new or self-education. Then we can step back and realize our illness is only part of who we are. We are not our diagnosis, nor are we only our symptoms.

In this process of learning, we find out that it's possible to recover — to define our own lives — and our journey toward recovery truly begins.

Just for Today
Today, identify one of those barriers — one you've held on to for way too long and that causes you to have while-knuckled fists. What is one first step you can take to try and move forward? Remember you are not your diagnosis, symptoms or negative experiences!

Being Gutsy

"I've learned that I am important and I do have something to share…
It can be a challenge to start over, but then again, I'm gutsy.
I'm a new person and I love it."
~ Pat Schwartz
Pathways to Recovery, p. 349

How often can we say these?

- We're gutsy because we've had the courage to start our lives over again when things got really tough.
- We're gutsy because we have the courage to get up each day and find joy in life — grateful to have it just as it is.
- We're gutsy because when we're feeling lonely, we can call a friend, pet the dog, watch a movie, play on the computer or find some other way to realize that loneliness is just a figment of our imagination.
- We're gutsy because feeling lonely doesn't stop us from enjoying life.
- We're gutsy because when we're feeling overwhelmed, we can take a break from what we're doing or thinking or feeling. We can rest for as long as we need to. We're gutsy because we can do this and not feel bad or guilty about pacing ourselves to stay healthy.
- We're gutsy because when we remember more good than bad things about life, we can let our souls sing and our bodies dance.

Being gutsy means we are important and we have something to share. Being gutsy lets us be a new people. Don't you love it?

Just for Today

How gutsy are you feeling today? If you suddenly had more courage, what would you do? Take a few minutes today and do something courageous. Remember, you can do it because you're gutsy!

Breaking through Barriers

"It takes courage to push yourself to places that you have never been before...to test your limits...to break barriers."
~ Anais Nin
Pathways to Recovery, p. viii

Many of us no doubt feel like we've been challenged with so many things — broken relationships, symptoms that grab hold of us in ways we would have never imagined, lost jobs and educational goals put aside — more barriers, changes and lost opportunities than any one person should have to endure.

But we are amazingly resilient. Think about it. Most of us have learned how to be good friends as we nurture our relationships. We've found all sorts of wellness tools to help keep our symptoms in check. We've gone after our dreams in new, unexpected ways that have taken us to places we'd never have gotten to experience had it not been for overcoming the barriers of what we've faced.

Recovery gives us the chance to unleash a new person — full of courage, hope and power. Our recovery gives us the chance to view all of our challenges as beautiful and life-enriching. It gives us the ability to test not only our limits, but to break down barriers we've held onto for way too long.

Just for Today

Start out slowly and simply today...change your routine. It could be anything — have breakfast for lunch or take a different way to work. Push yourself a little and test your limits. Change can break down barriers!

A Good Time For Laughing

"A good time for laughing is when you can."
~ Jessamyn West
Pathways to Recovery, p. 365

It has been well-documented that laughter is important to our ongoing health and happiness. Laughing helps to reduce our stress, lower our anxiety and increase our sense of well-being. It can lower our blood pressure, help us breathe more deeply and block negative thought patterns.

Laughter is one of the things that can help move us through the difficult times of a mental illness diagnosis or trauma. The comic, Bill Cosby, once said, "If you can find humor in something, you can survive it."

Finding the "good time for laughing" in all our life's experiences gives us a greater opportunity to take control over those experiences, allowing us to move forward as survivors and people who can thrive.

Just for Today
Look for laughter throughout the day. Find a person who makes you laugh and spend time with them. Pay special attention to how you feel when you're laughing. Doesn't it feel good?

Taking Chances

"If your life is ever going to get better, you'll have to take risks.
There is simply no way you can grow without taking chances."
~ David Viscott
Pathways to Recovery, p. 42

Taking chances means doing things differently than how we're used to doing them. Taking chances means thinking about things differently than how we're used to thinking about them. It means shaking up your routine a bit, and feeling excited about what might happen.

Taking chances means doing one thing differently each day than how you usually do things. Taking chances means choosing vanilla instead of chocolate, smiling instead of frowning, going to bed an hour earlier or later than usual, taking a walk around the neighborhood, or inviting a friend over for dessert.

Taking chances means moving life from *wishful-thinking* mode into *happening* mode. Taking chances can be scary—but taking chances means growing into the person you know you can become.

Just for Today

Today is the day to do something different, to take a chance. How about trying the first thing that pops into your head? What will it be?

The Truth Is Today

*"I am in the present. I cannot know what tomorrow may bring forth.
I can only know that the truth is for me today."*
~ Igor Stravinsky
Pathways to Recovery, p. 49

Most of us know all too well how to live in the past. It's often a place full of regrets, packed with a bunch of coulda-shoulda-woulda's or broken expectations our family or friends have held for us.

Although we can't predict it, the future most likely holds at least a few possibilities and the hope that things will change or get better. We may sometimes choose to look ahead in fantasy or imaginative dreams.

But being in the moment? That's pretty hard for most of us to do. In fact, some studies have shown that we spend less than 5% of our time actually living in the present!

Learning to live in the present begins when we notice we're trying to alter our current moment into the past or future. Once we can begin to let go of the past, we gain self-confidence, even in new situations. Once we start to purposely plan for our future, we can begin to make better choices and fully experience the people and things around us in more meaningful ways.

Just for Today

Technology has brought many wonderful things into our lives — but these things can also distract you from enjoying what is right in front of you. Today — go unplugged! Turn off the television, put away the headphones and don't check your e-mail. Notice what's going on around you. Take it all in and enjoy every minute of the day...you may find you actually like it!

Seeing Our Strengths

"Part of my journey to recovery is finally seeing my own strengths."
~ Vicky Walter
Pathways to Recovery, p. 73

Each of us has strengths within us. It's what has brought us through adversity to where we are today. We are strong in the fact that we have survived and are moving on with our lives.

We must take an honest inventory of ourselves to see what our strengths are. In doing this with someone else, they might see strengths we can't see for ourselves. If we can find someone we trust to begin making that list, we'll be amazed by what we find. In gaining an inventory of strengths, we can begin to see the possibilities in front of us.

Recovery thrives on possibilities, just as a waterfall needs the strength of the river behind it to exist, flourish and fall abundantly. So we too are like the river, full of strength and possibility, flowing toward the waterfall that leads to a happy and fulfilling life.

Just for Today
It's very true that others probably see your strengths when you can't. Today, can you find three people who will answer you honestly when you ask, "What strengths do you see in me?" Make sure the people you ask are trusted friends or family members.

Everything with Passion

"Nothing in the world has been accomplished without passion."
~ George Wilhelm Friedrich Hegel
Pathways to Recovery, p. 358

Passion is...

- What makes us want to get up in the morning
- What makes us look forward to meeting with friends
- What makes us want to go to work
- What makes us love to read a book
- What makes us love the smile of a child, a partner, a parent or a friend
- What makes us spend the day working on a hobby
- What leads to the greatest of all inventions...electricity, medical miracles, space ships, computers and so much more

Passion is our motivation. Passion is the key to what makes the heart come alive, the soul want to dance and the mind open to overcome anything that tries to stand in the way of living life to its fullest. Passion is what shows up when we paint the world in vivid colors, laugh out loud, and say yes when we're told no!

That's what passion is...and that's how all things accomplished in this great world are supported, pushed, prodded and nudged along. By passion. Simply, wonderfully, wholesome, heart-felt, soul-felt passion.

Just for Today

Many people express their passion by collecting something they enjoy. Do you collect anything? If not, why not start today?

A Thought More Powerful

*"Put love first. Entertain thoughts that give life. And when a thought
of resentment or hurt or fear comes your way, have another thought
that is more powerful – a thought that is love."*
~ Mary Morrissey
Pathways to Recovery, p. 360

Our thoughts are like many tiny particles, swimming through our
heads, some grabbing on, some continuing to swim, while others go
unnoticed.

One thing we can do for ourselves is to take some control of our
thoughts. This sounds difficult, and it is. It takes practice and focus.
Overcoming hurtful thoughts takes action.

That action can be done in a number of ways, like memorizing positive
affirmations about ourselves. We can choose a positive statement
like, "I am worthwhile." When we start to have hurtful thoughts, we
replace them with a positive affirmation instead. The more of these we
have, the more they're available for us to use and the more powerful
our thoughts become!

Just for Today
*Ever seen those refrigerator magnets that include lots of words to
create your own poetry, affirmations, lists, etc. What are some of
the words that best describe what you're looking for in life? Take
those words and create your own positive slogan. Put it on your
fridge for some daily inspiration!*

Wandering and Wondering

"If a man can keep alert and imaginative, an error is a possibility,
a chance at something new; to him, wandering and wondering
are part of the same process and he is most mistaken,
most in error, whenever he quits exploring."
~ William Least Heat Moon
Pathways to Recovery, p. 266

Sometimes we feel lost because of all that
has happened to us. We experience the
loss of hopes, dreams, predictable health
and the ability to do all the things that
others get to do. Sitting in that loss might
feel like depression. We might be told to get
over it — and to not think those things that bring
our spirits down. But we sit there anyway,
because many of us really do experience true loss.

This isn't the same as depression. It's about coming face-to-face with
something real. And we can always take steps to make it better.

When we do, we really can wander into new territories, full of
wonder.

Just for Today
Grab a piece of paper and some markers. Draw your own
pathway, giving it some hills and challenges and places to
explore. What are some ways you can wonder and wander along
it today?

That Which Is Yes

*"Thank you God for this most amazing day: for the leaping
greenly spirit of trees and a blue true dream of sky; and for everything
which is natural, which is infinite, which is yes."*
~ e e cummings
Pathways to Recovery, p. 354

Have you noticed lately how awesome and wonderful life is and what
a miracle it is each time we take a breath? In, then out, then in again —
without having to think about it — steadily, as we rest, play and work.
It's not anyone else's breath. It's ours...marvelous and miraculous.

We are incredible and beautiful people. How intricate we are with
all the physical parts of ourselves...the shape of our fingers, toes,
muscles, eyes, nose, mouth...the color of our skin, our eyes, our hair...
our brain and its wisdom, knowledge and creativity. The beauty of
our honesty, our spirituality, the connection we may have to our
friends and family.

When we ponder things about life, this reflection brings us a sense
of awe, wonder, and gratitude to our spirit. Something inside of us
awakens and the darkness of depression fades away. We start saying
"yes." We start enjoying that "which *is* yes."

Just for Today
*Throughout today, for every time you want to say "no" to
something good, try saying "yes" instead. Move your thoughts
to positive ones when you can. Feel the beauty around you!*

Receive the Gift In Joy

"If it is a quiet day, trust the stillness. If it is a day of action, trust the activity. If it is a time to wait, trust the pause. It if is a time to receive that which we have been waiting for, trust that it will happen clearly and with power, and receive the gift in joy!"
~ Unknown
Pathways to Recovery, p. 332

We never know exactly what our day will be like when we get up. While some are routine, other days can change our lives in a flash.

There are days when the things we think will bring us happiness, don't. There are other days when our lives seem loaded with heartbreak yet the wisdom gained from these experiences teaches us more about ourselves than we would have ever expected.

Learning to trust the moment—whether it's quiet, busy or a time of reflection—also means learning to trust in ourselves. It means giving up the fear of the unknown and the pain of the past, allowing ourselves to feel and experience the richness of the now.

As we learn to receive the gifts each day brings, we can allow ourselves the opportunity of receiving joy. And what greater gift could there be?

Just for Today
Today is the day for you to just be. Don't plan a lot of things. Trust that your day will unfold in the way you want it to. Enjoy each moment. All you have to do is step outside your door and see what happens!

February

"The February sunshine steeps your boughs and tints the buds and swells the leaves within."
~ William Cullen Bryant

The Soul and Ordinary Life

"The spiritual journey is the commingling with ordinary life."
~ Christina Baldwin
Pathways to Recovery, p. 240

The thing about life is that we really don't know what's coming next. We wake up and usually do the same thing day after day. Sometimes we feel rather bored with it all. Sometimes, things are really rough and we aren't sure we're going to see a bright day again.

Here's the deal about life: We really don't know what tomorrow will bring. We don't even know what today will bring. But the exciting thing about the unknown is the mystical part of life which really happens *right now!* We can look around to discover beauty, joy and wonder, anticipating the realization of our hopes and dreams as they come true.

As we do this, we start to realize what a miracle our lives are—just as they are. The fact that we are here, breathing and living life today—just as it is and *because* of who we are—is something we start appreciating in new ways. And when that happens, we know we're living life from the depth of our souls, fully engaged in the journey, instead of avoiding it out of pain and fear. And at that moment, we'll know that it's really enough.

Just for Today

As you move through the day, pay close attention to the responses you have to what is going on around you...at that moment. Are you responding out of pain and fear or are you doing your best to enjoy what is happening right now?

Create the Future

"The best way to predict the future is to create it."
~ Peter Drucker
Pathways to Recovery, p. 344

Often we wonder what's in store for us. What does our future hold? Will we be ready for it when it happens? Or will it overwhelm us?

Our future is much like a glass jar, empty and clear. There is nothing to see when we look into it. But within seconds, we have put something in it, just by existing. Our very existence shapes our future.

If we can remember that everything we choose to do goes into that glass jar, then we can take hold of every moment. Every way in which we react to what happens to us determines the memories that will fill our glass jar. We can consciously put hurtful things in that jar, or we can fill it up with positive thoughts, actions and good things to remember. It's our choice what that jar will look like when it's full.

Just for Today
Stop. Close your eyes and ask yourself, "Is this what I really want?" If your answer is yes, do it! If you're not sure, go ahead and do it but check how it makes you feel. If your answer's no, stop! You probably don't want it after all.

Facing Our Fears

"With my strengths of courage and determination,
I faced my fears."
~ Sandy Lewis
Pathways to Recovery, p. 118

One of the toughest things for many of us to do is to look into a mirror and really see our faces. The negative voices probably arise just by thinking about doing this. We can be our worst critics!

Ever felt afraid to look in the mirror to see yourself? How about placing your fingers on your face and feeling your eyes and the softness of your eyebrows, the slope of your nose, the slant of your cheeks, the curve of your lips, and the shape of your chin? Your face is what the world sees as you move forward with courage and determination.

We are truly unique on this planet. And while sometimes it might feel daunting to face the world, we are doing it in our own distinctive way. The world sees our face, and our friends get to know what lies behind our eyes and our smile. We are courageous. Determined. Able to face our fears. There may be days where we need to tell ourselves this 100 times a day—but we can tell ourselves this because it is true.

Just for Today
Pick one fear you have and challenge it. Is it real or imagined? If your fear is real, then take action to change it. If it's one you've just imagined, give it up...you have the strength of courage and determination and you can face that fear!

Living and Growing

"There are as many ways to live and grow as there are people."
~ Evelyn Mandel
Pathways to Recovery, p. 5

One of the exciting things about recovery is that there are so many ways to do it—every person's journey is different.

For some, the journey is a slow, step-by-step-by-step path with not all the steps moving forward. We may struggle for years, trying to find our way, gently making as much progress forward as possible.

For others, the "aha" moment seizes us, and we quickly find ways of making changes. Everything becomes new and exciting; every moment becomes an opportunity.

Regardless of how recovery happens, we can build a life that is distinctly ours. We alone have the ability to change, to learn and grow as we want. We can "get a life" that is just as exciting, just as meaningful, just as important as anyone else's. What a comfort it is to know we already have this ability to change within ourselves!

Just for Today
How do you define recovery for yourself? What does it look like? What words do you use to make it real for you?

More Than Before

"You have to let go of the pain and the old ideas of you as you
let in the new images you have to give yourself permission
to be someone different than you used to be…"
~ Suzette Mack
Pathways to Recovery, p. 158

A big part of having mental health issues is a loss of our former identity. We often let go of — or lose — our jobs, sometimes our families or a safe place to live. This causes us to question who we are now compared to who we once were. It's certainly a time of great loss, anger and indecision.

In order to go on with our lives, we eventually must let go of our old ideals and create new ones. Our symptoms and experiences don't make us non-human. We are still full of talents, hopes and aspirations. Nothing can take that away from us!

In letting go of our pain and anger, we free ourselves to the possibilities awaiting us. There's no doubt that we're different now, but in this difference are new ways of being, and new ways of creating ourselves. We must take the risk of becoming more than what we once were. We must take the risk of being who we really are.

Just for Today
What are your dreaming and hoping for? Do you think it's too risky or would you be willing to try it?

Tough Enough to Follow Through

"You have to have confidence in your ability,
and then be tough enough to follow through."
~ Rosalynn Carter
Pathways to Recovery, p. 47

What is it in life that seems most appealing? Finding someone to love? Taking sculpture classes? Learning to play soccer? Maybe raising a puppy or trying tai chi?

It can be hard to feel confidence in our abilities. Identifying our strengths can be just as difficult. Sometimes it's a whole lot easier to hold ourselves back, to keep from moving forward. But what does that get us? Same thing we put into it—not much.

Finding confidence in ourselves and our abilities doesn't have to be difficult. Sometimes it's simply a matter of taking small steps. And as we push forward, we gain confidence. As we gain confidence, we're willing to take more chances. And as Rosalynn Carter—a long-time supporter of mental health recovery—says put on that armor of toughness and follow through!

Just for Today
Do something today that requires you to make a decision...then
follow through and do it! Trust yourself!

We Have a Voice

" Our hearts are not merely pumps…we are people…Those of us who
have been diagnosed are not objects to be acted on. We are fully
human subjects who can act and in acting, change our situation.
We are human beings and we can speak for ourselves.
We have a voice and can learn to use it."
~ Patricia E. Deegan
Pathways to Recovery, p. 379

At some point in recovery, it becomes impossible to be a passive
recipient of services. It may feel comforting at times to be taken care
of by others; in fact, we may truly need that direction as well as a place
to feel safe. But in time, we realize we're not always in the middle of
a crisis, or that we're not experiencing stressful symptoms at all times
and in all places.

It's when we begin to realize we're a bit bored with mental health
services, or we disagree with what others are telling us to do, or we
have an inner desire to do something different or new with our lives
that we begin a new step on our road to recovery. Our voices become
stronger. Our thoughts and wishes become whispers, and then words
spoken aloud. Others can hear us and understand
better who we are—recognizing the new places
and spaces in which we're beginning to live.

Just for Today

*As you begin to share your voice, try
keeping a success log. Include your
accomplishments and breakthroughs. You
can change your situation when you learn
to share your strengths!*

Hard Knocks and Soft Touches

"If you can learn from hard knocks, you can also learn
from soft touches."
~ Carolyn Kenmore
Pathways to Recovery, p. 181

Recovery urges us to learn from our "hard knocks." And for most of us, there surely have been many bumps along the way. Not only are these experiences easy to identify, but we can sometimes begin to feel that the hard way is the only way.

But learning doesn't always have to come from getting beaten up. Can't we learn just as much from the "soft touches"—those things that also shape our lives, often gently and quietly? How often do we look for and take the time to enjoy those?

Every day there are soft touches around us—trees budding in the spring, a hug from a dear friend, walks along the beach, the laughter of children playing, a good book or a favorite song. These experiences are also bumps in the road, just softer ones.

Each of us travels our own path. It's up to us to reach out and grab both the hard knocks and the soft touches, listening to and learning from the gifts each has for us.

Just for Today

Learning from both hard knocks and soft touches requires you also pay attention to caring for yourself. It's kind of like the phrase we hear when flying, "Put your oxygen mask on before you help others." What can you do today to experience some learning from those hard knocks and soft touches?

Hearing Our Own Truth

"If you do not ask yourself what it is you know, you will go on listening to others and change will not come because you will not hear your own truth."
~ St. Bartholomew
Pathways to Recovery, p. 78

How many of us have spent years living by someone else's expectations? How many of us have settled for a life that is less than we thought it would be? How many of us have listened to someone else's voice and not listened to our own?

It's time for a change! We've got to move forward, giving up on what "could have been" and listening to what it is we really want in our lives…now! Our own truth can be blocked by listening to the voices of others and not paying attention to our own.

Let's open wide the spaces and let our truth in—our ears ready to hear the jubilation of our voices! Let's open up the spaces, open up our hearts, open up our minds to the glory of all we are!

Change will come then and we will be ready!

Just for Today
Do you have one thing you've been wanting to change? What is it? Sometime during the day, put yourself in motion and do it! Open up your heart and mind to all you can be!

True Belonging

"True belonging is born of relationships not only to one another but
[also] to a place of shared responsibilities and benefits.
We love not so much what we have acquired as
what we have made and whom we have made it with."
~ Robert Finch
Pathways to Recovery, p. 156

It's fun to buy new things for ourselves. A short trip to the store for a snack, a new outfit, a book, a basketball or something for our home... getting these are always a lot of fun and a good way to chase away our boredom. We bring our new things home and savor them for a while. But soon, the newness wears off and we start thinking about something else we want.

It's different with friends. Our loneliness fades when we're connected with others, and we find that just being together is enough to spark contentment, joy, and a true sense of belonging and it lasts longer than the pleasure we get from buying things. We may think we have no friends, or that we don't belong anywhere, but that isn't true.

Deep down, we're all passionate about something that makes us smile and motivates us into action. When we join with others, our shared passions and interests connect us in exciting ways. In these relationships, we find we can truly belong.

Just for Today
Finding a relationship can be more difficult when your life experiences have been a struggle. Check out www.trueacceptance. com — it's a dating and friendship web site developed specifically for individuals with mental health issues.

Dare to Begin

"All glory comes from daring to begin."
~ Anonymous
Pathways to Recovery, p. 263

Daring to begin? It starts by just taking the first step.

We have to try doing something new. We have to learn that change is not always bad and that fear can be a good motivator. We have to dig deep inside ourselves for our hidden courage. We have to trust our values and set our goals high.

Daring to begin is all we need to do. Once we take the first step, the next one will come. And the next one. We can't just accept where we are, who we've become or what others think we should or shouldn't do.

We take the first step because if we don't dare to begin, we'll never get to where it is we genuinely want to be.

Just for Today
What 'first step' can you take today? Try joining something or going somewhere you haven't been before. One step is all it takes!

Saying Grace

*"You say grace before meals. All right. But I say grace before…I open
a book, and grace before sketching, painting, swimming, walking,
playing, dancing and grace before I dip the pen in the ink."*
~ G. K. Chesterton
Pathways to Recovery, p. 58

Gratitude brings a deep sense of well-being. Instead of seeing the
negatives, we see the positives and start to realize how much we have
and how wonderful and beautiful our lives are. Everything becomes
a gift— something to be taken care of, something valuable, something
treasured.

Saying thank you for each thing we own, each meal we eat, for the
way our bodies can move, for each breath we take in and for each
one we release back into the universe—we begin to live in a state of
peaceful appreciation. We see what we have and forget about what
we lack. We see beauty and have the sense of wonder, manifesting
the curiosity of a child.

Being thankful takes practice. It requires us to quiet our minds, to live
more fully in the present and not be so concerned with worries of the
past or concerns for the future. We notice more new things—sounds,
smells, tastes, textures, people, feelings—than we do when we forget
to just slow down and be thankful for what we have, and know that
it's enough.

Just for Today
*Find a stone or special item to carry with you during the day.
As you hold it and feel it, think of something for which you are
grateful. The more you do this, the more practice you get at being
thankful.*

A Reason for Living

*"Your distress about life might mean you have been living
for the wrong reason, not that you have no reason for living."*
~ Tom O'Connor
Pathways to Recovery, p. 58

How many times do we have this *all-or-nothing* concept about our lives? We make one mistake and then think everything we do is a mistake. We do something embarrassing and focus on it for the rest of the day — or longer — reliving the horror of the situation in our minds over and over and over again, totally missing out on all the wonderful things about ourselves and the world around us.

Did anyone ever mention that living requires purpose…and that the way we perceive things really is — in the end — our own choice? So what if we make mistakes, forget appointments, do something embarrassing or live our lives very differently from others. What matters is that we live our life proudly but never feeling less important or special than anyone else. We've got to hold onto the good and know that we absolutely have a purpose and a reason for living!

Just for Today

Many forms of meditation use a 'mantra' — meaningful words said over and over. There is great power in using the voice. Try creating your own mantra that has meaning for you. It could be something like "I am enough," "I love myself" or "I love my life." When your mind starts to focus on the negative, repeat this mantra to support your own purpose and reason for living!

The Road Comes Into Existence

"Hope is like a road in the country; there was never a road,
but when many people walk on it, the road comes into existence."
~ Lin Yutang
Pathways to Recovery, p. 31

Finding hope when it's been taken away from us can be one of the hardest things to recover on our journey.

Joining with others—those who walk the path with us—makes the road strong and wide and easier to travel. And as we walk with others, we find our own hope, we find our true purpose and we find our own way. We find the direction for our life. And the road becomes real.

Just for Today
If you're not part of a peer group, make some calls to see if your community has a peer center. There are also lots of places online that include forums and chat rooms where you can 'meet' others who are also on a journey of recovery.

At It's Own Speed

"Gratitude softens us. If we begin to acknowledge these moments and cherish them, then no matter how fleeting and tiny this good heart(edness) may seem, it will gradually, at its own speed, expand."
~ Pema Chodron
Pathways to Recovery, p. 347

Sometimes we spend a lot of our days being unhappy or concerned about what has happened to us or what might occur in the future. One way to overcome these thoughts is to seek something for which to be grateful.

Gratitude is recognizing something has been received and we feel more positive because of it. Being grateful helps us feel better about everything.

To be grateful for something, no matter how small, we begin to put into our minds warm, positive thoughts that can change our attitudes about life. If we can pinpoint something to be grateful for each day, we'll begin to feel better about the world around us — and ourselves. Our experiences will take on a more healthy perspective, and eventually gratefulness will become second nature to us.

Just for Today

Try being grateful by starting a gratitude journal. At the end of the day, write down the things you noticed during the day for which you were grateful. Some days, you may only be able to think of one thing...That's okay. Just start. After a while, you'll begin to notice things you'll want to write down later...which means you stopped for a moment to appreciate and expand your life!

On Being Loved

*"Just because someone doesn't love you the way you want them to
doesn't mean they don't love you with all they have."*
~Truman Capote
Pathways to Recovery, p. 235

There may be nothing as intense in life as love. When we experience love, it fills our entire beings, our every thought and action. Life is more exciting, colorful, and meaningful when we are in love.

When love fails us in some way, as it often can and does in all sorts of relationships, it can be devastating. When the dynamics of love in a relationship change, we can feel lost, rejected, unable to find our way. Being disappointed in love happens to a lot of people. Many great poems, songs and books are written about this very thing—which means, of course, it's a *normal* part of living!

When someone doesn't love us the way we want them to, we can choose to be grateful for the opportunity we've had to love and to be loved. We can choose to look beyond and to see who else may need our love, which has endless potential.

We can know, deep in our souls, that when love disappoints us, it isn't because we're not lovable. Neither does it make the other person bad. We can learn to appreciate what we've had and slowly move forward, with a spirit of hope, trust, and forgiveness, toward new opportunities for love.

Just for Today

Is there someone who has failed you in love? Consider writing them a letter that includes your feelings and what you may have learned from the loss. No need to actually send the letter – in fact, you probably shouldn't do that! You have said what you needed to say. Look instead for new opportunities to love.

Power of the Heart

"In every community, there is work to be done. In every nation,
there are wounds to heal. In every heart, there is a power to do it."
~ Marianne Williamson
Pathways to Recovery, p. 154

Because of our life experiences and symptoms, we've often sold ourselves short. We've taken jobs no one else would want and then find those jobs are unacceptable or substandard, generally quitting them sooner or later. We've settled for less-than-satisfactory experiences and — not surprisingly — found ourselves wanting more.

Our mental health concerns shouldn't mean we're given a sentence to spend time in miserable careers. It *isn't* the end of our lives and we *can* make the best of it. Many people with these challenges have become advocates, business owners, nurses, artists, politicians — even therapists and psychiatrists.

We each have many talents of which we may not be aware. It's in our awareness of what we enjoy doing, and what we do well, that we'll find our way to contribute to our communities.

Just for Today

It's important to do a self-assessment of the things you are capable of and enjoy doing. Doing this assessment on our own, or with others, can bring light to your hidden talents and open up avenues to new careers.

Paint a Bold Stroke

*"Life is an immense mural that
requires each of us to pick up the brush
and paint a bold stroke."*
~ Holly Near
Pathways to Recovery, p. 49

Negative thinking can be our worst enemy. It often comes from long-ago abuse or difficult experiences. Patterns that create such feelings often start with negative self-talk.

We have control over how we talk to ourselves. It's a matter of being aware of the things we say to ourselves, and changing them to positives as needed. We can alter the way the world looks to us and how we interact with it by changing what we think by substituting positive self-talk for the old conversations.

What is important is that we practice replacing our negative self-talk with positive affirmations. It can take a lot of practice — picking up the brush and painting a bold stroke — but it's so worth it!

Just for Today

One way to paint your own "bold stroke" is to begin using your own affirmations. We can find affirmations in many places: your own collection or affirmation cards, self-help books, magazines, spiritual writings, friends or family and on many web sites.

Celebrating Our Life Stories

*"Celebration of passages provides an opportunity for people to
remember stories of the experience being observed
and to draw new insights from them."*
~ United Church of Christ Book of Worship
Pathways to Recovery, p. 367

When we think of a birthday, what is it we think of? Perhaps ice cream and a cake. Maybe presents. Maybe getting to do something we didn't get to do the year before when we were younger.

Many people celebrate the passages of life. Birthdays are just one way we recognize our growing older. Other passages might be religious — such as a first communion. Some might be cultural activities like the quinceañera — a special party for girls turning 15. There are passages for children who graduate from elementary, middle and high school. We celebrate weddings and new babies. As we get older, are we as good at celebrating the different chapters of our lives as when we were younger?

Are we still able to celebrate our accomplishments? Can we realize that each thing we do — no matter how large or small — is another wonderful chapter in the story of our lives that is worthy of celebration?

Just for Today

*Today is the day to celebrate something small in a very big way!
It doesn't matter what you're celebrating...bake a cake, blow
up some balloons, invite your friends...then sit back and enjoy
whatever it is you have accomplished!*

A Loaf of Bread and a Lily

"When you have two pennies left in the world,
buy a loaf of bread with one, and a lily with the other."
~ Chinese Proverb
Pathways to Recovery, p. 321

This ancient proverb tells us that practicality and beauty can go hand in hand. We often forget this truth when we're struggling, trying our best to make it through each day.

Being practical—taking care of the necessary things in our lives—is vital for us to keep our lives on track, to keep us moving through each day with common sense and consistency.

But how many of us also seek out beauty at the same time? It could be a beautiful flower—a lily—placed in our home that we see each time we walk past. It could be a few minutes spent writing or drawing or creating something. It might be watching an old movie on a lazy Sunday afternoon or cleaning out the extra room that collects all our stuff.

Do the every day things but don't forget the beauty. There's not a better way to spend those two pennies.

Just for Today
It doesn't take a lot to add some beauty to your life. Try dining by candlelight!

The Only One

*"I am the only one who can tell the story of my life and
say what it means"*
~ Dorothy Allison
Pathways to Recovery, p. 376

How do we define our lives? Let's think about this for a few minutes:
If someone asked us who we were and what our life was about, how
would we answer?

Would we answer with definitions given to us by a health provider?
Many of us have some sort of diagnosis for something. Does this
make up all of who we are?

Would we answer with things our friends have said about us? Perhaps
they'd say we're funny or quiet or outgoing. Does this make up all of
who we are?

What really defines us? What are all the things that tell the story of our
lives? Is it something deep inside that guides the way we live—like
being honest, caring for others, wanting to make a difference in the
world, or having a special talent for something? Is it the memories we
have as our lives unfold? Is it the essence of our hearts or the wounds
we have healed?

Our stories are an expression of the very essence of our lives. And
remember, we are the only ones who can tell them!

Just for Today

*Today, why not design the cover of your autobiography? What
will it look like? What colors will you use? How about giving it
a title? It's your life – your story – so only you can create it the
way you want it to be!*

Making Footprints

"It's your body, mind and spirit: Develop a wellness lifestyle.
Don't follow in any footprints; make your own prints.
Because you are the future of tomorrow."
~ Jackie Joyner-Kersee
Pathways to Recovery, p. 174

The path to wellness looks different for everyone. There are no magic, fixed ways to become healthier than we are. Often, it's a road not yet traveled. We can try to learn from others, but ultimately it's up to us to create ourselves, our habits, our patterns of being.

We are amazing creatures and able to build our own lives. We may often feel incapable of becoming who we want to be, but as long as we have that vision, there is possibility. As long as we have a goal and strive toward something, the road will broaden and our lives will become more than they once were.

We can choose the path. We can make our today brighter by challenging ourselves to new experiences, and new ways of being. We can change possibilities into probabilities. We can make our own footprints.

Just for Today

Find your own footprints to wellness! Try to take time each
day for a bit of meditation — even for five minutes. Taking time
to clear your thoughts can help you better center and balance
yourself.

A Different Environment

*"There is electricity about a friendship relationship. We are both more
relaxed and more sensitive, more creative and more casual,
more excited and more serene. It is as though when we come in
contact with our friend we enter into a different environment."*
~ Andrew M. Greeley
Pathways to Recovery, p. 227

Our friendships often provide us with some of the greatest joy we'll
ever experience. Our friends accept us for who we are. They make
us laugh; they challenge us, encourage us and can be brutally honest.
They are there when things fall apart and they're there when we
need to take action. They help us set our dreams higher, they give us
courage to make changes and they allow us to be our true selves when
we're together. Our friendships give us the opportunity to provide
the same for them.

It's no wonder there's a lot of research that supports the value of
friendship. We're happier, our health is better, and there's even
evidence we live longer if we've had good friends. Friendships
add a fabulous dimension to our lives—a different and electric
environment—that leaves us feeling loved and
supported.

Just for Today

*Can you identify someone in your life who you
admire? Why do you admire them? What is
it about them that seems special? Are these
traits or talents that you also possess?
Or are these things that you'd like to
learn to enhance your own life?*

Deep Ruts

"My ruts were so deep they had their own tunnels."
~ Julie Bayes
Pathways to Recovery, p. 27

How often are we hidden by our own routines? Is our lack of taking risks so dark that we can't see around us? These are questions we must ask ourselves constantly. If we don't, we're in danger of losing our perspective.

Routines can be very good for us. They help stabilize our days. But doing the same thing over and over again, without thinking about why and how we're doing it, can be self-defeating.

Only when we take risks can we see ourselves for who we really are. It's like turning on a light and allowing ourselves to experience change. And in that change comes a new way of being that allows us to grow and move past the ruts.

Just for Today
Do something today that will take you out of your ruts. You could shower in the evening instead of the morning or sleep with your head at the foot of your bed. Don't let those ruts grow tunnels!

I Am a Stronger Person

"In my recovery, I have become a stronger person."
~ Catherine Scruggs
Pathways to Recovery, p. 167

Recovery is a journey that focuses on overcoming something with which we've been struggling. Recovery is a process that can take months…years…a lifetime…to reach.

Recovery is a journey that takes us to new places, and as we do this, we realize we're becoming different people. Through recovery, we gain tools that help us be gentler to ourselves, and that help us to find more satisfying ways to live.

Recovery is a journey that teaches us how to let go to forgive, even if we can't forget. Each day that passes brings us the ability to live with gratitude and contentment, even when there are still things we want.

Recovery is taking a journey during which we sometimes have to look back. But when we do, we realize we're no longer the same person we used to be. We have new tools to use. There is joy in the future and we're motivated to keep walking forward. We are more confident and we are stronger.

Just for Today
Recovery pushes you to move forward; feeling stuck can only make you feel miserable. What is it in your life you need to think about in a different way that can help keep you moving forward?

Everything Is Possible

"When nothing is sure, everything is possible."
~ Margaret Drabble
Pathways to Recovery, p. 45

When we were ourselves first diagnosed or if we experience a relapse, our world is turned upside down. We can't see which way is up or in what direction we may be going. Nothing is certain and everything's a risk.

This may seem like a time of uncertainty when, in all actuality, it's a great opportunity, a time for an ending and a new beginning. With that ending we can let go of old habits or ways of being which wasn't really who we were to begin with. We can replace those things with something new, and it's up to us what that will be.

This is a time to reach out to others who have been through the same experience but are now on the road to recovery. In this way, we can begin to see new possibilities, new ways of existing that are healthier than the old ones. We can begin to let go of our past in search of our true selves.

Just for Today
See if you can get to the highest place in your community...like a building or a hill. Sometimes it takes seeing things from a different perspective before you can understand that everything... everything...is possible!

Things to Be Believed

"Some things have to be believed to be seen."
~ Ralph Hodgson
Pathways to Recovery, p. 240

Ever get up in the morning, read the newspaper about some outlandish feat and think, "Well, I'll believe that when I see it!" Don't things have to be seen *first* in order for us to believe them? After all, our eyes don't deceive us. If only we can see the unusual, odd or amazing thing, then — and only then — will we be able to truly believe.

But if we take that view — overlooking the possibilities — then we would have missed out on some of the more amazing inventions and beliefs of our time. Orville and Wilbur Wright believed people could fly before they actually saw themselves accomplish the first flight. Martin Luther King, Jr. proclaimed his belief over sight when he made his famous, "I Have a Dream" speech. His belief in peace and equality shaped his behaviors, even though he lost his life before seeing much of what he fought for actually accomplished.

If we are to make changes in our lives, if we want to create new systems of care, if we hope to get rid of stigma and discrimination against us, then we must first believe these things can happen. We must have a vision and we must have faith. Because when we believe — *truly believe* — we will see.

Just for Today
What do you truly believe? Start today by giving voice to your dream. Write it down. Post it around your home. Let those negative thoughts move right out of your mind and let your faith in!

A Precious Jewel

"Sweet are the uses of adversity, which, like the toad,
ugly and venomous, wears yet a precious jewel in his head."
~ William Shakespeare
Pathways to Recovery, p. 348

Living with mental health issues can be a serious challenge in our everyday lives. Sometimes we may feel that having these symptoms is all our life is about. Our world seems small and unrelated to the rest of society.

It's when we can look at ourselves as survivors, as warriors of our limitations that those challenges become our strengths. Living with adversity has made us stronger, more resilient human beings. It has given us gifts that far exceed our experiences. We have the choice to find the positive in our less than perfect situations and to share those thoughts with others. Ultimately, they become our best allies.

Just for Today

What is it you have learned from your adversities? What are the gifts you have gained from your experiences? What is the precious jewel you hold today?

Birds and Church Bells

"It's not a bad thing [in life] to be serenaded by birds and church bells."
~ Alexandra Stoddard
Pathways to Recovery, p. 195

Our spirituality gives our lives backbone, supporting us when things go wrong, helping us celebrate those things that go well.

As our spirituality grows, we are often drawn to others with like beliefs. For us, knowing others believe in similar things can be a warm welcome from being seen as an outsider in the world. If we can connect with others, then we are not alone. If we can connect with that central part of ourselves called "spirit," we will find strength and the will to go on. And then, we'll look forward to a wonderful serenade. Can you hear it?

Just for Today

How are you using sound to find your spirit and beauty?
Listening to wind chimes, bells or your favorite music is one way to do this.

March

*"March is a tomboy with tousled hair,
a mischievous smile, mud on her shoes
and a laugh in her voice."*

~ Hal Borland

Increasing the Speed

*"There's more to life than
increasing its speed."*
~ Gandhi
Pathways to Recovery p. 314

Living with mental health issues can take a lot away, especially time. Many of us have lost months and years; regaining some of that lost time can be a highly sought after goal. But there is more to life than trying to regain what's been lost.

There's also more to life than always looking ahead, rushing to make up missed opportunities and broken dreams. Speeding ahead only causes us to miss the moment—which is where most of life happens. Increasing our speed to reach goals can cause us to miss important steps in the process, steps that are needed for us to succeed.

In our recovery, it's important to find a pace that works for us. Not too slow or we miss the joy of being challenged. Not too fast or things will become a blur. We need to find our pace, the one that allows us to move forward to reach our hopes and dreams.

Just for Today

What pace is your life going? Is there something you'd rather be doing? Is there something you'd like to give up? Today is as good a time as any to begin setting your own pace.

Pursuing Our Hopes

"We should not let our fears hold us back from pursing our hopes."
~ John F. Kennedy
Pathways to Recovery, p. 305

We all have fears about failure and success. It's part of life to fail at times, but it's also part of life to *fear* success. Why? Because we're creatures of habit and to do something different than we're already doing, to try something new, is scary. And to think of ourselves beyond our current situations, possibly succeeding at something, means we must adjust our point of view.

How many times have we said, "I think I could do that," then told ourselves, "but I wouldn't be very good at it?" In order to counteract our fears, we must be aware of them. If we're aware of our fears, they can be overcome. If we can begin to see they can be overcome, then we can get past them.

Getting over fear isn't easy. But getting to where we are today wasn't easy either, and yet, we did it.

Just for Today

Listen to yourself today. Are you telling yourself there's something you can't do or are you letting your fears – of failure or success – jump in and take over your thoughts? When you have negative thoughts, write them down. Later in the day, look at those and replace them with more positive ones. Seeing how you think and talk can be a powerful way to stop those behaviors!

Don't Block the Blessing

"My fear of change caused me a lot of anguish and heartache
until I learned to accept some simple facts of life:
change is the only constant — the trick is to learn to see it as just another
opportunity to grow, a chance to transform yourself from the person
you are into the person you want to be. When you fear it, you fight it.
And when you fight it, you block the blessing."
~ Patti Labelle
Pathways to Recovery, p. 330

Every one of us has experienced change that we weren't prepared for — life just happens. There are so many things in which we have little, if any, control. Yet we fight these experiences. We blame. We feel angry and lost. We tell ourselves that we must have done something to cause these hurts.

But while we're focusing on feeling bad, why not take the same amount of energy and use it to find the blessings in our experiences? We'll never be able to change what has happened in our lives — no one can. But we do have all the power in the world to look at our lives and recognize what these experiences have taught us, what they have given us and what these experiences mean in our lives. We alone have the power to transform ourselves — to mold and define our lives in a way that gives us greater meaning and purpose. What a blessing that can be!

Just for Today

If you find yourself having a hard day, you don't have to continue down that path. Stop whatever you're doing and simply start your day over...even if you have to do it several times! You don't want to block the blessing that might be headed your way!

Dearest to the Heart

"Peace can…be reached through concentration upon that which is dearest to the heart."
~ Patanjali
Pathways to Recovery, p. 355

That which is dearest to the heart…how often do we really pause to figure out what matters to us? Do we take time to identify what our passions look like? Could we tell someone what our values are if they asked us?

It's pretty easy to get caught in the trap of just moving through each day. Our lives can pretty quickly become routine. It's at that point that we get bored or discouraged or just plain unhappy. Peace—that sense of calm or serenity—gets pushed aside.

Taking time—through study, meditation, prayer or conversations with others—can get us started. Through finding—and trusting—that which is dear to our heart, we can find the way to a more beautiful—and peaceful—life journey.

Just for Today

Peace can elude you very easily, especially when you get caught up in all the daily things you feel need to be done. What is it that gives you peace? You might try going to a place with a fountain or a waterfall. Listening to water flow is often soothing, beautiful and peaceful.

The Result of What We Think

"All that we are is the result of what we have thought.
The mind is everything. What we think, we become."
~Gautama Buddha
Pathways to Recovery, p. 108

Are we really the result of what we think? Try this.

When we think about something we enjoy, something that makes us really happy, something that we look forward to doing, how does that feel? Usually these things make us feel relaxed, self confident and joyful. We smile. We feel good as we experience happy memories.

But what about the not-so-great moments? It could be a time when we felt embarrassed, angry or sad. As we think about those times, how does that make us feel? Do we tense up and feel a knot in our stomachs? Do we feel frustrated and hurt? Do things from the past start surfacing that we don't like to think about? Most likely, all of these things happen.

Thinking better thoughts really does make a difference in the quality of our lives. We all carry negative stuff from our pasts, and while there's not much we can do to change what was, we can take control of the future by thinking about things that give us life!

Just for Today

Look in a mirror. Start to say the things to yourself that you wish you could hear from others, not what you expect someone to say. You can begin to take more control of your future by thinking – and saying – better thoughts!

The Secret of Discipline

"The secret of discipline is motivation. When a man is sufficiently motivated, discipline will take care of itself."
~ Alexander Paterson
Pathways to Recovery, p. 59

We sometimes find ourselves without discipline, letting our lives drift at will. At those times, motivation seems like a fleeting idea, not something we can find. But however fleeting, each of us has motivation within us. We must tap into it to make it a part of our lives.

Motivation can be found through others, listening to their stories of how they found the will to go on. Often the stories of others will inspire in us the will to do things of which we are already capable. There are things that we have asleep within us that just need to be sparked.

We can also find motivation from within. We can do an inventory of our dreams, our hopes and aspirations, no matter how distant they may seem. In this discovery, we can find the energy to get going. We can begin to take the small steps toward recovery. It's in those small steps that we gain motivation which moves us to accomplish our dreams.

Just for Today

It's your choice to live your life as though it's a full glass in front of you. Take one of your challenges and see if you can solve it by using a positive attitude. It might help to make a list of the possible actions that you can take to move forward. You might even find yourself motivated to actually do some of them!

The Longest Journey

"The longest journey is the journey inward."
~ Dag Hammarskjöld
Pathways to Recovery, p. 198

The journey of recovery can be a long one.

How do we make sense of our lives since we've been impacted by our mental health? How do we reframe relapse, or stop all the negative messages we give ourselves? How do we let go of self-stigma or the fear of success? Can we really live the life that we want? Yes, yes, yes!

We must be willing to dig deep within ourselves to realize that the longest journey in recovery is the distance from our head to our heart.

Some people do this by exploring their creativity. Others find solace in seeking more spirituality. Many of us find meaning by giving to others or trying to change broken systems to enhance our communities.

The journey from head to heart is indeed long. Learning about recovery is one thing; but it's in *living* recovery that we find peace.

Just for Today
Try this. When you face a difficult decision, put your hand on your heart. Can you tell how your heart feels? Remember, your heart decisions are the ones that usually bring you the most peace.

Be Brave

"Let me follow a path that will allow me to demonstrate
I am a survivor of life's most difficult journey."
~ Kathy Shinn
Pathways to Recovery, p. 38

This journey of recovery we're on isn't always easy, but we can do it if we just remember to be brave.

Be brave. Remember what matters. Forget the messages that restrict us.

Be brave. Do something we don't want to do. Face something we don't want to face. Claim the losses that are ours, but then let them go.

Be brave. Say something kind to a perfect stranger. Try something new that we thought we never would.

Be brave. We can do it by ourselves, even though we'd rather do it with someone who is no longer in our reach.

Be brave. Take a risk because it might make a difference. Don't let fear rob the future.

Be brave. Life is sometimes mean—embrace what it hands us, and learn what we can. Reclaim a lost wish. Have the conversation that might scare us, for it might mean making something better.

Be brave. Look for love if we want to. Express love when we have it.

Be brave. Face your journey without a detectable moment of defeatism.

Be brave.

Just for Today
About what do you need to "be brave" today? Go ahead...you can do it!

Our Behavior Affects Others

"I realized I couldn't stay deeply depressed and couldn't continue to harm [myself] because I was part of a family…Thinking about how my behavior affected my family got me onto a path of recovery and keeps me focused on improving my life and mental health."
~Anonymous
Pathways to Recovery, p. 67

Struggling with our health issues can be a full-time job. We feel victimized by our symptoms. We deal with medication side effects. We face losses that many others don't.

There are many of us who say the thing that finally pulled us into a different way of living with our mental health issues was when we realized we could still affect the lives of others in a positive way. Some of us realized being well was better for our families. For others, it means we found a passion in life—like helping at an animal shelter, volunteering with children, doing art or helping others through a rough spot.

We've can try to be at our best in order to do these things well.   We can recognize how much better we feel each day when we don't give in to our symptoms, but more forward in hope.   Each day we can continue on our journeys of recovery and recognize how different it will feel to be part of something more.

Just for Today

Have you ever volunteered for something? When you find what you feel passionate about, you naturally want to get involved…and volunteering is a great way to do that. It's hard to give of yourself without seeing how your caring is helping others! Make a call today and lend a hand!

If We Listen

"No one on earth can do what you alone are called to do,
can give to the world what you alone were sent to give through your
authentic gifts. The call may be so faint you can barely make out
the message, but if you listen, you will hear it."
~ Sarah Bon Breathnach
Pathways to Recovery, p. 67

So often we think we have no purpose, or we find ourselves always searching for the meaning in our lives. However, when we listen to our hearts and to the people who care for us, we can learn our truth.

No one has the same exact gift as another, that's why they're true gifts. They come from the universe, from our spiritual beliefs, from our culture and from our ancestors. We listen. We hear the message.

We are each called to do what only we can do in the world. We are each a part of the puzzle of life, offering what only we can. We can believe in and enjoy our path and our purpose; it's part of our recovery.

We each follow our own path in recovery, we all hear a different drummer and we all have a distinct dream. Listening to that drummer, walking that path and living that dream defines who we are. We just have to listen to our own wisdom.

Just for Today

Ask yourself today, "What do I really need?" Is that enough for you?
Can you listen and hear the message?

Risky Business

"Any life truly lived is a risky business, and if one puts up too many fences against the risks one ends by shutting out life itself."
~ Kenneth S. Davis
Pathways to Recovery, p. 40

It takes courage to live our lives to the fullest. After having painful experiences, taking risks seems out of the question. Even so, we take risks every day — getting up in the morning, taking a shower, going for a walk — all these involve risk.

It's the bigger risks — getting a job, starting a relationship, buying a house — that really stump us. We have been taught early on that it can hurt badly to take big risks. To love, to hope, to dream, is simply scary. But if we don't take those risks, what does life really come down to? Existing? What about thriving? What about trying to enjoy life and experiencing it to its fullest?

We deserve these things. We have worked so hard to get to where we are. What could be more rewarding than knowing we will live our lives to the fullest? It's our choice to take down the fences and let life in.

Just for Today

Create an adventure today...a really big adventure! Yes, risks can be tricky but you deserve to let the fences down. What is it that you've always wanted to do? Go on a cruise? Climb the highest mountain? Get a full-time job? Find a partner? Make a commitment today to a big adventure and let life flow in!

New and Lasting Strengths

"There are the stories that never, never die,
that are carried like seed into a new country,
are told to you and me and make in us new and lasting strengths."
~ Meridel LeSuer
Pathways to Recovery, p. 381

A woman told stories to her young granddaughter from the time she was old enough to listen. Despite only having an 8th grade education, the grandmother was wise, playful, ornery and humorous. Her stories were wildly creative.

She began to record her family history so that the stories would live on.

At age 99, the grandmother died. Now the granddaughter is the teller, passing on the stories and memories of her wise grandmother—like seed into a new country—to relatives and friends. She continues to write and speak and tell the stories she has collected throughout the years. She feels pride, strength and mastery when connecting to others through storytelling. Her grandmother gave her a gift that would live on.

We all need to know the story of our lives. It gives us a place in the world—one that gives us great strength in our recovery that will never, ever die.

Just for Today

Telling your story can be a very healing activity. Your struggles have, no doubt, been difficult, but in getting through the challenges, you have gained strength and resiliency. Today, spend time thinking about—and planning—how you'd like to share your story. What parts are important? What have you learned? Where or with whom could you

A Series of Small Things

*"Great things are not done by impulse
but by a series of small things brought together."*
~ Vincent Van Gogh
Pathways to Recovery, p. 277

Recovery rarely happens because we wake up one day and decide we're now on a new journey. Chances are, there's been a series of small things done to help realize a different perspective. New risks have been taken. We recognize ourselves in the story of our role model and we get involved with our peers to do some community advocacy. Each individual act combines with the next one to show us a new way of living.

Have you ever thought about hiking the Grand Canyon? This walk is quite literally one step at a time—all the way down and all the way back up. It's not the kind of trip you can just start without a plan.

You must do some exploring and questioning of those who have gone before. As a hiker, a firm foundation—like a good pair of hiking boots—is a must so as to avoid injury. You have to decide how to keep your load light yet still have the right equipment. You've got to carry your own weight, being prepared for anything. Joining with others to make the hike definitely makes the trip easier, as well as more enjoyable.

Before you know it, you've made the climb down and back—a great and memorable thing indeed!

Just for Today
You don't have to know all the facts about how to do something. Learning too much can distract you, bring on your fears and keep you from moving. Get the knowledge you need to feel safe but move a little... step-by-step. Great things will find you!

Just Celebrate!

"Celebrate anything you want. Celebrate the start of something, the end of something. Dance and sing, give speeches, take pictures, finger-paint…squeeze your own lemonade and bake a pie.
Celebrate early, celebrate late, and celebrate often. Celebrate."
~ Rachel Snyder
Pathways to Recovery, p. 333

We don't often think about life as a celebration. For so long, we've looked at life as a constant challenge, a reason to worry. But it's never too late to get started. If we start today by celebrating the little things — such as the sunrise, a smile from a stranger or a passing away of something we didn't enjoy — we can literally change our lives.

Celebrating can be as simple as eating our favorite food, talking to a friend or taking a ride on the night bus. It doesn't have to be elaborate, just fulfilling. Celebration is a good way to put one foot forward as we begin recognizing the things for which we can be grateful.

Just for Today
Celebrate today! Invite a friend to join you for a spontaneous meal… just because! It's the little things each day that give you the most comfort, not just the big moments. Thank yourself for a job well done!

Mystery and Wonder

*"If your heart is pulling you in a direction that has mystery
and wonder, trust it and follow it."*
~ David Wilcox
Pathways to Recovery, p. 341

To trust one's heart requires a mix of courage, a willingness to accept change and more than a little bit of faith in oneself. Often fear creeps in, and uncertainty flutters: "Surely this idea I'm having isn't a good one! What am I thinking?" Our thoughts race into us and tell us to stop. But should we?

When we begin to trust that which is in our own heart, we take a giant step forward in our journey of recovery. We can start by taking a chance with the simple things, getting our feet wet, feeling connected to what we believe. As we trust these small things—and take the risks—it becomes easier to make more life-changing decisions. And when we do—when we accept and trust the mystery and wonder presented to us—life as we once knew it changes.

Just for Today...

Is your heart pulling you in the direction of mystery and wonder? How do you know you can trust what your heart is saying?

Turn Back

"No matter how far you have gone on the wrong road, turn back."
~ Turkish Proverb
Pathways to Recovery, p. 13

We are resilient, strong people. We have survived many things in our lives that we were told weren't survivable—distressing symptoms, trauma, self-stigma and discrimination.

So many of the roads we have traveled led to more discontent, but it's never too late to turn toward the road to discovery.

Recovery is not a short street, but a long road, taking us in many directions, challenging us in various ways. We each travel that road with our own unique steps, defining for ourselves a life worth living. It's never too late to turn back and change the road we're on.

Just for Today

Make a list of your thoughts about not doing something you wish you could — perhaps you've been on the wrong road. Beside each thought, put a 1 for "I can do this now," and put a 2 for "I might not be able to do this now, but someday I will." Remember, you can always turn back!

Embrace Your Creativity

*"Being creative is seeing the same thing as everybody else
but thinking of something different."*
~ Albert Szent-Gyorgi
Pathways to Recovery, p. 340

Creativity is a wonderful thing. We all possess a measure of it, even those of us who say, "I'm not at all creative."

We all have special gifts and talents for doing things in ways that no one else can: dressing in original ways, being artistic, building things, cooking, finding ways to help someone else. The list goes on and on. These all are creative ways of living.

Recovery offers a special opportunity to be creative.

Many of us have had experiences that have hurt our self-esteem. We may feel like we're not good at anything. We may struggle at times, believing that we don't have the inner tools to recover. Because of that, relapse may feel like an option.

Take courage! We can recover! We can recover because we are creative! This means we can rethink our lives—pushing away any negativity—until we think of something different for our recovery.

Just for Today

Spend your day asking lots of questions, even though some of them might seem silly. Questioning things gets your creativity going and can lead you to take more action in your recovery!

A More Complete Wellness

*"We live in our minds so much of the time
that we have almost forgotten our bodies."*
~ Ray Kybartas
Pathways to Recovery, p. 172

When we see our life as a struggle, we can spend too much time analyzing, thinking about, dissecting and evaluating what's going on in our minds.

Physical illness can be a symptom of mental health concerns and vice versa. Because of this connection, people searching for mental wellness must always be aware of how their body feels as well.

To be effective, we must be able to separate our physical symptoms from our mental ones. We must listen again to our inner voice, the one telling us about our body. It's a matter of simply sitting down in a chair, clearing the mind and then listening to our body—to the information it's trying to tell us. It will strengthen our recovery and promote more complete wellness.

Just for Today

Make a line down the middle of a piece of paper. Label one side "mind" and the other "body." List any symptoms you experience in one of the columns. Listen to your entire body and be clear about your symptoms and how they impact your life. Take the list with you when you visit your doctor. Help him/her better understand how the two are different, the same or if they overlap.

Our Mission in the World

"Being a witness is my mission in the world,
and this is what I do when I tell stories."
~ Isabelle Allende
Pathways to Recovery, p. 382

We all have a calling in life. For some of us, it's to work behind the scenes, making our contribution to the world. For others, it's to lead and be seen. But some of us — *if we can tell our stories* — find ourselves contributing a great deal to society.

So often people aren't knowledgeable about mental health issues and how they affect us. They don't understand our lives are no different than anyone else's; it's an arduous journey, but we can recover.

This message is important to share with others, to allow them the privilege of hearing from us what our life is like and to give them an understanding so they can be empathetic with other people in their lives.

In telling our stories, we become more whole and more content with where we've been. In telling our stories, we find our mission in the world.

Just for Today
Write down your significant life moments — good or bad. What do you see? Is there someone you need to share your story with so they may better understand you? You have been a witness to your own life and your story is important!

Getting Our Feet Back

"Help me if you can; I'm feeling down, and I do appreciate you being
'round. Help me get my feet back on the ground. Won't you please,
please help me?"
~ John Lennon & Paul McCartney
Pathways to Recovery, p. 230

Recognize the lyrics above as one of the Beattle's famous songs, "Help"? It's become a classic that brings back memories for many who hear it.

It's hard to read the lyrics of a favorite song and not start to feel a bit like singing…or a lot like singing…or maybe to burst right out in song, right where we are! Music is a special tool. It's next to impossible to hear a favorite song and not do something…like tap your foot, hum, smile, sing, snap your fingers, drum on the table, pick up an instrument and play along.

That's what it's all about—this thing called recovery. It's about moving—however we can—forward, to the side, in a circle, hopping up and down, stepping back a bit to see what comes next. It's like dancing to a favorite song. It doesn't need to look smooth; we don't need to win a prize for our moves! We simply respond with intention.

Once we're moving on the recovery dance floor, it feels so good we don't want to stop! Sometimes we might stumble, uncertain of what to do next. That's when we can ask for help—even from a favorite song.

Just for Today

Take a few minutes today to dance! Put on some music and move.
Don't worry how you do it or what you look like…just dance and see
how good you feel!

Looking Fear in the Face

*"You gain strength, courage and confidence by every experience
in which you really stop to look fear in the face.
You must do the thing which you think you cannot do."*
~ *Eleanor Roosevelt*
Pathways to Recovery, p. 18

Every day in recovery, we face fear head on. Recovery takes strength,
courage and the confidence in yourself that you can get up every
morning and live your true purpose rather than giving in to illness
or symptoms.

Fear is a distressing emotion, but we can become skillful in controlling
our "imagined" fears by looking those ideas "in the face." We can
change our response to fear, to those times that torment and immobilize
us—because those thoughts are simply in our heads. Whatever the
fear might be, we can challenge it.

Real danger happens in real time, in the moment. It's not something
we can reflect on beforehand; it's something we must be courageous
against as it happens. It's up to us to let go of imagined danger. We
can discover a life of strength and peace. We can do the thing which
we think we cannot do.

Just for Today

*Do something wild today, something you've never done before! Use hot
sauce instead of mild or take the long way to get somewhere. You can do
it; look your fear in the face and grab on to your courage!*

Relying On Ourselves

"Our remedies oft in ourselves do lie."
~William Shakespeare
Pathways to Recovery, p. 306

We are in charge of our own dreams and desires!

Ask 100 people what we should do with our lives and we're likely to get 100 different answers. It's ultimately up to us to decide these things.

We can travel the world looking for advice on what we should do to live a good life, how to reach recovery or how to find happiness. We'll eventually end up back home again, filled with new memories and new wisdom, but we still come home to ourselves.

Lots of us have spent time with a therapist — asking questions, seeking advice and getting support on our journeys. We learn new things and set goals for our lives. But it's up to us to make real changes.

Asking for support from others is a good thing…but we need to remember the real answers for our lives will eventually come from within ourselves. We have to have faith and believe we have those answers. Because we do.

Just for Today

Being able to recognize your feelings is often the first step toward change. Trust yourself today and what you're experiencing. You've got all the answers you need within you!

See the Funny Side

*"Seeing the humor in difficult situations really helps me heal.
It helps me see that I have at least one strength – the ability
to see the funny side of what could be seen as the end of the world."
~ Amy Stiefvater
Pathways to Recovery, p. 366*

How simple it can be to laugh!

Many of us spend our days going through the hard stuff—pressure from work, stress at home, not enough money at the end of the month, locking our keys in the car. You name it, we can probably find a way to concentrate on life's struggle.

But laughter—and finding humor in situations—can actually lift us up to give us a whole new perspective on the difficult moments in life.

Humor helps break old patterns to see our experiences more lightheartedly. Laughing helps reduce stress, boosts our immune system and makes it easier to fight off illness.

So next time the hard stuff hits, laugh. Laugh more and laugh harder. See how finding humor—especially when life seems too tough—can simply make things easier.

Just for Today

Look for a little help today to lighten your mood. Maybe it's a favorite movie or special music. Keep it handy for the next time you need a lift!

Becoming So

"If you constantly think of illness, you eventually become ill;
if you believe yourself to be beautiful, you become so."
~Shakti Gawain
Pathways to Recovery, p. 75

Ever have one of those days when you wake up, see it's a beautiful morning and decide to skip whatever responsibilities have been set for the day? You've been working hard, so it's time to take a break.

When someone decides to call in sick, they've probably been up for awhile before work or whatever they have to do. So they begin to develop what they're going to say, how they will sound, how serious their 'illness' is or if they will see a doctor.

All of this thought and planning goes on for maybe an hour until we know someone is finally there to call. Raspy voiced, coughing feebly, we carry on about how we've been ill all night. We've done brilliantly, getting many "get well's" from the individuals we've called.

It's rather amazing, though, that when we hang up the phone, our throat starts to hurt. We begin to wonder if we're feverish and, instead of feeling excited about having a *play* day, we crawl back under the covers.

This is the power of our minds. We can use it to remain ill—or we can believe in ourselves and our beauty. Which will it be?

Just for Today

Ever find yourself having a bad day? Try taking a bath or shower when you get home. Watch the day go down the drain!

Our True Colors

"Vocation…would include finding out the place where
the need of the world coincides with our own gifts,
where that which you can give is joyfully received."
~ James Carroll
Pathways to Recovery, p. 151

We often are led to believe that our value lies in fitting into what the world needs from us. We take on roles—child, student, friend, employee, parent and so many others—along our particular life's journey.

Going through recovery is really a lot about "discovery." It's about discovering our true colors—focusing on things about us that make us feel good inside, instead of focusing on what's wrong with us.

Getting to this place of discovery requires a lot of exploring. We get to try new things out—such as a hobby, food, relationships, jobs, places to live and lot's of other things, as we discover who we are. When we get to the place where we're living our lives while doing what we enjoy—and what we're good at—we automatically start giving our gifts to the world. We not only feel joyful doing this, but also we

Just for Today
Are you listening to your own true voice today? What is it telling you? Try to identify a couple of your "true colors" and then share them with someone else.

…true colors…

It Takes a Lifetime

"It takes only a minute to get a crush on someone,
an hour to like someone, and a day to love someone,
but it takes a lifetime to forget someone."
~ Unknown
Pathways to Recovery, p. 230

Exploring new relationships can be very exciting *and* very frightening, all at the same time. We know in the past we have made mistakes in relationships, and those mistakes led to loss. It's that loss which leads to our feelings of not being worthwhile, or of being hopeless. So we think to ourselves, "Why would we go there?"

We go there to find ourselves. We make friendships to learn about ourselves and to learn about others. We can't grow without relationships.

But we can make a difference to others in our relationships. No past mistake is large enough to keep us from reaching out, testing the waters again. It's only human to give and receive from those around us. After all, don't our memories of people help make us better than who we were?

Just for Today

Is there someone in your life with whom you need to say you're sorry?
The person you choose isn't as important as your ability to forgive
them. When you learn how to forgive, you open up the opportunity for
healing.

Replenishing the Soul

"In the darkest hour the soul is replenished
and given strength to continue and endure."
~ Heart Warrior Chosa
Pathways to Recovery, p. 6

Without a doubt, we have all experienced our own "darkest hours." These times of despair may have come in various forms—ongoing depression, trauma, devastating losses, troubling symptoms or relapse, changes in relationships or the need to alter our life plans.

But our greatest opportunities for learning and growth also come in that darkest hour. Think about it. Because of depression, we learn how to experience the beauty of each day. Were it not for the experience of trauma or loss—as devastating and painful as it may be—our compassion for others might not be as strong. If it weren't for our symptoms or periods of relapse, we might never learn how to dig deep inside ourselves to find our wellness. And face it, we've all had to "blow up" relationships and alter our lives in ways we never imagined.

All the "darkest hour" experiences of our lives stand as testaments to our strength and resilience. While these times challenge us, test us and run us down, they also leave us with so much more—the ability to continue on our journey with hope, compassion and a true sense of purpose.

Just for Today

Remind yourself today that you are doing the best you can! Nobody gets through life without a few "dark hours." Stop blaming yourself and see your soul refreshed!

What No One Can Take Away

"The most marvelous mentor in my life was my Dad. He always told me that education was the one thing no one could ever take away from me."
~ JoAnn Howley
Pathways to Recovery, p. 137

The knowledge that we each possess is ours alone.

We learn something new each day. We read, watch TV, use the Internet, listen to radio, talk to our elders or go to a crafts class, a technical school or university. There are as many ways to learn as there are students to study.

In recovery, knowledge is power. Being masterful at something that is solely yours—and cannot be taken away from you—is a way of feeling whole, of being connected with your inner self. It's a way of expressing and enjoying your true purpose.

Education—whether formal like attending a class or informal learning on our own—is one way to help ourselves. We can learn who we are, what we know, how we know it, where we will share it and often, why we're the ones who have chosen it.

Throughout our recovery, our knowledge helps us stay well. We must always be learning to keep our minds focused, our bodies healthy and our lives balanced.

Just for Today
What have you always wanted to learn? There are probably free classes in your community that you could take. Check it out!

Living Life Twice

"To write about one's life is to live it twice, and the second living is both spiritual and historical, for a memoir reaches deep within the personality as it seeks its narrative form."
~ *Patricia Hampl*
Pathways to Recovery, p. 391

You may be thinking…there's no way to live life twice. Aren't we sort of stuck here in the present, headed into the future?

Telling our stories is a way to go into the past to relive what we've experienced. There will be happy things we remember. There will be sad things, traumatic things and things with little emotion at all. We've probably even forgotten things about our lives, and there are other things we'd like to forget. But no matter what, our pasts are valuable because we've lived them, and we have important life stories to tell.

For some of us, the past will bring up unpleasant things. But we are *not* those things, nor do they have control over us anymore. For some of us, the past might be too unpleasant to think about. That's perfectly okay—because we have many more stories ahead just waiting to be lived.

Just for Today
As you look at sharing your recovery story, don't look back with regret but rather look to see what you have learned. Remember to be gentle with yourself!

The Eye Begins to See

"In a dark time, the eye begins to see."
~ Theodore Roethke
Pathways to Recovery, p. 194

As we face our challenges head on, it's easy to lose our way as the darkness forces us to lose our footing. It seems like we've fallen off the path, losing control of our very own lives.

The symptoms and repercussions we have can make us feel hopeless. Dark times fill our nights and seep into the daytime, making everything seem cold, scary and lonely. Trying to find the light—the purpose and joy in living—might feel impossible when our bodies, souls and minds are bogged down with the darkness of despair.

But nature is amazing. If we watch, we'll see the sun always returns to replace nighttime darkness with light. Sometimes the day is cloudy—but there's still light. Sometimes the day is stormy—but there's still light. Sometimes the night grows long and the time for daylight is short. Nonetheless, the sun always returns.

When we experience darkness on our journey, we can hope for the light, knowing it will come. When that darkness makes us stumble and fall—causing us to lose our way a bit—we can ask for help from others, from our spirituality, from ourselves.

Then what? We'll begin to see the light again.

Just for Today

Take a walk and enjoy the sunlight! Breath in, taking in everything that's around you. Look for things you haven't seen before because you've been too busy or are moving too fast.

The Best Bet

"The best bet is to bet on yourself."
~ Arnold Glasow
Pathways to Recovery, p. 100

Why give our lives over to our family, our medical providers, our neighbors or friends? As much as any of these people may care about us, or feel they are doing things in our best interest, we're really the experts on ourselves. We're the ones who know who we really are, what we want for our lives, where we'd like to go and how we think we could get there.

Betting on ourselves is really the only way to get what we want. Developing greater self-responsibility enhances our confidence and gives us the inner power to set, and complete, goals we may have for our lives.

Betting on ourselves requires us to figure out what our strengths are and how we can best use them to make our lives better.

Betting on ourselves also means we have no one to blame when things don't work out as we wish. It also means, however, that we can celebrate our accomplishments with joy and delight. After all, we've got ourselves — and that will always be enough.

Just for Today

Try to trade roles with someone today, even for a few minutes. Being able to see how someone else lives can give you a boost as you work to "bet on yourself!"

April

*"April hath put
a spirit of youth in everything."*
~ *William Shakespeare*

Things that Don't Work Out

"I have grown from my problems and challenges.
From the things that don't work out, that's when I've really learned."
~ Carol Burnett
Pathways to Recovery, p. 289

Bracing, stepping out and being touched
By our fears, our heartaches,
By our anger, by our instinct to survive,
We live.

Learning, taking the chance
Whatever comes our way, we are courageous.
We are miners in a field of solid gold.
We grow.

Complaining, we go through life
Until we see that it is how it should be;
it is for the best.
We become.

Just for Today

Maybe things don't always work out the way you want them to. But what is it you'd really like to see? Try decorating a window in your home with pictures of what you'd like to see happen in your life. Remember, you can live, grow and become who you want to be!

Love Made Visible

"Work is love made visible."
~ Kahlil Gibran
Pathways to Recovery, p. 155

Is it possible to see love? If we could see love, what would it look like?

Love is hard for some of us. We might have had experiences with love that negatively impacted our lives. We might feel like we can no longer love—or that we are no longer lovable.

Part of walking the path of recovery is giving a little bit of ourselves to others—with boundaries that we learn—so we can have full lives, with real relationships, so we can give and experience that wonderful thing called love. Part of walking the path of recovery is trusting others, and letting them into our lives for as much as we are comfortable.

We can work to make love more visible in our lives, no matter how much we've been hurt by it. If we try little things—like smiling at someone in the store, calling a friend to see how he is doing, volunteering at a pet shelter, or sending a card to someone for a special occasion—we can begin to let love enter our lives. We can begin to extend love to others and make it visible.

Just for Today
Try to do something today that will make someone's life easier. It's a great way to let your love be more visible!

Anticipate the Good

"Anticipate the good so that you may enjoy it."
~ Ethiopian Proverb
Pathways to Recovery, p. 308

Anticipate the good? How do we do that?

Too often, we make excuses for having a bad attitude. "But I have a horrible illness...I don't have a job...My family doesn't believe in me...I have to take these medications. How in the world am I supposed to find the good in any of these? How am I supposed to enjoy my life when I have all these things that hold me back?"

But we *can* find the good in our lives. Many of us have found a strong resiliency and power in the face of our experiences. As we look for work, we find we can volunteer or go to school to further develop a passion we might have. Family a struggle? Remember, we don't choose our kin but we can create a family of our own that does support us. And medications may help us past the difficulties until we can find other wellness tools that relieve our symptoms.

We can spend too much time worrying and blaming and anticipating the bad in life. If we're going to spend time and energy on those things, doesn't it make sense to anticipate good things? We might just find we enjoy it!

Just for Today
Ever get frustrated when you miss doing some of the daily things that are important and make your life better? Try to pair those tasks with something you might not forget. For example, keep your dental floss by your remote control. Once those tasks become routine, you'll have more time to take on some of the good things!

A Better Understanding

"Self-knowledge is the beginning of self-improvement."
~ Spanish Proverb
Pathways to Recovery, p. 79

We may live each day with emotions that cause us more harm than good. Feelings of sadness, anger, grief or fear are reflected in how we interact with the rest of the world. When asked how we are doing and we reply, "okay," it isn't the same as being happy. Okay is better than bad, but it doesn't sit with us the same way as contentment can when it fills us up.

Satisfaction is a wonderful feeling and, in life, the motivating power in what we experience is emotion. It's easy to see how this works when we watch other people. What they complain about or what they praise is pretty much a reflection of their lives.

This is true for each of us as well. We need to listen, to hear and spend time paying attention to what we choose to complain about and what we praise. In doing so, we have an opportunity to discover the feelings that fuel what happens to us. This is the first step in changing our perspective, improving our thoughts and ultimately, what happens when we interact with others.

Just for Today

One thing to be aware of when you interact with others is your own posture. How you carry yourself and the body language you have lets others see how you feel about yourself and ultimately, how they will see you!

Don't Become Normal

*"The task is not to become normal. The task is to take up your journey
of recovery and to become who you are called to be."
~ Patricia E. Deegan
Pathways to Recovery, p. 65*

Our journey of recovery is part of who we are called to be. We were
given these challenges to rise to the occasion, to decide that we will be
who we're meant to be—regardless of illness or wellness.

Being *normal* is different for each person. There are varying states of
normalcy depending on our identity, our culture, our education, our
traditions and the place we live. "Normal," someone once said, "is a
cycle on a washing machine, not a state of being."

We each find our own sense of who we are by continuing to follow our
own heartbeat. Becoming who we want to be and what our authentic
gifts call us to be—that's our task of recovery.

Just for Today
*At some point today, take a few minutes to do whatever it is you feel like
doing – as long as it isn't hurtful. Take up your journey of recovery!*

When the Tide Will Turn

"Never give up, for that is just the place and time that the tide will turn."
~ Harriet Beecher Stowe
Pathways to Recovery, p. 286

There's something amazingly comforting about having the sunrise after a long, dark night. Depression, anxiety, fear, loneliness, the urge to engage in an addictive behavior—these are some of the things that can happen during the night when most people are resting and dreaming. Yet they are things that leave us wide-awake and miserable.

We might think over and over—"Will I get through this? Will this night ever end? Will the sun ever get here?" And then it does— because it always does. This miraculous thing called the sun—it rises in the east and wakes up the world. It shines in the sky and brightens the day, and it can turn its rays to shine in our eyes and brighten our souls. It leaves at the end of the day to give us rest.

Nature is amazing like that—the sun, the moon, the stars, the seasons—they always return, giving us something familiar. We can hold onto their steadiness when we feel ready to fall. Giving up—no matter how hard things might feel—is not an option when we can look forward to the rising sun and the beauty of each day.

Just for Today

Sometimes we miss the things that may help us change our lives. Take ten minutes today to sit in silence. Be still and listen to all that is around you. What are you missing that might help you turn the tide?

Dream Lofty Dreams

"Dream lofty dreams, and as you dream, so shall you become.
Your vision is the promise of what you shall at last unveil."
~ John Ruskin
Pathways to Recovery, p. 106

Stained-glass windows are beautiful when the light shows through them and we can see the patterns and fusion of the glass shining outward.

Dreams are like light. They direct us and give us hope. To have a vision of something we want is like putting the sun behind our window, letting it cast the many colors of our experiences into the air around us, revealing who we are.

How can we take our vision, letting the light shine through? By deciding today what we want our life to look like tomorrow. We let our light shine by embracing our vision as we begin to have control over what we do and what we dream.

Just for Today

Create a "dream board" today. Find pictures or objects that represent your dream. Combine those things in one place — like on a poster board or a small table. When you see them, you'll be reminded how your dream looks. If you can see it, you can do it!

Resistance to Fear

"Courage is resistance to fear,
mastery of fear — not absence of fear."
~ Mark Twain
Pathways to Recovery, p. 260

Fear? What is fear but facing the unknown? Trying something we've never done before? What is fear but the pounding of our hearts when we put on a new persona and face a new drummer?

Courage can only come when we fear something. It's in fear that we find our strength and find ourselves in new places, taking new risks.

Seeking a life we rightfully deserve...now *that* takes courage. Looking fear in the face and deciding we can deal with it—even with all its ugly realities—is courage on top of a stick, ready to be pointed at any endeavor.

We can master our fears. We can find within us the strength we need to live courageously.

Just for Today

Try to identify five times in your life when you felt the most fear. In what ways were you courageous? What strengths did you use? Remember, the courage and strengths you had then are still with you now!

Still Going

"Standing is still going."
~ Swahili Proverb
Pathways, p. 331

Some days are nothing more than a struggle. Maybe water from the broken pipes flooded the kitchen or we tasted the sour milk only when we took the first sip of coffee. Maybe we haven't felt good, or things haven't gone the way we planned. Perhaps we were late for the bus, or the umbrella we thought we had for the downpour was nowhere to be found. Maybe we burned dinner or spent more money at the grocery than we had in the bank.

Nevertheless, at the end of the day, we are still standing! At the end of the week, we are still standing! Throughout the struggle, we find we can continue to stand.

And standing? That is all that truly matters.

Just for Today

Sometimes it's important to stop for a while. Maybe it's a good day for a long afternoon nap. Get some rest and prepare to start again...standing!

A Hearty Meal of Chili

"Everyone uses visioning without even thinking about it. If you go grocery shopping, you are using visioning techniques to buy the foods you buy. If you buy tomato sauce, kidney beans, hamburger, onions and peppers, you probably are envisioning a hearty meal of chili."
~ Chris Shore
Pathways to Recovery, p. 105

Imagine a recipe for wellness and recovery. What are the ingredients?

- Working to have happy, positive thoughts
- Taking time for ourselves
- Setting goals and checking them often so we stay on track
- Getting enough rest
- Taking any medications as prescribed and with our consent
- Having a list of people to call if we need support
- Keeping a gratitude journal, recalling to be thankful each day
- Spending time practicing our personal spiritual or religious beliefs
- Asking for support when we need it
- Spending time as often as possible doing things we enjoy
- Knowing we are more than a "diagnosis"
- Spending time with others
- Taking care of our "whole" selves—mind, body and spirit

What items will help make our recipe taste good? What ingredients will we need to begin envisioning ourselves at our best?

Just for Today
Pick one of the ingredients above as your goal for the day. Is there one you're needing to do more work on than another? Make that one your first priority.

The Feeling in Your Stomach

"Butterflies mean 'a lot' in life. Remember how they live
in a cocoon before they thrive as beautiful creatures.
But never forget how they feel in your stomach."
~ Millie Crossland
Pathways, p. 184

Ever get that feeling in your stomach—that fluttery sensation of excitement and nerves when you anticipate something special? Sometimes that fluttery feeling comes when there's something we have to do that we don't really want to do. That fluttery feeling can become such an overpowering ball of anxiety that we stop, unable to move forward.

It's not possible to know what the inside of a cocoon is like. What we do know is that remarkable work occurs in its silken sleeping bag. This has to be done before a beautiful butterfly can break through to fly freely into a whole new world and way of living.

Recovery is like that. At some point, we stop what we've been doing that isn't working. We stop because we've reached a point where we need some protection from the world we've been living in. Then we take as long as we need to—just like the activity within the cocoon—to rest and nourish ourselves so that one day the butterfly will emerge: A beautiful butterfly.

When we're facing that "fluttery" feeling in our stomachs on our steps to recovery, we can think of the butterfly, becoming gentle with ourselves, yet still moving forward. The world is ready to see our beauty take flight!

Just for Today

What's one simple thing you can begin today that will help you connect to your inner beauty and true self? Think about how you can "take flight!"

Just Being

*"I have learned that I have to pat myself on the back
and reward myself in small ways for my accomplishments.
I reward myself for just being me."*
~ Julie Bayes
Pathways, p. 331

What is the definition of a "reward"? When should someone be rewarded? Do we ever take time to reward ourselves?

Perhaps we resist the whole self-reward thing. Maybe it's just hard to see how special our lives really are—and to realize that *special* doesn't have to be a big world-changing event for us to make a difference. There are so many things we do that are opportunities to smile with a sense of satisfaction, even saying to ourselves, *"Yes! I did it!"*

Do we realize that each day is filled with all sorts of moments of accomplishment that fully warrant taking a bit of time to say to ourselves, *"Wow! I did it! I am amazing!"*

Let's take time to reward ourselves every day—in big and little ways—just because.

Just for Today

Reward yourself today by having—or making—your favorite meal, the one that warms your stomach and your soul!

A Purpose I Didn't Know

*"I began to have an idea of my life, not as the slow shaping of
achievement to fit my preconceived purposes, but as the gradual
discovery and growth of a purpose which I did not know."*
~ Joanna Field
Pathways, p. 81

I searched and searched, my life to be,
just who I was, my identity.

I tried to fit, where I had before,
but like a glass slipper, I fit no more.

"My purpose?" I questioned, at the top of my lungs.
Then softly, I asked, "What's my direction?"

Though I fought to be who I wanted to be,
I finally realized that I must do it gently.

I opened my eyes, my heart and my mind,
and there stood purpose...my own kind.

"Thanks," I said to the powers that be.
I'll honor my purpose, eternally.

Just for Today

*Open your eyes, heart and mind today. See if you can identify one step
you can take to find your purpose. Feel like you've found it already? Look
deeper and see where it takes you!*

One Must Do Something

"One starts an action because one must do something."
~ T.S. Eliot
Pathways to Recovery, p. 61

Every great accomplishment began as an idea, a dream, a vision. Most of us have dreams of things we want to accomplish.

Maybe it's writing a book, being a good parent, owning a home or inventing something that changes the world. Even when there are setbacks in life, our dreams are the things that keep us motivated and hopeful.

When there's something to reach for, getting up in the morning isn't quite so hard, even during the times we're discouraged or not feeling well. When there's something to reach for, we know our lives matter—and suddenly there's so much to do as we look forward to the day ahead!

Some days we might do more than others, but we're moving forward when we set goals and commit to following through on them. When we continue to do something, a little at a time towards accomplishing our dreams, we are amazed and excited when we see our dreams come true.

It takes action steps to transform our dreams and inner hopes into accomplishments. All we need to do is start, one step at a time.

Just for Today

Life never gets better if you don't make changes. Today, tell yourself you have the ability to handle any situation. What positive thing can you do to make sure you get the result you want?

To Benefit by Giving

*"It is expressly at those times when we feel needy
that we will benefit the most from giving."*
~ Ruth Ross
Pathways, p. 160

It's hard to capture in words what it feels like when we just need someone to be there to make things better. So often in the past, no one was there when we needed them the most. We felt alone and scared, unable to grasp onto anyone who could give us stability.

Yet we have grown from needy children to self-sufficient adults. We have gained the maturity of growth and the wisdom that comes with it. Sometimes, though, we get that feeling of needing someone to just be there.

When that's not possible, how do we deal with the feelings of loneliness? One way to overcome this need is to step outside of ourselves by reaching out to help someone else. In giving, we find that we're not so alone. We actually feel a sense of well-being, because to give is to receive.

Just for Today

Benefit by giving today! Instead of asking someone if there's something you can do for them, think of something and then do it!

First A Dream

"Nothing happens unless first a dream."
~ Carl Sandburg
Pathways to Recovery, p. 114

Remember sitting in grade school class, on a nice spring day, staring out the open window, daydreaming about what life would become? Remember wondering where you could be instead of in that stuffy boring class? "Things will be better when I'm an adult," you claimed.

We thought then that we knew how we would catch our dreams, and that we were ready. We would dream big; it would be so.

Even though many of us have felt stifled by the symptoms of illness or the experiences we've had, it's never too late to dream again. Look out the window today, and let yourself dream. Right here, right now, dream. We can start anew by letting today's dream guide us.

Just for Today
Anticipate the good today by spending at least five minutes daydreaming. Let your mind roam. You just might find some great ideas!

If We Didn't Have Strengths

"If I didn't [have some] strengths,
I wouldn't have survived for so long."
~ Linda Endicott
Pathways, p. 74

If we didn't have strengths, we wouldn't get out of bed in the morning. Life's too hard.

If we didn't have strengths, we wouldn't be advocates, educators, peer specialists and directors of nonprofit agencies.

If we didn't have strengths, we wouldn't be able to determine goals for our true purpose.

If we didn't have strengths, we wouldn't help one another when life's pain gets us down.

If we didn't have strengths we wouldn't be able to express ourselves honestly.

If we haven't discovered our strengths, we can still find them because we are survivors!

Just for Today

Make a list of what you like about yourself. These things are your strengths and the ones you likely have used the most in your survival and ongoing recovery!

Getting Anything Done

"Love yourself first and everything else falls into line.
You really have to love yourself to get anything done in this world."
~ Lucille Ball
Pathways, p. 301

Spinning out of control. This has to be one of the hardest things to face in recovery. It usually means we 're tired, overwhelmed, have uncertain goals or are confused with what to do next. Anxiety can trigger our symptoms or cause us to feel afraid—with both feet on the brake pedal—even though our minds are screaming, "Keep on going!"

Much of what we encounter during these times is simply our own overwhelming thoughts and emotions. We can learn to have control over them! Even when we can't change a situation, we can learn to change how we respond to it.

A big first step in doing this is learning to love ourselves. We must tell ourselves that we are deserving, that we are on a wonderful path in life. We must believe we can overcome any fear, doubt, bad memory or overwhelming emotion that may arise.

By loving ourselves, we can see all the things we did today are now the stepping stones which lead to a successful tomorrow! We take the journey slowly, moment-by-moment, loving ourselves every step of the way. We're steering in the direction we want, instead of spinning out of control.

Just for Today
Forget about your "to do" list for the day. Instead, create an "I did" list.
Let yourself recognize all the things you accomplished, loving yourself
and setting out on the direction you want to go!

Keeping Our Eyes Open

"Seeing is of course very much a matter of verbalization.
Unless I call attention to what passes before my eyes, I simply won't
see…It's all a matter of keeping my eyes open."
~ Annie Dillard
Pathways, p. 386

Shush…
        Notice — touching
                fingers, toes, shoulders,
                        describing.
Be quiet…
        Surroundings — seeing,
                hearing, smelling,
                        becoming.
A moment…
        Emotions — calling,
                saying, regretting,
                        praying.
Minutes…
        Engaging — evoking,
                promising, saving,
                        staying.
Shush…
        Notice.

Just for Today

Are you keeping your eyes open to the message you send to the universe?
What would it take to make that message a more positive one?

Looking Around

"Stories move in circles. They don't move in straight lines.
So it helps if you listen in circles. There are stories inside stories and
stories between stories, and finding your way through them is as easy
and as hard as finding your way home. And part of the finding
is the getting lost. And when you're lost,
you start to look around and to listen."
~ Corey Fisher, Albert Greenberg & Naomi Newman
Pathways to Recovery, p. 390

We each have a story to tell. A story of triumph and growth. A story of coming from behind and catching up. Our stories have movement, sometimes going forward, sometimes spinning around and around.

Yet our stories are the coats of our experience, made of vivid colors and interesting designs. How we design these coats is up to us.

In telling the story of who we are, we find new ways of wearing them. Not wearing our multi-colored stories is like telling the world we haven't been rebellious or rambunctious in our determination for life. We must wear our stories proudly, so others can listen and learn. We must wear our stories—the inside stories and the stories between stories—so we may listen and learn.

Just for Today
If you find yourself struggling, spinning when you don't want to, try watching a movie about someone who did something hard and made it through. Let their story help guide your own!

Letting Our Light Shine

"And as we let our own light shine,
we unconsciously give other people permission to do the same.
As we are liberated from our own fear,
our presence automatically liberates others."
~ *Nelson Mandela*
Pathways to Recovery, p. 8

We each have an inner light. Each of us.

When we're not reacting out of fear, we can show our light freely, letting it heal us from our own fears and letting it calm the fears of others.

A young woman was scared to death to speak in public. She dropped college classes she had to speak in. Her constant anxiety made her afraid of people, especially about what they would think of her.

Later—as this woman grew older—she challenged her fears. In doing so, she found her true purpose. She began to speak in public about recovery. She spoke of not being afraid of life—that life is to be cherished, not feared.

In giving her own inner light permission to shine, she sees the light of others shining, too.

Just for Today
Sometimes we need a little help and support as we challenge our fears. Seek out a good teacher or mentor that can help you let your own light shine!

What Does Recovery Mean?

"What does recovery mean to me?
To have hope… to feel needed…to use my abilities…to help others…
to have a positive attitude… inner healing…spiritual wholeness…
living effectively…giving back…forgiveness…believing
in yourself…overcoming obstacles in achieving my goals."
~ Sheila Hill
Pathways to Recovery, p. 6

How do we define recovery? It's a really important question because, if we try to follow the plan someone else lays out for us, there's a high chance we'll have trouble staying on the road.

Relapse is a normal part of this journey—but staying on course long enough to get to a better place in life, is vital to what recovery is all about.

Recovery is on-going. It's a time to find inner healing and transformation. Recovery is about learning to live well, in spite of some obstacles we may face with our health. It's about living beyond our diagnoses, integrating them into our lives instead of focusing on the disruptive force they may have on us.

There are many people in the world who are on a journey of recovery. We are each at different stages on the journey. But the thing we each share is an ability to learn how to take control of our journey, seeing it as a path of exciting discovery.

Just for Today

One of the things that's important in moving recovery forward is to feed your mind. Stretch yourself to learn something new. Make it simple and something in which you're interested.

The Last Key

"Don't be discouraged.
It's often the last key in the bunch that opens the lock."
~ Anonymous
Pathways to Recovery, p. 331

How many times have we almost given up to once again find ourselves soaring among the clouds? Sometimes when we let go, we succeed.

Too often we're searching, looking for that perfect solution, trying to find what we've lost. We may feel stress, we may press ourselves further into despair by looking, yet not seeing.

It's only when we stop that we notice what's already there. It might take trying every key we have on the ring, but when we get to the last key, we can open the door and move forward.

Just for Today

It takes time to move through recovery but things do eventually happen! Get a key today and put it in a place where you will be reminded to unlock your own door!

Coloring Outside of the Lines

"Live life to the fullest. You have to color outside the lines once in a whileif you want to make your life a masterpiece. Laugh some every day, keep growing, keep dreaming, keep following your heart. The important thing is not to stop questioning."
~ Albert Einstein
Pathways, p. 307

Live the dream. Walk the path.

Belly laugh, snort and laugh again, harder.

Always be curious. Keep questioning.

Enjoy one another. Feel peace.

Plant the seeds to grow.

Take healthy risks.

Learn when to use a different color and when not

to pay attention to the lines.

Just for Today

Color is a very strong part of life...whether we're coloring inside the lines or not. Find something that's your favorite color and surround yourself with it today. Why do you like this color and how does it make you feel?

Choice Is the Rudder

"Choice is the rudder that guides each person's destiny."
~ *Peter Megargee Brown*
Pathways, p. 259

Making our *own* choices is key to creating the life journey we desire. Although there may have been times in our life when it was necessary for others to take on this responsibility for us, recovery actually encourages us to take a conscious step toward accepting self-responsibility.

Learning to make our own choices might be daunting at first, especially if we've had a recent relapse or lots of stress. Sometimes we test the waters by doing things a little differently than how others might do them. We might think about things differently, shaking up our routine a bit until we can feel the excitement of the positive changes that have occurred because of our decision-making.

Being able to make our own choices takes us from just wishful-thinking into happening. Making our own choices can definitely be scary — but when we can do it, we get the opportunity to grow into the person we're sure we can become.

Just for Today
How are your choices guiding your journey? What would you do if today were your last? Laugh, love and be happy. You are in control of your own life!

Courage to Continue

*"We are always called upon to have the courage to continue on
our path toward greater and deeper feelings of self-worth."*
~ Sue Patton Thoele
Pathways to Recovery, p. 75

Ever noticed how children love to draw attention to the things they're
doing? They say things like "watch me" or "see what I drew today."
They take a lot of pride in being independent, saying, "I can do it by
myself." With beautiful smiles on their faces, they bring us dandelions,
knowing we will appreciate their gifts. And we treat them with
gentleness and gratitude, embracing their spirits and encouraging
them as they live and grow.

Some of us have received messages telling us we were to be quiet,
not to brag, or that we were somehow less important than others.
Messages like this cloud our thoughts and experiences, making us
focus on negative things. We start to compare ourselves with others
and feel like we don't stack up to them. We may set up standards that
are unrealistic to meet; these messages get in our way and act as huge
roadblocks to recovery.

It's possible to learn how to recognize these messages and reframe
them into positives. We can learn to move from a problem-oriented
perspective to a strengths-oriented one. Being positive gives us the
courage to keep walking the journey of recovery to a place of health,
wellness and joy!

Just for Today

*If you're struggling with negative thoughts, try laying some bricks of joy
today. Write down your sorrows — and then your joys. How different do
they feel?*

Living Intensely in the Present

"The future belongs to those who live intensely in the present."
~ Anonymous
Pathways to Recovery, p. 83

So many times we have lived waiting for the next shoe to drop, the next problem to emerge. We have let our lives go by, not really experiencing them with full curiosity and exploration.

To live intensely in the present is to take in every minute of every day. It's to believe enough in ourselves that we reach out and touch what's in front of us. To ask questions and to expect answers which make sense and allow us to embrace the "now" of the present.

When we walk with a determined step, when we hold our head up, we are taking control of our lives. We are living with purpose, knowing that every day has a special prize waiting for us to find.

Just for Today

Go ahead and enjoy the day! Practice walking with a long stride and keep your head up so you can see as much of the present as possible.

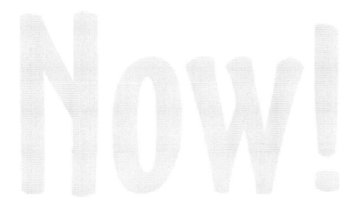

Three Descriptions

"Don't fear failure so much that you refuse to try new things.
The saddest summary of a life contains three descriptions:
could have, might have, and should have."
~ Louis Boone
Pathways to Recovery, p. 304

Failure is a state of mind. We cannot let ourselves get caught up in this mind-set without letting go of who we have become. So we don't get what we started out to accomplish—so what! We did get something out of the adventure; we just need to look at it from a different perspective to see all the good that came from it.

New understanding, new adventures or the beginning of a sweet relationship can all come from taking chances. It does us no good if we don't at least try. We must give our lives the chances we deserve.

Just for Today

It's time to get rid of those coulda — mighta — shoulda's. Write all of yours down and then get rid of them. Burn them, shred them or throw them away. You don't have to keep those with you any longer!

Now Feel The Joy

"The most difficult thing in life is to know yourself."
~ Thales
Pathways to Recovery, p. 81

It seems to me,
We always see
The things that we just aren't.

But I believe,
There's more to us;
There's good that makes us up.

The good we may yet know,
Our own true selves,
Helps us on our path.

It's all we need
To really succeed;
Now feel the joy of that.

Just for Today
Create a list of "101 Things that Bring You Joy." If you can't make your list that long, just start and add your joys as you experience them!

With Each New Day

"With the new day comes new strength and new thoughts."
~ Eleanor Roosevelt
Pathways to Recovery, p. 9

Those of us on a recovery path wake up each day to continue on our journey. But some of us continue to be told we are "sick" by others. Some of us will still receive the message that we're only going to be able to manage our symptoms and that the hope for anything more in life is impossible. And, while being able to manage our symptoms is a positive thing, there is much more to our journey.

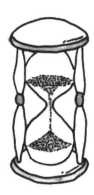 We can wake up every day a little different than we were the day before. We can take advantage of the new day, reflecting on how great it feels to be in recovery, realizing that it's a process, not something that just happens.

Life holds more and more—it's never just "as good as it gets." Remember this, and take courage in knowing there are others in recovery who have broken free from their limiting ideas. And if we just look, "with each new day comes new strength and new thoughts."

Just for Today

Imagine you've been granted three wishes. What would they be? Are you holding on to the past, wishing it would change? Or are you so focused on the future that you're missing the present? Let this be your "new day!"

May

*"All things seem possible
in May."*

~ *Edward Way Teale*

Look, Listen and Say

"Everyday...look at a beautiful poem, listen to some beautiful music, and if possible, say some reasonable thing."
~ Goethe
Pathways to Recovery, p. 325

We struggle with the blues so often that we forget to look for the simple joys in life.

Joy is not just some huge grandiose moment that we only experience once in our lives. Joy happens every day, but we must look for it and allow ourselves to feel it.

Using our senses can help us notice joy. Hearing and seeing a child's gleeful laughter, feeling a gentle touch, tasting our favorite recipe — these may be simple, but they are personal joys. Noticing these can help us feel good. They can bring us pleasure.

Happiness is a feeling we deserve to experience fully. If we stop now, and let the joy wash over us, we'll feel good the next time we recognize something to celebrate.

Just for Today

Today, start paying attention to how your senses bring you joy. Make a list by using this prompt..."These things in my life I have seen...I have tasted...I have touched...I have heard...and I have smelled..."

Things for Which We Must Hunger

"It seems to me we can never give up longing and wishing
while we are alive. There are certain things we feel to be beautiful
and good, and we must hunger for them."
~ George Eliot
Pathways to Recovery, p. 60

Longing and wishing is a part of our daily lives, regardless of whether we're feeling good or bad. The trick is to get moving and make our wishes come true.

There was a man who approached recovery slowly, but hungrily. He understood the need to see the beautiful things in the world. So he planted a garden—a wonderful garden of recovery.

As the plants grew and grew, so did the man. Each and every day he appreciated the beauty of nature...and eventually, people.

As he sought for the beautiful and good things, his recovery continued growing. He appreciated the beauty. He felt true joy. He felt healing occur. He felt good.

Just for Today
Getting outside is a good way to put things into perspective. Take a walk in your neighborhood. See if you can find a spot where you can go to see beauty, find peace and feel your joy.

That Single Moment

"A friend of mine said to me one day, 'You don't have to believe your diagnosis; it's only a label.' I thought I'd been given a death sentence from the medical 'experts' which I had no choice but to accept. That single moment changed my life forever...years later, I'm working full-time, living on my own...and starting my own business."
~ Author Unknown from Kramer & Gagne
Pathways to Recovery, p. 65

Too many of us have been given this same life-altering message. The message that our challenges—with its symptoms, its barriers, its stigma—is all we have to look forward to in life.

But the message of recovery is so much more than this! We can learn how to live with symptoms by finding our own tools for wellness. We do have strengths to use in moving our goals forward. We can understand our experiences and use its lessons to help ourselves and others.

Our lives don't need to revolve around a diagnosis. We can take these positive messages instead, knowing that we are the experts of our own lives. We do matter and we do have the power within ourselves

Just for Today
What does the diagnosis or label you've been given say about you? Take a few minutes to really listen to your body. What is it telling you to do?

The Small Things

*"Often we allow ourselves to be upset by small things we should despise
and forget. We lose many irreplaceable hours brooding over grievances
that, in a year's time, will be forgotten by us and by everybody. No, let
us devote our life to worthwhile actions and feelings, to great thoughts,
real affections and enduring undertakings."*
~ Andre Maurois
Pathways to Recovery, p. 299

Sometimes we feel upset by the littlest things. Maybe someone looks
at us wrong or annoys us in traffic. Maybe the neighbor's music is too
loud or the phone won't stop ringing.

When we don't let the little things bother us, we feel more light-hearted
and forgiving. We use our energy to pursue things that matter more to
us. We might have more time for a hobby, relationships or self-care.
We just feel better emotionally, physically and spiritually.

When we are more joy-filled — with clear goals and enjoying activities
that make us happy — we are less likely to brood about the little things.
Sure, we still might feel upset at times, but we're more likely to focus
our energy and feelings on worthwhile endeavors that will matter far
longer than our bad moods and hurt feelings.

Let's learn to "choose our battles," making the decision to see less of
what's wrong, and focus more on what's going right.

Just for Today
*Are you being burdened by the little things? Think back to a time when
your values were questioned. Are you feeling stuck on the little things
from these experiences? Are you choosing your battles correctly?*

Becoming Who We Really Are

"It takes courage to grow up and become who you really are."
~ e e cummings
Pathways to Recovery, p. 39

Growing up changes our perspective. Having courage to be who we really are changes our entire lives.

Letting go of illness, sadness, depression, the past, the pain, the limitations and the all the negativity is just a part of facing life courageously. To move forward, we must find our courage, dumping the baggage that keeps us from being who we are.

We have purpose; we must be brave adults and grab hold. We'll play later…with courage.

Just for Today

Is there something you need to dump out of your life? Grab hold of your courage and purpose. You can make the changes you want to see!

All the Connections

*"Although the connections are not always obvious,
personal change is inseparable from social and political change."
~ Harriet Lerner
Pathways to Recovery, p. 298*

One-by-one, person-by-person, we see change happen.

At first, it's just one or two of us. Then there's ten or twenty of us. As our numbers grow through our own personal change, we begin to speak out.

We start to demand change. We become active in our treatment and our lives. We start to participate more fully in our community. We begin to get more comfortable with the changes.

Finally, many of us begin to get involved in the greater recovery movement. We begin advocating for ourselves and others. We talk with each other. We talk with our local legislators. We register to vote and we speak up for what we need.

It's because of positive personal change that we're able to work toward social and political change. Our movement will continue. Our movement will survive. We will see change!

Just for Today

Change does happen! If you look back even five years from now, can you see how your life, your community and our mental health movement has grown? Are you making connections to that growth? Try getting involved in an advocacy group and make some connections!

Hopes, Dreams and Aspirations

"Everyone, regardless of their current situation or their personal characteristics, has hopes, dreams, and aspirations and may fulfill those only if they use their talents, abilities, and skills and the resources available to them."
~ Alice Lieberman
Pathways to Recovery, p. 107

Whether it's to love someone, to build something, to create something or to see a child grow up, we have inside of us a spark which can light even the darkest corner.

No matter what we do for a living, where we live, what we eat or how we do it, we have something we'd like to see happen or changed. We find our passion, our talents, abilities, skills and resources will help us reach our hopes, dreams and aspirations.

Life is full of some powerful sparks. We must live to make them shine.

Just for Today
What's the spark in your life that gives you energy? Light a candle today as a reminder of your own hopes, dreams and aspirations.

A Road Built in Hope

"It has never been, and never will be, easy work! But the road that is built in hope is more pleasant to the traveler than the road built in despair, even though they both lead to the same destination."
~ *Marian Zimmer Bradley*
Pathways to Recovery, p. 76

How would our lives change if we were told — and really believed — that the only moment we really have is now — the present — this very moment that we're alive? What if we were told this road could be joyful — even when it gets rocky? What if smiling a bit and enjoying today would help us feel better tomorrow? Would that make a difference in the way we live?

Would we be more likely to take time to sit back and enjoy the day? Would we be less likely to complain or spend time lost in negative emotions we can't change? Would we be less prone to feel hurt or anger toward others who don't agree with us or who may have hurt us.

Since this path we travel isn't always perfect, we can choose to have a positive perspective. We can choose to be more concerned about making a difference in our world instead of dwelling on the bad things. We can be grateful for what we have right now, instead of feeling upset about the things that haven't gone so well before today. When we actively focus on learning, growing, changing and appreciating our lives, we have less energy to focus on the problems. And that just makes things feel lighter *and* easier.

Just for Today

Be sure to move toward positive perspectives. Need help with that? Put positive reminders or notes around your home of your goals.

The Riskiest Choice

"Many of us have played it safe for so long and wonder why we are miserable. Playing it safe is the riskiest choice we can ever make."
~ Sarah Ban Breathnach
Pathways to Recovery, p. 306

How do we know which risks to take and when to step back and let them go by? Only after we go through a process of learning and reflection on our experiences—and maybe those of others—can we be confident that a risk is truly worthwhile.

While we don't want to take risks with our health or our safety, we do want to risk uneasiness if it will allow us to form new relationships or take us a step closer to our dreams.

Staying safe doesn't always mean comfort. Taking risks doesn't always mean failure. Taking risks is uncomfortable, no matter how we try to avoid it. If we don't take risks, though, our lives will become stifled and drab.

To really live, we must take well-chosen risks.

Just for Today

Practice taking risks! Do something today that is completely out of character for you!

Our Real Blessings

*"Our real blessings often appear to us
in the shape of pains, losses and disappointments."*
~ Joseph Addison
Pathways to Recovery, p. 200

How in the world can we ever get to the place in life where we see our pains, losses and disappointments as blessings? How could we ever even imagine that to be true? And who would dare to even think that?

Pain can teach us to be gentle with ourselves. The hurts can force us to slow down a bit, to feel more, to understand others with more compassion.

Losses often help us see what we have before us — the people, places and things that mean a lot. Losses force us to look at what's important, to be more forgiving and to open ourselves up to what's before us.

Disappointments lead us to see the good in things — if we let them. Disappointments can bring us determination, a strong will and a desire to move forward on our journey

Experiencing pain, loss and disappointment guides us in our search for a different life and, when we dig down deep inside ourselves, we grasp our own resiliency and strength. Because our lives — even with the difficulties — are blessings.

Just for Today
If you're feeling confident about your recovery journey and the blessings it has given you, why not share your hope with someone else today? Send a card or leave a note that says, "I believe in you."

Looking at My World

"I am not limited by any past thinking. I choose my thoughts with care.
I constantly have new insights and new ways of looking at my world.
I am willing to change and grow."
~ Louise L. Hay
Pathways to Recovery, p. 362

Willingness is the key to all success.

The willingness to be open to looking at our world, as though for the first time with the curiosity of new eyes, promotes positive growth and change.

Willingness to choose our thoughts with care is also a good step forward. It's one of the kindest gestures we can do for ourselves.

Since we would never say to someone else all the negative things that we think about ourselves, why not stop saying them to ourselves? Instead, we can think of ourselves with gentleness. This kindness toward ourselves changes our lives in momentous ways.

Be willing to think with "care." Be willing to let go. Be willing to change and grow. It'll be the first step to a whole new world.

Just for Today

When you're limited by your past thinking, it's often hard to hear others say nice things about you. Today accept a compliment by simply saying "thank you."

On The Wings Of A Dragon

"To attract good fortune, spend a new penny on an old friend,
share an old pleasure with a new friend, and lift up the heart
of a true friend by writing his name on the wings of a dragon."
~ Chinese Proverb
Pathways to Recovery, p. 225

Many of us have withdrawn from friendships because of our illness or life experiences. We may fear stigma or worry what someone will think of us. We might feel like we don't fit in anymore. We see people sharing and laughing, but we don't seem to know how to fit in.

Sometimes we've been sick for a long time and our lives have changed; we feel like we've drifted away from our old lifestyle and friends. Withdrawing from people is something we do when we need to protect ourselves.

It's normal to feel vulnerable when trying to make friends. People sometimes hurt us. Not everyone will hurt us, though, and not everyone *has* hurt us. Making friends takes time and trust and courage. Gaining inner courage and hope is a big step on the road of recovery. We can find hope in knowing that, in time, we'll be able to trust someone to share our lives with — first with the little things — and eventually with the big things.

In time, we'll find those true friends. And we'll take the time to write their name on the wings of a dragon.

Just for Today
Make a mental list of your friends today. Which ones are your true
friends — the ones who love and care for you just because of who you
are? Give one of them a call and tell them how you feel.

The Greatest Good

"The greatest good you can do for another
is not just to share your riches, but to reveal to him his own self."
~Benjamin Disraeli
Pathways to Recovery, p. 91

We can create within ourselves an image so honest that others can see who we really are. And in seeing our honesty, others can actually find within themselves their own strengths. We can become a mirror for others.

One of the richest gifts we can give to someone else is to actually be ourselves, aware of our own strengths and weaknesses. We need to come out from under our insecurities to find and express our authenticity, our true self.

To do this, we'll need to assess our strengths so that we're aware of them. In doing this, we can appreciate what makes us strong, letting others in on the truth.

It isn't our ability to hide which is our strength. It's our ability to be ourselves.

Just for Today

Are you sharing your greatest good? Today, stop hiding and accept yourself for who you are and who you've become. Your strengths — not your barriers — make you who you are. Celebrate you!

An Untold Story

"There is no agony like bearing an untold story inside you."
~ Nora Zeale Hurston
Pathways to Recovery, p. 380

There are lots of things that happen for which we have no explanation. Trauma, illness, loss and unbearable grief. We find ourselves in difficult circumstances and we find ourselves weighed down by negative experiences, many of which we had little or no control over.

Often, we find ourselves pushing these to the side or burying them deep within ourselves, afraid to share them with anyone else. The older we get, the harder it is to talk about some of these experiences, yet they continue to have a strong hold over us.

There are many ways to let our stories out—with an understanding peer, a trusting therapist or maybe through writing, art or music. However we find to share our story, we cannot hold it inside of us. We must share who we are in order to heal. We must open our hearts to let our experiences be told.

In telling our story, we will find our strength and resiliency. And what happens? We find we can be whole again.

Just for Today

Sharing your experiences with others can be one of your greatest healers. Don't let your story go untold. Is there someone you can share your story with today?

Be Ye Merry

"Be ye merry; you have cause. So have we all of joy."
~ *William Shakespeare*
Pathways to Recovery, p. 205

Above all, to feel validated, worthwhile and full of our own purpose, we simply must, *must* celebrate our accomplishments! Rewarding ourselves helps us carry out our goals.

We don't have to achieve big tasks to celebrate. Maybe we're having trouble getting out of bed. So when we *do* get up and going, we need to reward ourselves with a nice cup of tea or a home-made breakfast.

Maybe we experience some of life's greater accomplishments, like a job promotion, mending a broken relationship or we finally grasp how to live a healthier life. While these may seem to be events when celebration is sure to occur, we still need to remember to do it!

Whatever accomplishment we have—be it big or small—we can reward ourselves! We can celebrate—*we have cause*—and then what? We can feel the joy!

Just for Today
Be merry! Maybe you could spend a few extra cents today on something that makes you feel good!

Ending Among the Stars

"Shoot for the moon. Even if you miss, you will end among the stars."
~ Les Brown
Pathways to Recovery, p. 361

Yes! Let's "shoot for the moon"! But let's get a little help as we do it!

Creating affirmations is a great way of getting support and encouragement as we seek new adventures. It's like giving ourselves a little hug and a pat on the back each time we use them. Affirmations tell us positive things. They help direct our thoughts and emotions as we seek to move forward.

How about trying one of these affirmations:

- I love and accept myself and I am worthy of love.
- I am a unique, peaceful and free being.
- I am safe and protected.
- I am joyful...grateful, loving...
- I am a forgiving person.
- It is safe for me to give and receive love.
- I am talented and successful in all that I do.

Some people say affirmations before each meal. Some start their day with a new affirmation. Others end their day with a positive thought. The more we use affirmations, the more we'll find ourselves in a positive place that will support us, especially when we find ourselves "among the stars."

Just for Today

Develop a bedtime ritual for yourself that is positive and affirming. Listen to favorite music, meditate, enjoy a relaxing bath or light a candle. Incorporate this routine into your daily activities.

A Good Time

"Life is about enjoying yourself and having a good time."
~ Cher
Pathways to Recovery, p. 166

Are we enjoying ourselves and having a good time? Or are we finding ourselves heavy—loaded down with burdens we can't put down?

We can all list the hard things we've been through. And, if we've taken the time to better understand these experiences, we're able to put those difficult times in perspective.

But what does it take to enjoy life? A little bit of adventure, a caring community to support us, a home where we feel safe, participating in meaningful activities and a sense of purpose.

Enjoying ourselves and having a good time refreshes us, makes us feel better and helps us heal. Cher's advice certainly stands the test of time. Enjoying ourselves...why wouldn't we grab on to advice like this?

Just for Today

Create a bulletin board with things that are fun for you to do. Include funny stories, pictures, cartoons or buttons...anything that makes you happy. Keep adding to it and keep it in a place where you and visitors to your home can see it.

Going Too Far

*"Only those who will risk going too far
can possibly find out how far one can go."*
~ T.S. Eliot
Pathways to Recovery, p. 43

Taking risks is often one of the hardest things we'll ever do. It takes guts to step into something new, not knowing fully what the consequences will be.

Actually, *not* taking risks is what we need to avoid. "I'll just play it safe right here," we say. And then we wonder why our lives never change, why we never feel happy, why we find ourselves bored.

Taking risks is what challenges us. It's what helps us grow and change. It's how we find out we can be happy with ourselves. Taking risks gives us the opportunity to make mistakes, learning important lessons along the way. Taking risks—even those that take us too far— lets us see just how much we can be.

Not taking risks? Well, that's our *greatest* risk.

Just for Today
Challenge yourself to do something difficult in the next few days or weeks. Sign up for a local walk or bike race. Try volunteering or looking for a job. Push yourself...you never know how far you can go unless you take a risk!

A Gift to Be Opened

"…life is not a problem to be solved, but a gift to be opened."
~ Wayne Muller
Pathways to Recovery, p. 380

Do we wake up each day looking forward to what may happen? Or do we wake up with fear instead?

No matter our troubles, traumas and tribulations, approaching life as a gift, savoring each moment and thriving each day, *is* pursuing happiness.

Do we fall into drama and chaos more often than peace and calm? Problem-based lives are the hardest lives to live. We don't need to work that hard!

We can open each day like a present, the biggest one ever, with all the excitement and joy of getting what we've always wanted in our lives. We deserve to feel that good each day.

Just for Today
Think about opening your own present! In the next month or so,
try creating a topic for each week that you'd like to focus on...maybe
something like cooking, reading or getting more exercise. Open the gift
of you and enjoy the present!

Sending Forth Ripples

"Each time a man stands up for an ideal, or acts to improve the lots of others, or strikes out against injustice, he sends forth a tiny ripple of hope, and crossing each other from a million different centers of energy and daring, those ripples build a current which can sweep down the mightiest walls of oppression and resistance."
~ Robert F. Kennedy
Pathways to Recovery, p. 15

Those of us with serious health conditions have many rights—the right to quality housing, meaningful employment and educational opportunities. We have the right to ask questions and to be treated with respect and dignity. We have the right to love and be loved. We have a right to our own voice.

In the past, we may have felt we had no voice. We may have had our rights disrespected or decisions made for us—without our full involvement. At times, we had no equal access to things those with other disabilities had.

Thankfully, the disability rights movement has made big changes in the way people are now viewed and treated. With the push for equal treatment, and for the upholding of dignity and respect for all human beings, the rights of all people are being better regarded.

Each of us can make a difference by standing up for ourselves—and for others by seeking what is true and by being intolerant of that which takes away the rights and dignity of ourselves and others. Standing up for ourselves brings light and hope and makes the world a better place for everyone.

Just for Today

Are you standing up for yourself? What issue is important to you? Get involved and send out your own ripples!

The Germ of Happiness

"Growth itself contains the germ of happiness."
~Pearl S. Buck
Pathways to Recovery, p. 263

Germs are contagious, and so is happiness.

When we surround ourselves with upbeat, happy people, it wears off on us, leaving us feeling happy, which is growth.

Do we have an accurate view of what happiness really is?

Happiness is a child's smile and wonder.

Happiness is in being with our pets and receiving unconditional love.

Happiness is seeing a flower blooming brilliantly in the middle of a chaotic, complex world.

It's in our nature to be happy. Happiness is inside of us. Let the contagion spread—a happiness outbreak to all around!

Just for Today

How do you define happiness for yourself? Is there something you've been wanting to enjoy but haven't made time for yet? Make plans to do it and grab on to your happiness!

Smoothing the Edges

"Success can make you go one of two ways.
It can make you a prima donna — or it can smooth the edges,
take away the insecurities, let the nice things come out."
~ Barbara Walters
Pathways to Recovery, p. 368

We all strive to be successful even as we face the fear of failing. It's natural to celebrate those successes and to feel good about ourselves when we succeed at something. But we don't want to become conceited and forget those who have helped us along the way.

We need to find ways to celebrate our successes without being a prima donna. We need to be open to other ideas and other points of view and to celebrate other's successes as well, when the opportunity arises. None of us can achieve success without the help of other people. We can celebrate together our mutual successes.

Take time to smell the roses, smooth the edges and let insecurities fall to the wayside. When we do, we can bring along a friend. That's just how success happens.

Just for Today

Celebrating yourself helps smooth your edges. Revel in your own way of being! Renew your commitment to knowing yourself and accepting your own uniqueness.

The Question of Stopping Me

"The question isn't who is going to let me;
it's who is going to stop me?"
~ Ayn Rand
Pathways to Recovery, p. 368

So often in life we have looked to others to find encouragement. Too long we have sought the acceptance of our peers and families. We've often been disappointed. If we stop asking who is going to let us and decide no one can stop us, we then find strength within.

We're not children waiting for our parents to give us permission or animals looking to be petted. We are adults ready to tackle whatever comes next. We are people who are capable of challenging ourselves.

No one else can give us the will to live; only we can give ourselves the hope to thrive. Who's going to stop us?

Just for Today

Think about creating a goal journal. This is a place you write down your goals and keep a record of your accomplishments. Don't let anyone – including yourself – stop you!

Parade Through Each Day

*"The victory of success is half won when one gains the habit
of setting goals and achieving them. Even the most tedious chore
will become endurable as you parade through each day
convinced that every task, no matter how menial or boring,
brings you closer to fulfilling your dreams."*
~ Og Mandino
Pathways to Recovery, p. 269

What if each day was one we looked forward to with excitement and enthusiasm? What if each night, as we fell asleep, we found ourselves anticipating the new day ahead, thinking about all the things we were going to do and how much fun we were going to have?

Our lives are a gift, and we have so much to look forward to, so much to do and so much to share. There are new opportunities and adventures in each step we take.

Even our routines become exciting when we realize what a gift our lives are. Walking to get the mail becomes an opportunity to whistle a tune. Dinner becomes a chance to try a new recipe. Going to school becomes an opportunity to learn new things and meet new people.

When we start turning our boredom and dissatisfaction with life into attitudes of joy and gratitude, we get closer and closer to reaching our dreams. And then, we can hardly wait to get up in the morning. We start to know we have enough—today—just as things are.

Just for Today
Making each day a cause for a parade will be easier if you're having a good time doing it! Make a commitment today to smile at everything you see and everyone you meet.

Giving of Ourselves

"They who give have all things; they who withhold have nothing."
~ Hindu Proverb
Pathways to Recovery, p. 162

Volunteering is one of the best ways for us to give ourselves to others. When we give and expect nothing in return, our lives are opened to opportunities we would never have seen coming.

Giving our time, our knowledge, our care and effort is the stuff of which dreams are made. It's only in giving that we receive. If we give nothing of ourselves, then we can expect nothing in return.

But if we look around, we can find something of ourselves to give that will, in turn, lead to something we give to ourselves.

Just for Today
Give some time today to a passion in which you believe. Go to a meeting or an informational session in your community.

Blooming Flowers of Hope

*"It wasn't easy at first, but with practice I really began to see
how the little seeds of affirmative thinking really started to grow
into beautiful, blooming flowers of hope…My thoughts set the tone
for how I live today — as well as how strong my hope is for the future."*
~ Suzette Mack
Pathways to Recovery, p. 364

Using positive words and thoughtful quotations can lift us up mentally, spiritually and physically.

Changing our negative thoughts into positive ones is life-altering — as one woman discovered after being institutionalized many times.

This woman had a complete lack of self-esteem. It was hard for her to think of anything positive. At the suggestion of her hospital roommate, the women started hanging positive, uplifting quotations all over their room. They both began to feel better.

When she went home, the first woman continued to post signs around her home. Now she challenges negative thoughts and she now has the courage to become a leader in her community. Her new found courage gives her hope for her future!

Just for Today
*Has someone helped you through
a difficult time recently?
Write them a letter today
and tell them how they
were helpful.*

A Single Event

*"A single event can awaken within us a stranger
totally unknown to us."*
~St. Exupery
Pathways to Recovery, p. 83

A stranger within got out of bed for the first time in a week — and took a shower.

A stranger within went back to work after 10 years of being disabled.

A stranger within helped someone in crisis.

A stranger within made the commitment to face fears head on.

A stranger within spoke publicly for the first time and found their voice.

A stranger within communicated boundaries effectively to another person.

A stranger within sees opportunities to grow, making changes gracefully.

The stranger within is actually the person inside each of us, just waiting to awaken.

Just for Today

What single moment in your life changed you? What did you find out about yourself? How were you awakened to the real you? Welcome the stranger inside you!

Just Do Them!

"You can't try to do things. You simply must do them."
~ Ray Bradbury
Pathways to Recovery, p. 247

"Maybe tomorrow I'll do all the things I thought I'd do today. Maybe tomorrow I won't run out of time or feel too tired to do what I want to do."

Does this sound familiar?

Is it sometimes hard to get things done? Are there goals that seem hard to reach because there's not a clear place to start? Are there projects that have been put off because we can't seem to focus on getting them done? Maybe there are things we can start working on, but can't seem to ever finish.

When we work towards recovery, a good thing to say to ourselves over and over again is: "Just do it!" If we don't commit to recovery, it will become more and more difficult to take the steps we need to take in order to change our path.

Recovery requires setting goals. Reaching these goals requires energy and movement. We can only move forward when we commit to reaching our goals. All it takes is to *just do it* – one step at a time.

Just for Today
Got a lot on your "to do" list? Take time today – or plan a day in the near future – to do all the little tasks that have been piling up. You'll be glad you did!

Friends Who Love Us

*"Friends love the person you were
and the one you've become."*
~ Anonymous
Pathways to Recovery, p. 217

So often it's difficult for our friends to see us change as we become someone different than we previously were. When we get sick, again in need after having been self-sufficient, this can really turn off our friends. Then when we get better—even finding ourselves becoming someone completely different—well, sometimes friends can't keep up with the change.

A true friend loves us no matter who we are at the moment, who we were in the past or who we are becoming. A friend sees the true potential in us and doesn't let disenchantment skew their view of us. They remain our friends no matter who we are or what we may become.

Real friendship is a gift that's holy and one to be treasured.

Just for Today
True friendships need to be nourished. Call someone today that you've been thinking about. Let them know they've been on your mind. Treasure your friendships!

What Makes Us Happy

*"It's a helluva start,
being able to recognize what makes you happy."*
~ Lucille Ball
Pathways to Recovery, p. 38

What's out there that makes us happy?

Often, it's not the big things that we need to be happy. Those moments are few and far between—a wedding, the birth of a baby, getting a dream job.

When depression finds us, it's a hard beast to drive away. It's also hard to grasp what it is that's the opposite of depression—does it mean we have to get to a point where we're *elated* about everything? That sounds like an impossible task.

No, the opposite of feeling down is not elation, but rather those moments when we realize we're happy. Moments like hearing kids singing or the rain softly hit the roof. Maybe we find ourselves happy when we enjoy a favorite movie or share a special meal with friends.

These are all moments of happiness, the times during the day when we stop—for just a second—to be thankful, to laugh, to listen, to wonder. Recognizing these times? Now that's where happiness finds us.

Just for Today
What are some of the small things that make you happy? Do what you want today for at least an hour. Just make sure it's not what you have to do or what others want you to do!

Discovering the Stars

"I haven't a clue as to how my story will end.
But that's all right. When you set out on a journey and night
covers the road, you don't conclude that the road has vanished.
And how else could we discover the stars?
~ Unknown
Pathways to Recovery, p. 377

Storytelling has been one of the richest ways that people have related to one another for centuries. It's much like a song or a melody carried on our breath, reaching out to others.

By telling our own stories, and listening to the stories of others, we are given the ability to reflect and to relate. In this relating, we find that we're human, that our stories aren't so unlike others' and that we can overcome even the darkest of nights.

Our stories give us pause to share our voice, our experiences. But it's when we learn to trust our own story, knowing we will find our way no matter what, that we discover our own road.

Just for Today

While the road gets dark, you can still keep going and discover the stars!
Write down the many roles you've had in your life. Which ones do you
want to keep and which would you like to change or get rid of? Now
make of list of the roles you'd like to have in the future. Use these lists
to discover your own road.

June

"I wonder what it would be like to live in a world where it was always June."

~ L.M. Montgomery

Find the Way

"Determine that the thing can and shall be done, and then…
find the way."
~ Abraham Lincoln
Pathways to Recovery, p. 265

We can find a way to do what we want to do. We are courageous. We are determined. We are strong. We are capable. We deserve success… and we know how to succeed.

Sometimes change is hard. Sometimes we aren't so sure we can continue on the journey of recovery. It gets tough, we get tired and scared and discouraged.

But we stay determined and, little by little, we find our way. We've set our goals. We've made up our minds. We can do it. We are doing it. We are determined and we are finding the way!

Just for Today

Want to find your own way? Stop comparing yourself with others. Be your own person! You have the courage, determination and strength to find your own path!

Go Into the Wilderness

"Be brave enough to live life creatively. The creative is the place where no one else has ever been. You have to leave the city of your comfort and go into the wilderness of your intuition. You can't get there by bus, only by hard work and risk and by not quite knowing what you're doing. What you'll discover will be wonderful.
What you'll discover will be yourself."
~ Alan Alda
Pathways to Recovery, p. 337

What is creativity? It's when we take some ideas and put them together in ways that are different than how anyone else has ever done them before. We might create a sculpture or paint our home, write a poem or a song, build a birdhouse or a fence, or make up a recipe for a great dessert.

The list of ways we can be creative is endless. There's a state called "flow" that we get into when we're being creative. Flow is when we're so content and happy about what we're working on that we lose track of time. When we experience a sense of flow, we focus less on our worries and struggles, and instead, feel a sense of contentment and peace.

We can increase the amount of time we spend in the state of flow when we explore what our natural likes and talents are, and when we give ourselves permission to be satisfied and excited with our uniqueness. Being creative is more than creating new things. It's when we're open to our true selves and are excited about who we discover.

Just for Today
Go for a little inspiration today and schedule a visit to a museum, especially one you've never been to or one you think you won't enjoy. Then, let your creativity flow!

Try Again Tomorrow

"Courage doesn't always soar. Sometimes courage is the quiet voice
at the end of the day saying, 'I will try again tomorrow.'"
~ Mary Anne Radmacher-Hershey
Pathways to Recovery, p. 19

It's pretty easy to think of courage as some great big thing, something so massive that there's no way to really grab on to it. It's easy to pass it off to someone else, giving them credit for having courage, but lessening ourselves when we feel we don't have it.

We've all had days when courage was the last thing we felt. We drag ourselves home at the end of a day, tired and drained from all that has worn us down. We try to regroup, but it all feels too heavy, too hard, too real.

It takes a tremendous amount of courage to be able to start afresh each day. Some days we know will be hard; others, not so much. But to go to sleep at night, knowing that tomorrow brings new life, new ideas, new adventures—now that's the kind of courage to hold on to!

Just for Today

As you awake, take a deep breath...and then another. Close your eyes
and imagine a perfect day. Don't let anything else in. Today is a perfect
day if you need to regroup and start over!

Free to Sing

"Recovery means to be free to sing no matter how weak or quivery
your voice…I know I am on the road to recovery
because I start each day with a song."
~ Anonymous
Pathways to Recovery, p. 6

How do we start our recovery days?

We choose each day to place our feet on the pathway to recovery, or we can choose to walk a pathway that leads to symptoms, relapse or loss.

Choosing to work—yes, it takes work!—on recovering every day, instead of lying in bed depressed, or being impulsive with our feelings or thoughts, is an opportunity to once again show our authentic, true gifts.

"Music soothes the savage beast," someone once said, and it applies to recovery. If we can find *our* music, the notes and words that allow us to dance, to sing and to play, then we find a much more refreshing way to live our lives. It's all self-soothing and puts us in a much better place when we wake up each day to recovery.

Just for Today

Oliver Wendall Holmes said, "Many people die with their music still in them." So sing today! Sing in the shower. Sing in the car.
Sing wherever and whenever you feel the urge to let your voice out!

Don't Give it to Them

"They cannot take away our self respect if we do not give it to them."
~ Mahatma Gandhi
Pathways to Recovery, p. 16

Having respect for ourselves must come from within. No one can *give* us self-respect, although too often people can try to take it from us by saying and doing hurtful things. We actually give away our self respect when we give power to these things, letting them eat away at our hope and happiness.

When we realize we've been giving power to the negative things, we can start to stand up for ourselves. We don't do this by fighting or throwing insults and criticisms back at others. Instead, we do this by claiming our own power—the inner knowing that gives us a sense of peace and calm. We realize then that no one can make us feel inferior without our permission.

As we travel the pathway of recovery, we claim a bit more of our own inner power each day. We commit to recovery because we can commit to ourselves—because we know our lives matter. What others say about us starts not to matter so much. We are the heroes of our life stories, and we walk with our heads held high, focused on hope and the positive things ahead. We hold onto our power and acknowledge the good.

Just for Today

What are your most precious and deeply embedded values? How are you connecting these values to your recovery? Remember it's your journey. Don't give it away to anyone else!

Learning from Others

"Is there anyone so wise as to learn by the experience of others?"
~ Voltaire
Pathways to Recovery, p. 233

Our stories are vital and significant parts of our daily lives.

The stories of others are significant too. They can teach us much about life, if we reach out and allow ourselves to be touched by them. Others' stories can only help us on our travels to recovery.

Many times we've felt alone and challenged by our circumstances. It's only when we begin to hear the stories of others that we don't feel so isolated.

We realize that others have gone through the same or worse circumstances in life. We learn from history's lessons.

In this we can find solace and hope. In this, we can learn from the experience of others—and in that, we are wise.

Just for Today

Share your life with someone else today. Give up what you'd like to do in favor of doing what they want to do. Learn from them.

Everyone Needs Help

"Everyone needs help from everyone."
~ Bertolt Brecht
Pathways to Recovery, p. 162

None of us can make it alone in the world. None of us.

We need our family and friends. We need our local stores, churches and schools. We need our neighbors, and we need those who protect us, keep us safe and respond to life's emergencies.

It's likely we've had to rely on lots of individuals throughout our journey, maybe even more than most people. But we can also look at the help we've received and simply say, "Thanks."

We can take opportunities to give back, to help others who need it. We can find ways to repay the support we've received by sharing our own support.

Why? Because everyone needs help from everyone to make it in this world. Simple as that.

Just for Today

Everyone needs a little help...including you! Send a postcard to yourself today. And while you're at it, send one to someone else to say thanks!

Keep Going

*"I am not the smartest person or most talented person in the world, but
I succeeded because I keep going and going and going."*
~ Sylvester Stallone
Pathways to Recovery, p. 272

No one succeeds without first failing. That's why we need
G.O.A.L.S.

Get curious — hold curiosity about ourselves, our dreams, the world
and the people around us.

Open to the options — Be willing to open our hearts, our souls and
our minds. Experience the relief that comes.

Allow Joy — Find it all around us in the simplest things, just by
noticing.

Live — Live life out loud. Live enthusiastically, vibrantly and
brilliantly.

Strive to Thrive — Don't just survive. Find a way to thrive!

Set goals to succeed — and then keep going and going and going.
That's when we'll find success!

Just for Today

*One of the most common mistakes made when setting goals is to not give
them enough detail. Goals should be realistic and achievable, be done
within a specific period of time and have a plan for support. Review your
own goals today to make sure they're complete! Adjust them as needed.*

Received and Given

"Love received and love given comprise the best form of therapy."
~ Gordon William Allport
Pathways to Recovery, p. 185

Love can be hard to talk about. It's not uncommon for the whole area of love to get ignored by our providers.

It might be hard to talk about relationships and sex with a therapist or psychiatrist. But not being able to talk about it doesn't make our desire for love go away. Not talking about it doesn't take away the pain we may have about losing someone we loved, or from desiring love, but not knowing how to find it.

Maybe we think — or have been told by someone — that we can't have special relationships because of our mental health experiences. But intimacy, sexuality and love are a normal part of being a person. If we can't think about this stuff, we're going to get stuck, and a piece of what makes us whole will be missing.

Some people find love by having a close friend or by getting a pet. Others find it by volunteering their time to help others. Still others find love by being in a committed relationship with someone they trust.

Love takes many forms — friendship, intimacy, sexuality — and means

Just for Today
How do you define intimacy? How do you define love? Are they the same things or different? How can you share your own love and intimacy with someone today?

The Key to Happiness

*"To find out what one is fitted to do, and to secure
an opportunity to do it, is the key to happiness."*
~ *John Dewey*
Pathways to Recovery, p. 153

At one time, we gave into the belief that we were incapable of doing anything other than menial work. Perhaps we entertained that notion because, at some point, we probably ended up with a psychiatric label. We may have believed that a label was a life-long sentence to less satisfying employment and fewer life choices.

Today we know that what we do is not defined by any illness or label. What we do is defined by our desires, our hopes and our wishes for the future. Our abilities are not limited by a lack of self-esteem, but are guided by our strengths. We are strong because we are resilient and because we have capabilities that others may not have.

We are especially qualified for tasks and jobs that appeal to our beliefs and knowledge of ourselves. We are capable of anything we want to be, any career we choose to go after and any goal we seek to accomplish.

When we know our strengths, life is not limited. Instead, our strengths become the foundation for success and a key to our happiness.

Just for Today

Which of your strengths gives you purpose in life? Use that strength today and see where it takes you!

Genius, Power and Magic

"Whatever you can do or dream you can, begin it.
Boldness has genius, power and magic in it.
~ Goethe
Pathways to Recovery, p. vi

What dreams lie just beyond reach? What goals have we given up on, convinced they're ones we'll never achieve? What ideas have we squelched, thinking we've lost too much time by now to work on them?

Why do we think we have to give up? We don't! Wherever our recovery journey has taken us, it hasn't left us without strengths and talents and skills. However many obstacles we've faced doesn't mean we haven't learned valuable lessons. Whatever time we've lost doesn't need to be lost forever! We don't have to give up on our dreams!

We will probably have to take some tentative first steps. We'll likely stumble a few times, too. But if we keep the dreams going, vibrant and alive, we will make it. Our boldness will carry us through. Our courage will keep us strong. We can be gutsy and spirited and determined. And before long, we won't have any trouble at all seeing our genius, our power and the magic we've brought to our dreams.

Just for Today

Pick out a time to create a weekly ritual that will soothe your spirit. Maybe it's getting together with friends, making a special meal or going to a religious service. Find the thing that will give you a chance to feel better each week about your genius, power and magic!

An Act of Faith

*"Adventures don't begin until you get into the forest.
That first step is an act of faith."*
~ Mickey Hart
Pathways to Recovery, p. 342

We don't always seek the adventure-filled path. Sometimes, we have to rely on faith.

On their first date, a couple went out to eat at a new sushi restaurant — for one, an adventure; for the other, not so much!

For the one who loved sushi, the meal was great. While she tried new things she'd never had, there was no fear, only excitement. But for the other person — the one who thought sushi would be awful — it took a step of faith to agree to try this new type of food.

But once that step was taken...once the couple headed into the forest together...sushi became their favorite meal to share!

Seven years later, they're still together...and they're still enjoying sushi! Had the one person decided not to take that first step, the couple might have missed out on many years of happiness!

That's how recovery happens, too. One step at a time into a forest of uncertainty. But if we're never willing to take the first step of faith, we might miss out on a lot of great sushi!

Just for Today

Do something that stretches your comfort level. Maybe there's something you wanted to do as a child but didn't. Perhaps there's a place you'd like to visit but not sure you'd fit in. Maybe you could try sushi!

Enabling the Future

"As for the future, your task is not to foresee it but to enable it."
~ St. Exupery
Pathways to Recovery, p. 264

"Enabling" is often a word that carries a negative meaning. We are told not to enable others and not to let others enable us. But what does this really mean, enabling? The dictionary defines it as "giving power, means or ability; to make competent or authorize; to make possible or easy."

So often we want to see what the future holds. We look for signs to help us prepare for what's to come. But it's exactly the future that we're capable of creating, of enabling. Choose what we might, it's in our power to make it possible. It may not always come out the way we planned it, but we have the satisfaction of knowing we're able to create it in all of its glory. We can begin enabling our future today.

Just for Today

As you move through the day, stop to ask yourself, "Where am I now? Am I stuck in my past? Or am I looking so far ahead that everything feels overwhelming? Are either of these influencing how you feel? Take one small step – today – to enable your future!

The Capacity to Love

"Recovery doesn't end with the telling and hearing of the story…
what finally renews people is the belief that their own
capacity to love has not been destroyed."
~ Unknown
Pathways to Recovery, p. 379

Telling our story and hearing others' stories is a great way to heal. Stories are rich in examples of how we have survived and come away better people because of our experiences. But this isn't the end to the recovery process. This is just one step.

So often love meant losing something of ourselves or creating friction because of our desires. But it's only when we realize in ourselves the ability to love that can we set again upon the path of discovery. Believing we are not toxic to others—but fully capable of giving and receiving—makes the path more worthwhile.

Just for Today

Your ability to feel self love may need a change in perspective. Instead of loving yourself for what you do, try thinking about self love as the ability to love yourself simply because you exist!

Choosing to Live

"No matter what befalls me, I feel commanded to choose life. You cannot give in to despair. You may hit bottom, but then you have choice. And to choose life means an obligation not merely to survive, but to live."
~ Nessa Rapoport
Pathways to Recovery, p. 283

How much easier is it to give in to our life's despair than to choose to live our life to the fullest? Some days are much easier than others, right?

Regardless of the bumps, roadblocks and wrong turns, each of us has to find our own way to move past mere survival.

For some, that's finding a job or career that brings us meaning and purpose. Others focus on relationships that nurture and bring much needed support. Many of us find ourselves turning our efforts toward others, especially to those who may just be starting this journey of recovery. We become advocates, we start families, we move forward to define — or redefine — the goals in life that bring us joy.

We choose a life beyond the expectations others have for us. We let go of despair and take command of our lives.

The choice is up to us whether we just survive — or fully live.

Just for Today
There are probably people in your life who have been through major challenges but who have remained positive and upbeat about their lives. Talk to one of them today to see how they were able to live the life they wanted. Ask them to share their ideas with you.

Put it Down on Paper

*"A goal isn't a goal until you put it down on paper,
say it loud, tell others about it, learn it by heart."*
~ Judy Molnar
Pathways to Recovery, p. 117

When we want to stop a habit — like maybe smoking — we aren't really serious until we write down our true goals. While being able to stop smoking is really big, the true long-term goals are based on how we will change — breathing better, tasting more things and not smelling bad because of the smoke. These are the true goals.

Saying our goals out load — to ourselves and others — is also key to our efforts. Saying our goals out loud keeps us honest and on track to actually reach them. Even creating a mantra like "I will quit smoking" becomes easier when we're accountable to ourselves and others.

As we reach out for support and work toward accomplishing our goals, change in our heart becomes easier. And that is where true change happens.

Just for Today
If you keep your goals to yourself, it might not matter so much if you don't reach them. Instead, share your goal with a supporter and ask them to send you a friendly reminder each week with encouraging words!

Giving Time

*"You must give some time to your fellow [human beings].
Even if it's a little thing, do something for others — something for which
you get no pay but the privilege of doing it."
~ Albert Schweitzer
Pathways to Recovery, p. 159*

Giving our time to others comes back to us in many ways. Helping others improves our overall health. We feel better. We find new strengths and nurture our souls. We make a difference, not only in the lives of others, our community or world, but in ourselves.

There are lots of ways we can be of help, most of which require very little time, money or effort on our part. Sometimes that help is as simple as a kind word or a "Thank you!" voiced sincerely.

Helping others is not something we generally need to learn how to do; it's really part of our better human nature. It's part of us, something we can do automatically, without hesitation. But the more we do it, the more its benefits increase.

Helping others is a privilege. We get to do it. We want to do it. We need to do it.

Just for Today

Let everyone go ahead of you today! It's a simple thing but see how good it makes you feel to give to others.

We Are Worth Telling

*"It's very strange, but the mere act of writing anything is a help.
It seems to speed one on one's way."*
~ Katherine Mansfield
Pathways to Recovery, p. 386

For many years we've listened to the stories of others. We've gained knowledge from them and taken their lessons as our own.

How many times have we shared *our* stories with others so they may learn from us? It's a huge risk to tell our stories—for we never know what people will think. It's a bigger risk, however, *not* to tell our stories. Because within them are nuggets of truth that go beyond who we are and stretch into the lives of those around us.

Writing down our stories not only helps when they are read, but the writing itself is a healing mechanism—a way for us to let go of the past to accept it for all it's worth. It's a way to stand up and be proud of all that we have accomplished, even though the odds were against us.

We are worth telling! We are worth sharing! Let's start!

Just for Today
Sometimes it's easier to begin sharing your story in a more anonymous way. If possible, look on the internet to see if you can find a place to share your story. Read what others have posted to give you more ideas.

Ain't Nothin' to It

"Ain't nothin' to it but to do it."
~ Maya Angelou
Pathways to Recovery, p. 157

Sometimes that's all it takes—we just have to DO it.

There are times when we think and plan and prepare, and things still don't turn out like we want them to. We can take calculated risks—measuring the difficulty of each step in the process—and still, things don't work.

Trust. Believe. Understand that jumping into something does not always mean failure. But if we just jump right in—letting go of our fears and worries and doubts—then when we're in that situation again, we'll just go for it...and there will be "nothin' to it!"

Just for Today

Use the power of "one deep breath." When you feel anxious about taking a risk, take one deep breath, then another and another if you still need it. Step out and do something! Let go of your fears, worries and doubts by breathing. You'll feel better and have greater courage to take those risks!

A Long Time

"I was raised to sense what someone wanted me to be and be that kind of person. It took me a long time not to judge myself through someone else's eyes."
~ Sally Field
Pathways to Recovery, p. 128

Do we build our worth on what someone else thinks of us? Are we crushed when someone is disappointed in us or judges us? That's because when we base our feelings about ourselves on the acceptance of others, we suffer.

Our society's vision of success is very narrow. Few of us fit that picture. Success comes from within our hearts. Our strong hearts must love who we are, just as we are. Each of us is a worthy and unique individual. We don't ever have to judge ourselves through someone else's eyes.

Just for Today
What have others told you that you should do...or could do...or ought to do? What is it you'd like to change about yourself? Trust your heart as you move to make personal change.

Unfolding Our Stories

"Don't be satisfied with stories of how things have gone with others.
Unfold your own myth."
~ Rumi
Pathways to Recovery, p. 377

Our lives gain deeper meaning as we explore and reflect on stories of recovery. These stories help us reflect on our own lives, and help us make sense out of things that didn't seem to have any meaning at the time. Hearing others' stories about recovery also helps us realize we're not all alone with our experiences.

We all have our own stories of recovery to tell. Each story is special and interesting. As we think about our lives, we find out how many obstacles we've overcome. We discover that we're survivors. We find our journeys have had some very interesting parts.

We also discover that recovery is truly a journey. We're not at all where we started from. We're moving forward toward new ways of living—reaching out for exciting adventures and making new memories as we go.

Each of us has a story. One that deserves to be told. Our story isn't like anyone else's and knowing that is empowering.

Just for Today

Struggling with how to share your story? Try writing a poem. There are no rules to follow; just share what you're thinking or feeling. If you don't feel you can write one, try re-writing one instead!

Claiming Our Strength

"When we deny our strength, we give up pieces of who we are."
~ Anne Wilson Schaef
Pathways to Recovery, p. 74

We all have strengths. From the time we were small babies, we've had the instinct to persevere, to keep going. As babies, we cried for our survival; as children, we learned to ask for what we needed. As adults, we can challenge ourselves by going after what we need, no matter what.

Every day we use our strengths. We challenge what has gone before and fight for what we want tomorrow to look like.

It's only when we realize these strengths within ourselves, and claim them as our own, that we're complete. We're giving to ourselves that which we really are—with an understanding that we are strong people. And with our strength, we can go anywhere and do anything we choose.

Just for Today

Claiming your strength is important to your recovery. A great way to do that is to teach something to someone you know well. What is it and with whom could you share it?

Where You Start

"Where you are is where you start from."
~ *Anonymous*
Pathways to Recovery, p. 13

No matter where we are or what we're doing at this moment, we have the gift of the future. We have the chance to do whatever we choose to make our future happen, to make it what we want.

It's never too late to start anew, to take the day by the reins and pull it to us in a positive way. It's when we realize this opportunity that we'll make wise choices, good decisions and healthy starts.

It's something to say, "I can do this." It's everything to say, "I *will* do this." To grab the future with gusto and fill it up with opportunity is a gift only we can give ourselves.

Just for Today

Need to start moving? Give something up that you know isn't good for you — just for today. Not only can you do it, you will be able do it!

Ideas of the Living

"Certainly, travel is more than the seeing of sights; it is a change that goes on, deep and permanent, in the ideas of the living."
~ Miriam Beard
Pathways, p. 330

There are moments in life that define a place and a feeling so solidly in our minds that change comes quickly and permanently. Just by taking that path, deep change in our character will happen unexpectedly.

Some of us take the journey, but our changes may come more slowly, yet they impact us just as deeply.

It's not always the destination. It's the journey and our observations along the way that matter.

Just for Today

Travel can bring changes to your life...so why not plan a dream trip? If you can't actually go, then go in your mind! Pick a place to visit; go to the library and get some travel books. Where would you go and what would you do? How do you think a trip like this would change you?

Live the Answers

"Be patient toward all that is unresolved in your heart and try to love
the questions themselves…live the questions now.
Perhaps you will then gradually, without noticing it,
live your way some distant day into the answers."
~ Rainer Maria Rilke
Pathways to Recovery, p. 300

As children we asked questions. We had a special awe for life, and we loved to learn.

Sometimes we lose that sense of awe as we go through rough times. We might feel burdened with depression, overwhelmed by anxiety or have difficulty focusing due to mania. We might spend so much time trying to feel well that we ask so many times, "Why me?"

However, when we take a few moments to quiet ourselves, we're able to use our senses to take in our surroundings. We begin to notice the world again through the eyes of our inner child. We hear the sounds of nature. We feel the gentle breeze. The food we eat tastes wonderful. Stars in the night sky twinkle and make us wonder, just as we might have as a child.

As we recover, we learn to resolve the hardest questions lodged in our hearts by gently accepting what was. We begin to ask new questions, learning to love what *is* and perhaps even finding the answers.

Just for Today

What are the questions you have about your life? Make a question jar. Write each of your questions on a piece of paper and put it in the jar. As you feel like it...perhaps on some distant day...pull a question out and see if you can answer it. Or do you simply need to re-write your question?

Getting Off the Old Road

*"The lesson of the crossroads is that we cannot get off the old road
and on to the new without going through this intermediate place...
disintegration always precedes reintegration."*
~ Robert Gillman
Pathways to Recovery, p. 193

Change is the sign of a new beginning. When
we come to that crossroads point in our lives
where change is inevitable and needed, we
must face what is being left behind and
embrace that which is becoming
clear to us.

Only in change can we grow,
can we come to another day
with arms wide open, hearts
accepting and minds full of
exploration.

To accept change in its flowing, ever-dancing self, is to accept life.
Living is change. If we can embrace this idea and hold on for the ride,
it will be the best journey we've ever taken.

Just for Today
*Worry is one of the things that can keep you from starting on a new
road. Practice not worrying...a lot of what we fear never happens. Do
your best to enjoy a new path!*

The Thing We Want Most

"We fear the thing we want the most."
~ Dr. Robert Anthony
Pathways to Recovery, p. 304

We all know what the fear of failure looks like. But do we ever think about how the fear of success holds us back?

There are lots of people who go through life, seemingly making one bad decision after another, keeping their life in what seems to be constant chaos and turmoil. But are they really making bad decisions? Are they lacking some knowledge or resources? Or could it be that they're fearful of the things they actually want in life?

We can live with our bad decisions—after all, we probably know the consequences, even if they're negative or cause us harm. But to take a risk, to step toward an uncertain future, can be is just as hard. When we can believe in ourselves and our abilities, then taking that step, although scary, is what we need in order to get whatever it is we truly

Just for Today
What is it that you truly want the most? What is one chance you can take today that will move you toward that goal? What can you do tomorrow? Next week? Next month?

Doing What Is Right

"The time is always right to do what is right."
~ Martin Luther King, Jr.
Pathways to Recovery, p. 157

Many of us have suffered a setback in our career, educational and personal goals due to setbacks in our wellness. But we must remember:

Never put off doing what is "right."

It's right to bounce back and to persevere.

It's right to expect a career or educational future.

It's right to ask for reasonable accommodations to achieve our goals.

It's right to speak up when we or others are being wronged.

It's right to expect a full, vibrant life where we thrive and we are happy.

It's right to search for happiness and not settle for less.

It's right to do what is right—for ourselves.

Just for Today

Identify your "right" thing today. Know that it is yours and you deserve it!

We Can Do So Much

"Alone we can do so little; together we can do so much."
~ Helen Keller
Pathways to Recovery, p. 232

Tough life experiences can change us. We are no longer the same. It can seem difficult to connect to other people. Will anyone understand? Is there anyone we can talk to on a deeper level? Will we be stigmatized if we tell someone we struggle with these symptoms?

When we can connect with our peers — those individuals who have experienced similar things — we find a powerful way to help deal with the stress and challenges we face. We also find a way to share our experiences, helping others along their journeys as well.

We can find peer relationships through self-help activities, attending group counseling and more. It can be scary to reach out and try something new. It can be hard to trust others. But life changes in positive ways when we connect with our peers.

Through peers we find mentors, advisors and friends. Our own recovery journey gets stronger and we realize how much more we can do than when we're isolated and alone with our struggles. Reaching out — together — brings us so much more.

Just for Today
Surprise someone today with a nice compliment and a small gift. Connecting with others shows us just how much we can do when we work together!

They Must Change

"I cannot say whether things will get better if we change;
what I can say is they must change if they are to get better."
~ Georg Chrisoph Lichtenberg
Pathways to Recovery, p. 48

Like the great sun that never stops going around — so we are forever evolving. No matter how hard we try to stay in one place, change comes without warning. Change is a given. We face it each and every day.

If it weren't for change, then how could things get better for us? How could new opportunities present themselves? How could we let go of the past? If not for change, we'd be forever floating in space, never beginning, never ending, only floating.

Change creates new adventures. If we can see the present and the future in this way, we can start each day with expectations of all the possibilities awaiting us. Changes are inevitable and it is safe to embrace them.

Just for Today

Are you stuck today, unable or unwilling to make or accept change? Remember change is the only constant but we all do our best to fight it! What's one change you can make in the next week? Do everything you can to make it happen!

July

*"I will paint July with
charming colour so that
she will be captured in delight."*

~ Niji Chrys

Extra! Extra!

"Equal rights are not special rights."
~ *Disability Rights Slogan*
Pathways to Recovery, p. 17

To be treated differently than others is not the point. The point is to treat everyone equally. The fact that we may have experienced the impact of mental health symptoms or trauma can cause us to need things that to others seem "special." But it's not special to be able to get where we're going. Everyone needs to do this, no matter what it takes.

We often wonder if what we need is really necessary. Often societal pressures can lead us to believe that we *shouldn't* need these things. But to think this way is self-defeating. We are not *special,* nor are our needs. We are human beings doing the best we can with the belief that everyone deserves the same chance, the same opportunities and the same choices — no matter what that may seem like or be.

Just for Today

If you're interested in learning more about the Americans with Disabilities Act (ADA) or for more information on reasonable accommodations, check out the Job Accommodation Network (JAN) at www.askjan.org. Sign up to get their newsletter and other resources.

Find A Way!

"We will either find a way, or make one."
~ Hannibal
Pathways to Recovery, p. 182

Being sexual is a vital part of life. It's close to us in a way nothing else is. When we lose our ability to be as sexual as we were, often because of the effects medications have on us — we can lose hope. We feel like things will never be the same again. But don't give up! Our sexuality does not have to become dormant; our sense of being sexual can still be there, but it just might be experienced in different ways than we might be used to.

We can be proactive with our sensual, sexual selves by being willing to explore other avenues of pleasure and stimulation. The human body can experience pleasure in ways we'd never guess. We can make our own paths to sexual fulfillment by experimenting and being open to new ways of expressing our sexuality.

Just for Today

Sometimes medications affect how we feel and respond sexually...which can have a great influence on self-esteem. If you find this a problem, talk with your doctor or other health care provider. You can make a way to experience pleasure. You deserve it!

Whatever You Desire

*"Whatever you desire, whatever change you want to occur,
whatever outcome you seek, remember that it's happening now.
The desire itself is already creating the outcome."*
~ Daphne Rose Kingma
Pathways to Recovery, p. 186

What is it our soul desires? What are those things that make us wake up charged, enthusiastic, excited and ready to face the day ahead? What is it we want for our life, for our family and friends and for the world we live in that would make us say, "Yes!" What is it that would let us know that we are strong, accomplished and purposeful?

We don't need to fear our dreams. We shouldn't have so many regrets that we get frozen in time. We can't have so many doubts we fail to realize how capable we are of working to make our desires come true.

Instead, we seek to believe in what brings us the greatest strength, courage and hope. We can use our higher power to go after what we desire. We can write it down and say it out loud. We can repeat it often to ourselves…to others…throughout each day, finding ways to get closer to realizing our deep and daunting desires.

Work it. Do it. Expect it. Experience it. Believe it. Know it.
Trust it. The changes we desire are happening now!.

Just for Today

*What is it that you most desire? Write it down
and say it aloud. Repeat it often to yourself and
others, including your higher power. You can find
ways to get closer to realizing your deep desires!*

The Future We Need

"If we only dwell on the problems we have,
we can never create the future we need."
~ Anonymous
Pathways to Recovery, p. 281

At times, we dwell on all the disappointments we've had or all the challenges we face. You know them. The disappointments are there when we say, "I didn't get to do that." Those challenges are front and center when we think, "I can't do that." We hold on tight to disappointments, playing them over and over again in our minds. We hold on so tightly we probably think we'll never be rid of them.

But let's face it. Everyone's had disappointments. We've all made mistakes or faced tough challenges. We're all trying to make it through the constant changes in life. But when we only see the problems, well, that's all we'll find...problems.

When we can accept our challenges, learn from them and know that we'll be okay—when we *trust* we'll make it through—then we can start to create our own future. A future that we want, that we need and that we desire.

Just for Today
Do you ever find yourself holding on tight to the past, to the problems and challenges you've faced? What will it take for you to let those experiences be, to accept what happened, recognize what you learned and find or create your own future?

Strength for Those in Need

"It was hard to utilize my strengths when my world was in chaos...
I believe, though, that strengths developed within me as I matured
and grew. My time of need began early, and strengths were
a step forward in my journey. I may not have been conscious
of the use of strengths, but I think they are there for those in need."
~ Anonymous
Pathways to Recovery, p. 127

Whatever we have survived in life, we have done so because we have many strengths. Our strengths kept us going, even though the odds were against us and we thought we couldn't go on. Our strengths are alive and active, and we can feel good about having them.

Strengths are tools that we've developed which have sustained us in life. Our strengths have kept us going, helped us to survive and have made us who we are today. We may not exactly be aware of our strengths, but as we journey down our road of discovery, they will show themselves to us and hold true wherever we go and in whatever we choose to do.

Just for Today

Using your strengths is an active process. It's not enough to just know you have them, you must use them. Act instead of react! Especially when times get rough, you can use your strengths to keep you from going back to any negative thoughts or painful feelings.

Transform the Whole

"Renew your energy, reclaim your fire and seize the power of your heart's desire. Rebuild your vision, restore your soul, transform the part, and you'll transform the whole."
~ Lyrics from The Fat Opera by JoAnn Krestain
Pathways to Recovery, p. 64

Many of us have been told that our experiences—whatever they are for each of us—is the "whole" of who we are. What's more, many of us have believed that.

But recovery tells us that isn't so.

As we find new ways of wellness, as we seek new passions, as we reclaim old goals and set new ones, we begin to understand ourselves better. And as we give our mental health struggles less power over our lives, we find it's only part of who we are. We find ourselves renewed and re-energized, ready to accept all the good we have within ourselves.

Just for Today

There are few things more important in recovery than to renew and re-energize yourself. Find time today to do whatever helps you feel alive and restores your soul...because when you transform part of you, you transform the whole!

Telling Itself in the Living

"Each person's life is a story that is telling itself in the living."
~ William Bridges
Pathways to Recovery, p. 385

Every morning, we rise to start a new day. A new day of adventure and the beginnings of a new page in our story!

But *how* are we living? Does the story we're creating tell others what we want it to? Are we showcasing our recovery journey for what it is? Or are we trying to live someone else's expectations for our life? Are we trying to live up to someone else's idea of what we *could* or *should* be?

Each day we have the opportunity to write a new page of our story, to share our truth and to give a hopeful message to those we meet. What does our story say today? How will we live so our story is truly our message?

Just for Today

What does your story say about you today? Are you living the way you want your story to be told?

Life and Choices

"Life is a process, choices are our tools."
~ Alexandra Stoddard
Pathways to Recovery, p. 259

We all need help along our path.

Helpful tools can take many different forms—eating well, exercising, taking medication, listening to music. Whatever it is we use, we alone should be the ones who choose the tool which helps us most. It's in our choice and use of positive tools that we find control in our life.

It's in discovering our choices and the tools that work for us, that we learn to live well.

Just for Today

Expand your tools! Abraham Maslow said, "if the only tool you have is a hammer, you will see every problem as a nail." What do you need to add to your toolkit today?

The Landscape in Which We Live

"Tell me the landscape in which you live,
and I will tell you who you are."
~ Jose Ortega y Gassett
Pathways to Recovery, p. 132

We spend much too little time and attention to the "landscape" in which we live. Paying attention to our environment is often just as important as the time we give to our physical selves.

House a mess? Unwanted noise and distractions constantly around us can disturb concentration. Living with things that have no meaning can keep us from exploring the everyday beauty all around us. And clutter in our living space simply clutters our whole life.

If we start to make a difference in our "landscape," then we begin the path to finding our way and learning who we really are. We can start by taking five minutes a day to pick up our living area. We can take steps to minimize the noise and distraction, replacing it instead with pleasant sounds and people who comfort us. We can bring in things that have meaning and purpose.

We can try to arrange things we enjoy so that they can readily be seen. And clutter? Well, this might take some time, but it can be done. As we start to clear our environment, it leads to finding our self.

What a wonderful landscape that is!

Just for Today

When you don't spend time nurturing your landscape, your whole environment can suffer. Take today — or plan a day soon — to clean your home top to bottom. Get rid of what you don't need. Let go of the clutter. Create a new landscape!

Potholes on the Road

*"Stop worrying about the potholes in the road
and celebrate the journey."*
~ Fitzhugh Mullan
Pathways to Recovery, p. 367

Of course, the impact of our mental health issues can create huge
potholes along the way. We didn't ask for this experience. We didn't
decide to take medications or see a therapist without good cause. We
didn't plan to change our life path or to experience misunderstanding
and stigma from our communities.

However, we do get to decide whether we remain inside the holes of
the road. Remember, we don't have any ability to change our past.
We don't get to go back and re-live things, making different decisions
for our lives based on what we now know.

So—while it may sound way too simple—we've just got to stop all
the worrying, cease making excuses and give up blaming. We've got
to take responsibility for what we need. We've got to recognize the
past but focus on today and tomorrow. Most of all, we each know
that who and what we've become is more important than any hole in
the road.

Just for Today

*How do you most like to celebrate? Take 10-15 minutes to move out of
your potholes and celebrate the journey!*

Beginning Where We Are

"Don't let life discourage you;
everyone who got where he is had to begin where he was."
~ Richard Evans
Pathways to Recovery, p. 43

Some days are routine, other days can change our lives in a flash. There are days when the things we think will bring us happiness, don't.

There are other days when our lives seem loaded with heartbreak that actually turn into the experiences that teach us more about ourselves than we would have ever expected.

Learning to trust the moment—whether it's quiet, busy or a time of reflection—also means learning to trust in ourselves. It means giving up the fear of the unknown and the pain of the past, allowing ourselves to feel and experience the richness of the now. As we learn to receive the gifts that each day brings, we can embrace the opportunity of receiving joy. And what greater gift to ourselves could there be?

Just for Today
As you learn to live more in the moment, try this. Sit in a chair and feel how it touches you and how you touch it. Do you feel pressure anywhere? Is it hard or soft? Feel the chair and nothing else for a few moments. As you go through the day, practice this in different situations.

The Secret of Success

*"To tend, unfailingly, unflinchingly, towards a goal,
is the secret of success."*
~ Anna Pavlova
Pathways to Recovery, p. 79

You can't get there until you go there.

Having goals in life can help us get to where we're going. If we just have one goal, it's enough. Living every day with a purpose can lead to fulfillment in ways we've never known.

Getting up each day with a purpose in mind—to help others, to do good work, to have fun—will bring us to a level of pleasure we never thought we could obtain. Purpose is what guides the things we do. If we have a goal, if we take a chance to go after a dream, what can it hurt?

Reaching for goals leads us on a path of exploration that we wouldn't go down otherwise. So why not give it a chance to see where the path leads? Be brave, explore and anticipate with joy what the next turn will be.

Just for Today
Reaching for goals can lead you on a path of exploration that you wouldn't let yourself go down otherwise. Why not give it a chance to see where your path will lead?

All I Have Seen

*"All I have seen teaches me to trust
the Creator for all that I have not seen."*
~ Ralph Waldo Emerson
Pathways to Recovery, p. 193

Each of us must find strength to heal: Something we believe to be our own personal spiritual connection can help us with the inner turmoil and hardships we've experienced.

We don't all have to believe in the same "higher power." Each person's spirit is different—which makes spirituality an individual experience. After all, what we're talking about is feeding the spirit. Nurturing the spirit is believing in a set of values that we continually reinforce. It's finding connectedness with other like-minded people. It's practicing our spirituality to help us get through the problems we face that we can't control or do anything about.

Whether we believe in God, Buddha, Jesus, Mohammed, the universe, love, a connectedness through activities, family ties, nature or anything else that uplifts our spirits, we can find some source of inner strength, a belief that keeps our hopes high and that keeps us going and growing. This belief can feed our spirits and help us to trust in things we cannot see.

Just for Today

*How do you express your spirituality? Are you connected with
a group of people with similar beliefs? If not, do you desire that?
What will you need to make this connection?*

connection

Dreaming, Doing, Trusting

*"To dream anything that you want to dream. That is the beauty
of the human mind. To do anything that you want to do. That is the
strength of the human will. To trust yourself to test your limits.
That is the courage to succeed."*
~ Bernard Edmonds
Pathways to Recovery, p. 37

To dream is to have the courage to step outside our doors and our
minds, taking risks and challenging ourselves with all that life brings
to us, no matter what we think or how we feel at the time.

Life goes on around us whether we have the courage to participate or
not. We can be on the sidelines—one of the unknown people—afraid
to come out of our houses, even for a better life, because we're afraid
of the first step, afraid to take the risk of stepping outside of our ruts.
They're not comfort zones; they're our ruts.

We must step up, out of the mire and into our courageous, fearless
selves. Success depends on our ability to face fear head-on. We can
do it.

Just for Today
*Once you're able to take risks, you really can feel your life
transformed. What's one fear you currently have? Make a "pro-
con" list...What are the benefits to me if I face this fear? What are
the negative things I may experience? Review your list and see
which list makes the most sense for you. Will you take a chance
at change or will you stay where you're at?*

Change Your Mind

"If you never change your mind, why have one?
~ Edward de Bono
Pathways to Recovery, p. 324

Sometimes we're told it's a sign of weakness to change…especially when we change our minds about something. Someone might say we don't know what we really want or who we really are if we change our minds.

As we look around, we'll see that life changes. If it didn't, we'd never grow up, start new relationships, celebrate birthdays, or watch the seasons change from summer into autumn…into winter and then blossom into spring once again. Even as we strive to stand still in this very moment, we'll notice changes. The wind will blow, the hands move on a clock, we breathe in and then out, and then in again. The telephone rings and we move to answer it. The night lightens when the sun comes up, and then the shadows lengthen as it becomes evening once again.

Change is good. It's a sign of life and living when things change — including when we change our minds. It means we're thinking, feeling, learning, and deciding things for ourselves. Maybe for the first time in a very long while.

Our minds are valuable. Each of us has a mind that is unique to us. So we can cherish it, use it, listen to it and change it whenever we want and need to. Just because we can.

Just for Today

Just as your body needs activity and exercise, so does your mind.
Keep your mind active through things like reading, puzzles,
math or anything that causes you to think and reason. You'll feel
better too!

Making It So

"Don't be afraid of the space between your dreams and reality.
If you can dream it, you can make it so."
~ Belva Davis
Pathways to Recovery, p. 28

The space between our dreams and our reality is found in the strength of our imagination—that ability we have to create a whole new world in order to look at any experience from a different point of view.

In our imagination, we can create anything we want. We can review what we've done in the past, taking the good points and leaving the negative ones behind. We can see ourselves in places that are exciting, ones that make us feel comforted. We can visualize how we might react in a given situation or how we'd avoid one we don't want. Imagination enhances our creativity and lets us begin to move toward our dreams.

This space between our dreams and the reality we want doesn't have to be so far apart. We can "make it so" with just some imagination.

Just for Today

Your imagination is a wonderful thing! Find a quiet place today; sit comfortably, close your eyes and try to escape into your mind and its imagination. Then practice, practice, practice! The more you use your imagination, the more it will freely come to you!

The Best Thing in Life

"The best thing in life is doing things people say you cannot do."
~ Jennifer Moore
Pathways to Recovery, p. 67

We've all heard someone tell us they don't think we'll do this or that. Maybe they've told us we'd never be able to work again or to go back to school. Others may have said we couldn't get married or be a parent.

Many of us have heard that our symptoms will never get any better and that we shouldn't aim our goals too high.

But look at us now!

Recovery opens up a whole new world full of possibilities, one that can be exciting, comforting and hope-full. We're taking back our own lives and doing all the things that matter to us. We're working and teaching and having families. We're joining our peers to help make a difference in the mental health system. We're exploring our spirituality, using lots of tools to help us stay well and finding a place in our communities. We're finding that life *can* be what *we* want—even though we may have been told not to expect this.

Being told you can't do something is a strong motivator. Shouldn't people tell us more often that we *can't* do something?!

Just for Today
What have you been told that you would never do? How did you...or could you...use that as a motivator to make your life better?

Learning is a Treasure

"Learning is a treasure that will follow its owner everywhere."
~ Chinese Proverb
Pathways to Recovery, p. 137

No matter what we learn in life, we take that knowledge with us wherever we go. But what one person knows is very different from what another person knows.

Consider this story: One woman completed two undergraduate degrees, a master's degree and now has the career she's always wanted. She's gone to school for years and finished each educational program on time. She always has the next step in mind. She loves school and values having each of her degrees.

Another woman has gone to college whenever she felt she needed to upgrade her career; she has a wide variety of class work. She has enough hours to have two degrees, but she doesn't really love school; she goes just to get fulfilling knowledge.

The first woman has a lot more school experience than a variety of life experiences. The second woman has diverse life experiences that enhance her schoolwork. The one thing the two women agree about is the importance of learning—no matter how or why they got it.

Learning in life is a treasure to hold. It will enrich us wherever we go.

Just for Today

Learning comes in 'formal' ways...like school or taking a class. Learning also comes in more 'informal' ways like traveling, reading or transforming life experiences. What treasures have you gained from learning?

Learning is a Treasure

"Learning is a treasure that will follow its owner everywhere."
~ Chinese Proverb
Pathways to Recovery, p. 137

No matter what we learn in life, we take that knowledge with us wherever we go. But what one person knows is very different from what another person knows.

Consider this story: One woman completed two undergraduate degrees, a master's degree and now has the career she's always wanted. She's gone to school for years and finished each educational program on time. She always has the next step in mind. She loves school and values having each of her degrees.

Another woman has gone to college whenever she felt she needed to upgrade her career; she has a wide variety of class work. She has enough hours to have two degrees, but she doesn't really love school; she goes just to get fulfilling knowledge.

The first woman has a lot more school experience than a variety of life experiences. The second woman has diverse life experiences that enhance her schoolwork. The one thing the two women agree about is the importance of learning—no matter how or why they got it.

Learning in life is a treasure to hold. It will enrich us wherever we go.

Just for Today

Learning comes in 'formal' ways...like school or taking a class.
Learning also comes in more 'informal' ways like traveling,
reading or transforming life experiences. What treasures have
you gained from learning?

The Person You Decide to Be

"The only person you are destined to become
is the person you decide to be."
~ Unknown
Pathways to Recovery, p. 361

"What do you want to be when you grow up?" Undoubtedly, we've all been asked this question as a child. But what happened to those early dreams?

Was it the symptoms of an illness that changed our answer? Was it trauma that we neither asked for — or deserved — that stopped us from thinking of our future? Were there a series of small losses that, when combined, seemed insurmountable? Have we done what we could to heal, or have others stepped in to stop us?

The journey of recovery is wide open to us! We can learn to manage our symptoms, and we can heal from our trauma. We can strive to make sense of the losses we've had. We can take charge of our lives — saying, "Thanks, but no thanks," to those who step in with their own expectations of us.

We can make our lives meaningful, happy and full of adventure. Our destiny is not to live a life we don't want. Our destiny is the life we decide. We get to design it. We get to change it. We get to live it!

Just for Today
Is there anyone or anything you need to say, "Thanks, but no thanks" to? How will you hold fast while you move forward?

Rushing Off

*"There are times in life when a person
has to rush off in pursuit of hopefulness."*
~ *Work for Justice Newsletter, Lesotho, South Africa*
Pathways to Recovery, p. 29

Sometimes we've waited around for so long, earnestly wishing that things were better.

We've waited to find the right medications. We've waited to find the right job. We've listened to everyone else tell us what they thought we should do. We've tried to please our family and friends. We've taken this class and gone to that group, in an attempt to get ourselves ready for life outside of the mental health system. We've tried over and over again to put all the pieces of our lives together—all at the same time—in order to move past early losses and disappointments.

But for many of us, there comes a time when we realize we're tired of waiting. We're tired of listening to everyone but ourselves. We're done trying to live up to someone else's expectations. We need to move…now!

That's when we find it's time to set our own goals and listen to our own hearts, to take steps away from the safe place where we've been resting and jump into life.

So grab on for the ride! Rush off, full of excitement, full of new adventures…full of hope!

Just for Today

Are you tired of waiting for your life to get better? Taking small steps in your life is a good way to begin. Why not rearrange your furniture to get started? A change in your environment can sometimes be the spark to take a powerful first step!

With All Your Might

"What one has, one ought to use; and whatever he does,
he should do with all his might."
~ Cicero
Pathways to Recovery, p. 247

In our multi-tasking society, we can put so many things aside that are important to us—our wellness, careers, education, children—that we forget to attend to our relationships "with all our might."

One of the things we often put aside is our circle of support—people in our lives who can have the most positive, healing affect on us. Better, stronger relationships can improve our mood, boost our immune system responses and decrease our stress.

It's important to remember to nurture our relationships, keeping the lines of communication open with our loved ones and being honest and gentle when disagreements arise. Doing nice things for our friends and family along the way will aid us in nurturing a helpful support system, one in which we can feel loved and a part of something greater than ourselves.

Our ability to create a positive support system is often our greatest asset. We should use those supports with all our might.

Just for Today

Spread a little joy today to someone who is in your circle of support. With all your might, do something nice for them!

Those Who Trust Us

"I wanted to live and shout from the top of my voice
that I am somebody! I wanted someone to notice me.
I wanted to feel wanted. I wanted to make use of my time.
In reality, I wanted to be able to trust someone."
~ Catherine Scruggs
Pathways to Recovery, p. 167

Trust. Many of us have trouble trusting. Maybe we've been hurt by others. Maybe the system has hurt us. Maybe a good friend turned his or her back on us. Maybe we've let ourselves down and just don't know how to regain trust ourselves.

Trust is something with which many people struggle. But if we remain afraid to trust—in ourselves, in others—we risk becoming bitter and unable to move happily through life. Not being able to trust means we stop moving forward, stop reaching out, stop setting goals and pursuing them. Not being able to trust means that, on some level, we stop learning and growing, because these require taking risks. And taking risks requires trust.

We have a life-time ahead of new opportunities that will require risk and trust. We are strong. We are likeable. We are lovable. We are courageous. We are willing. We are able to reach out and to trust, one step at a time.

Just for Today

Being able to trust is truly a step-by-step process. You may need to ease into relationships slowly. Start by sharing small confidences with someone and see what happens. As you see that person responding in a trustworthy way, your trust can grow.

Try and Try Again

"You may be disappointed if you fail, but you are doomed if you don't try."
~ Beverly Sills
Pathways to Recovery, p. 302

To fail isn't the worst thing that can happen to us. It may feel treacherous, but it's not the end.

On the other hand, we can look to see our accomplishments? If we can get up in the morning, we've succeeded. If we take a shower or make a sandwich for lunch, we've succeeded. If we get out of the house for a while, we've succeeded.

If we choose to do nothing at all, only then do we fail.

If we do nothing at all, we're not living, much like the dust that falls on our bookshelves, only to be moved by outside forces. When this happens, we've lost control of our lives, and who wants that?

To succeed, we must *do* something, even if we're afraid.

Just for Today
What are you willing to try today? Pick one thing you've been putting off, something you don't really want to do. Begin it today even if you don't finish it, you moved...and in that you have succeeded!

A Change of Self

"Very often a change of self is needed more than a change of scene."
~ A.C. Benson
Pathways to Recovery, p. 321

So many of us have asked ourselves questions like, "Why me? Why did I get this diagnosis? What did I do to deserve this?"

Actually, we could just as easily say, "Why not me?"

We can move around—jumping from job to job, house to house, relationship to relationship—but what does that get us? Nothing if we expect each move to bring us the life for which we've always dreamed. It doesn't work that way. When we keep moving, we simply take everything with us.

But what if we stop avoiding ourselves? What if we stop thinking things will just get better and actually move in ways that will make it so? We can spend the rest of our lives trying to figure out why we've had these experiences...or we can change our view of it. As we expect more from ourselves, we change ourselves. That's when we find our way.

Just for Today
Try daring yourself to change. "I dare myself to...get more sleep...to save more money...to lower my blood pressure..." Go ahead and dare yourself!

Honoring Us

*"The greatest and most healing service that can be offered to people
with psychiatric disabilities is to treat them with respect and honor them
as human beings. This means honoring us in our full humanity,
including our sexuality and our desire to love and be loved."*
~ Patricia Deegan
Pathways to Recovery, p. 180

Sadly, there are many people in society who still view us as a group of
people who should not be taught about sexuality or how to maintain
safe and intimate relationships. But we can change that.

We can start talking with each other about the hurdles we go through
to be intimate, even though it's not easy for some of us. We can
work with our doctors to change medications that interfere with our
sexual lives. We can ask for support in our desire to form positive
relationships. We can determine our own needs for sexuality and
intimacy, and we can seek ways to fulfill our desires. We might even
need to redefine intimacy and sexuality for ourselves.

Our healing is important—and that includes our need to love and be
loved.

Just for Today

*Don't be afraid to share your own love with
others. While being in love is exciting and
wonderful, it can also be scary. But don't
give up on love just because you think you
might get hurt. Love is worth it!*

In Ourselves

"Grab the broom of anger and drive off the beast of fear."
~ Nora Zeale Hurston
Pathways to Recovery, p. 305

Fear is a good thing, especially when it grabs our attention and helps protect us from danger. But fear can also hold us back, making it impossible to travel forward on our journey.

Can we really list the things we're afraid of? Are we afraid of what someone will think of us? Are we afraid we'll be laughed at? Are we afraid we won't succeed because someone has told us we can't? Are we afraid stress will cause a relapse? Are we afraid we'll let others down?

Remember that trying new things requires courage. But having some anxiety about the unknown is something everyone experiences. We can be resourceful and determined on our journey. We can find ways to overcome our fears, and then succeed at reaching our goals—even when we feel fear.

Fear has its place, and it can be useful. But when fear is holding us back, it's time to counteract it by focusing on our strengths and accomplishments. We can tell our fear about all the things we succeeded at today—then fear has less power over us. We can celebrate and reward our courage. We can tell fear we no longer need

Just for Today

What words would your friends, family or supporters use to describe you? Find time today to ask a few people this question. Do you see similarities in how they view you? Do they see you as fear-less or fear-full? Which description fits you best? Can you tell fear that you no longer need it?

We are More than Logical

"If we were logical, the future would be bleak indeed. But we are more than logical. We are human beings, and we have faith, and we have hope."
~ *Jacques Cousteau*
Pathways to Recovery, p. 30

Jacques Cousteau, the most famous oceanographer ever, must have been a logical man. How else could he have made the discoveries he did in studying about our magnificent oceans?

To be logical is a must in our world. How else could we go from day to day, completing everything that needs attention in order for our lives to move forward?

But life is more than logic. Life is full of discoveries to believe in. Life is filled with opportunities for happiness and joy. Life requires a little fun, a little adventure and lots of risk. There is hope — believable hope — to carry us through on our journey.

Just for Today

Do you ever find yourself thinking too much? While thinking is good, sometimes you just need to start doing. Stop thinking about all the things it will take to get you where you want to be. Once you decide what you want — and you add a little faith and hope — your journey can move forward.

The Things We Didn't Do

"The only things you regret are the things you didn't do."
~ Michael Curting
Pathways to Recovery, p. 62

Feeling regret is a big burden holding us down and robbing us of being true to ourselves. It also keeps us from exploring new ideas, places or people. Holding onto regret just brings us guilt, keeping us from feeling free to take risks or try new things.

Risking failure or maybe success—is the only way to make sure we don't leave this world with lots of regrets!

In fact, regret seems much worse than failure. If we try something and it doesn't work out, we can still be proud of the fact that we tried. We can still feel good about the chances and choices we made. Having tried, we may not even care later if something didn't work out or things didn't happen as we'd hoped.

One thing is certain: we will remember what we *didn't* do.

Just for Today

Imagine yourself celebrating a big birthday...60, 70, even 80 or more. When you get out of bed on that morning, what will be on the list of things you have done? Can you use that list to help move you closer to the success you'd like to have in your life?

Gifts in the Pain

"It isn't easy for any of us to transcend the past or pain we might have suffered. Yet there are gifts in those pains, and we can choose to let light into the dark places."
~ *SARK*
Pathways to Recovery, p. 383

One of the ways we can let "light into the dark places" is by being with others, sharing our stories of pain, turmoil, recovery and joy. When we connect with others through our shared experiences, we become more complete; we feel more whole. We accept ourselves a little easier, knowing other people have had similar experiences, too.

We are here as one teacher to another. Our connectedness shows through the flow of word-to-word and story-to-story, healing along the way. It's powerful, and it makes our recovery stronger, especially when we need to "let light into the dark places."

Just for Today
Have you ever thought about using your experiences – including all the gifts you've received from those pains – to become a peer specialist? Bringing your voice and skills into the mental health system is a powerful way of being able to share what you've learned with others who are beginning their own journey.

The First Peace

"The first peace, which is the most important, is that which comes within the souls of people when they realize their relationship, their oneness with the universe and all its powers, and when they realize at the center of the universe dwells the Great Spirit, and that this center is really everywhere, it is within each one of us."
~ Black Elk
Pathways to Recovery, p. 194

Many of us have used spirituality to find peace within ourselves. Spirituality can be a belief in a higher power. It can be practiced by participating in organized religion, such as regularly attending a church, synagogue or temple or worshiping with others. It can be practiced alone, free from traditions and directions from others.

No matter how it's practiced or viewed, many of us have found spirituality through a higher power outside of ourselves. It's that power which gives us peace and calm, as well as a place to go to for healing, comfort, answers and joy.

Spirituality is where our cherished values, beliefs and principles are found. These are often the guiding principles we use in the way we live our lives—personal attributes we practice, like being patient, forgiving, humble, kind, non-violent and faithful. These things provide a "frame-work" for how we live our lives. We find them within ourselves.

Just for Today
Anticipate the needs of someone else. Offer your seat on the bus, open a door or carry someone's groceries.

August

*"Remember to be gentle with
yourself and others...None can say why
some buds will blossom while others
lay brown beneath the August sun."*

~ Kent Nerburn

Making Changes

"We all know what we need to do, but it takes will, determination and even courage to face yourself and others and begin to make changes."
~ Judy Molnar
Pathways to Recovery, p. 44

Deciding to make a change is tough for all of us; actually making that transition can be very daunting. But in each one of us is a natural will to do so, to strive for better circumstances and to take necessary steps to follow our dreams.

Courage is also a part of who we are. If we didn't have courage, we wouldn't be where we are today. How much have we survived to get here?

Survival takes huge amounts of courage. Courage wells up in us like a river. All we need to do is tap into that river of courage and let it flow. As it carries us along, we find change is not as hard as we once thought it would be.

Just for Today

You already have incredible courage within you...you've grabbed your courage when you made difficult decisions that you knew in your heart were right for you! Connect to your courage today; make the changes you know you need to make!

Agreeable Friends

*"Animals are such agreeable friends;
they ask no questions, they pass no criticisms."*
~ George Eliot
Pathways to Recovery, p. 241

Unconditional love.

That's what the animals in our lives offer us. So often we search for it in human beings, only to find our hearts broken by the experience. Animals are companions that accept us no matter what we've done, no matter what we've said.

Some of us only feel confident and safe when our service or companion animals are with us. They help get us through the day. They heal our sorrows and make us feel love, laughter and connection, without rejection and abandonment. Some of them partner with us to make the challenges of our daily tasks easier.

Our companion's lives may not be as long as we like, but we are blessed that we get to know so many wonderful animals throughout our lifetime. They share many gifts with us and make us feel loved.

Just for Today
Find some time to share your life with an animal. Love them, appreciate them and give them a special treat! If you don't have a pet at home, visit a zoo or do some bird watching. Enjoy their unconditional love!

Feeling with Us

"We want people to feel with us more than to act for us."
~ George Eliot
Pathways to Recovery, p. 229

Generally people try to fix what we're unhappy about, when we really only want them to listen to us, without offering advice. We just want them to feel how we feel—just for a moment—so we know we are supported and validated.

Listening is a skill most of us need to improve so that we can better support one another. If we're really listening, we're supporting someone in the best way we can. And if we're really listening, it makes it easier for all of us to ask for support when we need it.

Don't do all the talking. Let's get out of our head and listen to others. That's one way we support each other and grow. We learn by listening. And as we listen, we heal.

Just for Today

Listening is a skill you can improve! Stop today and just listen. Turn off the television and the radio. Find a supporter and simply listen to them without interrupting. As you listen, you will learn...and you can heal!

Make a Commitment

"What we ever hope to do with ease,
we must first learn to do with diligence."
~ Samuel Johnson
Pathways to Recovery, p. vii

A star athlete practices his or her sport daily. There is always more for them to learn. There are always muscles to tone and strategies to work on in order to perform skillfully and competitively. A star athlete commits to his or her sport, knowing that practice promises they will get better and better.

Recovery is like practicing a sport. We commit to it, and this commitment requires daily practice as we modify our lifestyles. At first we might feel tired and worn out. Sometimes we might not feel like practicing recovery at all. But we continue to train, practicing and working towards recovery, because we've committed to making our lives the best they can be.

We commit to recovery because we want to—not because someone else demands that we recover. We commit to recovery because the journey is ours—and we know it's going to be filled with exciting discoveries, many new choices and endless opportunities to celebrate our accomplishments along the way.

We commit to recovery because we have hope for a better future. We deserve to recover. We deserve to meet the goals that we've set. We deserve to win.

Just for Today

Have you made a commitment to recovery? Remember, just as you would respect the promises of someone else, you also need to respect the commitments you make to yourself!

You Will Know What to Do

"When we live with a grateful heart, we will see
endless opportunities to give: a flower from the
garden to a coworker, a kind word to your child,
a visit to an older person.
You will know what to do."
~ M.J. Ryan
Pathways to Recovery, p. 352

Being thankful for what we have is a way of opening our hearts to others. When we come in out of the rain into a protective shelter, we're better able to see those around us who have also made it and give a part of ourselves to them.

When we see a starry sky and appreciate it, we must see it with joy, taking it in, making it a part of who we are.

By intentionally stepping into the shelter of gratitude, we find that we're more capable of giving to others. We can then sit back and take the load off long enough to share a smile or a warm handshake. It's in thankfulness and giving back to others that we find meaning in life.

Just for Today

Living with a grateful heart means you share your gratitude with those around you. Today, tell someone they were kind to you. You will know what to do!

Courage Is Being Scared

"Courage is doing what you are afraid to do.
There can be no courage unless you are scared."
~ Eddie Rickenbacker
Pathways to Recovery, p. 41

Eddie Rickenbacker was certainly a man who understood fear. Whether it was as one of the earliest stunt pilots, behind the wheel of a race car or through many of the near-death experiences he had in his lifetime, Rickenbacker never gave up.

So it is with our recovery — we must never give up. For some, recovery is a long and arduous trek as we go forward three steps, back four, over three, down two, around the corner and sometimes, back to where it was we started. But we must never give up.

Taking risks and being scared is normal. In fact, it's probably not good if you don't feel frightened! We just have to keep trying — as Eddie Rickenbacker did. Courage won't be far away.

Just for Today
Being scared is normal. You probably won't ever quit being afraid, you just learn not to let the fear control what you do. As you let your courage out, your confidence will build!

I Own My Excellence

"I accentuate my abilities.
I own my excellence by concentrating on the good in myself."
~ Sue Patton Thoele
Pathways to Recovery, p. 87

How easy it is for some of us to look at our deficits and not our natural abilities. We all have strengths; we just need to search our souls and spirits to find them.

We're all good at certain things, but we can have trouble identifying our strengths and abilities. Others often recognize or reflect on our personal excellence because sometimes they see them better than we do.

Finding our skills and abilities is part of the journey to finding our unique gifts and talents. Once we can see all those strengths inside of us, we can begin to accentuate our own abilities, finding the good in ourselves.

Just for Today

Identify one strength that you have today. It may be something you're good at or a skill that someone has noticed. Keep track of how many times you use this strength over the next week. Own your excellence!

Three Things to Crave

*"There is a wonderful mythical law of nature that the three
things we crave most in life – happiness, freedom and peace of
mind – are always attained by giving them to someone else."*
~ Peyton Conway March
Pathways to Recovery, p. 161

If we had the opportunity to deliver a speech to tell the world what
we believe would make it a better place, what would we say?

What is it we can do today to make that difference? Maybe it's smiling
at someone we see in our neighborhood. Maybe it's writing a letter to
the editor of the newspaper, complimenting someone for something
special he or she has done for the city. Maybe it's telling someone
we forgive them for something we've been angry or hurt about for
awhile. Maybe it's sharing a piece of our sandwich with a squirrel at
the park.

The ideas and opportunities for making the world a better place are
endless. We can all make a difference when we give positive energy
and love to others around us. Giving to others can give us a deep sense
of satisfaction. It can chase away the blues, and it can chase away our
loneliness. Giving to others can satisfy our cravings; it's an act that
brings happiness, freedom and peace of mind.

Just for Today
*What's one thing you bring to the world that only can give? Do you
love genuinely? Do you share your laughter freely? Do one thing
today where you share your "gift" with someone!*

Do it with Enthusiasm

"You may do foolish things, but do them with enthusiasm."
~ Colette
Pathways to Recovery, p. 123

It's time to celebrate all that we've done to get where we are today!
We can put on the goofy hat and bring out the bubbles, start the music
and sing along. It's time to celebrate!

Take off those lonesome blues, those achy hearts. Know that the miles
we have traveled have been worthwhile, for we know what we know
today and we have grown from who we were yesterday.

We must dare to do that which we usually don't do, like wearing a
wild pair of shoes or cutting our hair in a different style. It doesn't
matter what others think—we must celebrate any way we can. For
we have lived the nightmare and can say that daylight is here.

Just for Today
*Go ahead and do something wild today! Step out...why don't you
get a new haircut? You might be surprised how good it makes you
feel!*

Today Is the Day

"Today is the first day of the rest of your life."
~ Abbie Hoffman
Pathways to Recovery, p. 50

Some of us seethe with anger under the surface about being ill, being overwhelmed with the trauma we may have experienced or regretting the life we lost when we first recognized our symptoms.

We must come out of the struggle of rage and make peace—today. We must forgive our bodies and ourselves and get on with the important business of getting well.

Don't let the past keep us from being our authentic selves. Don't let the voices take over every shred of reality. Don't let the mania rage out of control. Don't let the depression stay around. Instead, sweep the anger and rage out the door. Then step onto the path to recovery—today—and start a new life.

Just for Today

Anger is something that can tear you down quickly and keep you from moving forward. If you find controlling your anger is difficult, look for ways to rid yourself of anger in a productive way...mow the lawn, lift weights, walk or run. Physical activity can be good for your body and your emotions! Start now...today is the day!

Live Every Day

"May you live all the days of your life."
~ Jonathan Swift
Pathways to Recovery, p. 123

If I cannot live as if the days were all gone,

If I do not take every day as it comes,

If I will not squeeze the juice out of life,

I will live all my days in awful strife.

If I cannot laugh every day out loud,

If I find myself always alone in a crowd,

If I will not reach out to others and speak,

I will only fulfill a little of what I want to teach.

If I do live each day as if it were my last,

If I gather my courage and leave the past,

If I face each day and find all the good,

I will live a life knowing I did all that I could.

Just for Today

What makes you say "Yes!" to life? Grab some colored markers and draw these things. Perhaps it's a favorite pet, the sound of rain or the calm of the ocean. Enjoy the fullness of your life today!

Leap After Leap

*"If your life is ever going to get better, you'll have to take risks.
There is simply no way you can grow without taking chances."*
~ Agnes de Mille
Pathways to Recovery, p. 42

Have you ever turned off the lights and used a flashlight to find your way around, noticing how different things look in the dark? Ever gone outside on a warm summer's night and noticed how many creatures in nature are buzzing, flying and hopping around, even though most of your neighbors are asleep?

The thing about living is that it's filled with so much we don't yet know. Sometimes we're searching for answers. What's the purpose of our lives? What are we supposed to do next? Will tomorrow be better than today? But all too often, we end up not knowing the answers to any of our questions.

The thing about living is that it's entirely okay not to have the answers to our biggest questions. It's okay not to know what the future holds. Sure, we can make plans and set goals, but it's in living life—in the now, in the present moment—that we can really experience the magic and mystery of this beautiful thing called life.

The next time life fills us with anxious questions we can't answer, and the moment starts feeling dark, we simply need to breathe in and breathe out and get the flashlights ready. They'll show us a different way.

Just for Today

Take one very small risk today. Taking a risk in one area of your life will spill over into other areas!

The Ultimate Reward

"The journey is the reward."
~ Taoist Saying
Pathways to Recovery, p. 68

At the end of the day, we all want to feel as though we've accomplished something worthwhile.

However, there are those days—sometimes weeks or longer—where we simply can't see the progress. If we have a 'to do' list, we've probably not marked anything off of it. Maybe we get to the end of the day and can't remember what it was that we hoped to accomplish—thanks to stress and interruptions and unanticipated changes.

Maybe our goals seem further away—like we can't achieve them—even though we keep trying. What do we do? We have to give ourselves credit for the 'job well done.' We must be willing to recognize the importance of the journey.

Reward those small achievements. Celebrate the daily push forward with understanding. Keep trying. Keep moving. The journey toward the goal is worth taking! The journey itself is—after all is said and done—the ultimate reward.

Just for Today

Do something excessive—but safe—today and do it without guilt!
Simply enjoy what you're doing without questioning yourself!

All We Have

"What we put into every moment is all we have."
~ Gilda Radner
Pathways to Recovery, p. 320

We never know exactly what our days will be like. While some are routine, others can change our lives in a flash. There are days when the things we think will bring us happiness, don't. There are other days when our lives seem loaded with heartbreak that turn into the experiences that teach us more about ourselves than we would have ever expected.

Learning to trust the moment—whether it's quiet, busy or a time of reflection—also means learning to trust in ourselves. It means giving up the fear of the unknown and the pain of the past, allowing ourselves to feel and experience the richness of the now. As we learn to receive the gifts that each day brings, we can allow ourselves the opportunity of receiving joy. And what greater gift could there be?

Just for Today
Try asking yourself these four questions each day:
1. *What are you proud of?*
2. *What are you grateful for?*
3. *What can you do to help someone today?*
4. *What can you do to have some fun?*

Stars Hidden In Your Soul

"Reach high, for stars lie hidden in your soul.
Dream deep, for every dream precedes the goal."
~ Pamela Vaull Starr
Pathways to Recovery, p. 120

We need to search deeply when we set goals for our lives, and we always need to remember the action steps we must first take to reach those goals.

So often, we give in to the goals others select for us. Our parents, our children, our partner, our work, our nurses, doctors and other providers, all have their own ideas of what they see as *our* goals.

But where are we in the planning of these goals? Are we behind the wheel driving or are we taking a backseat, sitting silently.

We need to personally identify our *own* goals to succeed. We must reach high and dream deep. We deserve it.

Just for Today

Are you working on your dream or just waiting for it to happen
on its own? If you're just waiting, your dream may pass you by.
Review your goals today. Do you need to do some more planning?
Maybe add or delete something? Remember the stars hidden in your
soul!

Taking Different Roads

"People take different roads seeking fulfillment and happiness."
~ Jackson Browne
Pathways to Recovery, p. 118

Are we able to celebrate our own lives, or do we spend too much of our time comparing ourselves to others, wishing we were more talented, wealthy, beautiful, successful…you know, more like someone else?

Each of us has a different path to live. The biggest part of our journey is to explore that path and to find excitement, fulfillment and joy as we go.

If we're comparing ourselves to others and seeing our inadequacies, we aren't able to discover much. If we're spending our time living in the shadows of someone else's journey, we aren't able to walk our own path, and then our way can seem unfamiliar and scary.

Focus on the happiness. Focus on what brings purpose and meaning to life. As we step out along our journey, with a smile on our faces, we'll be ready to go for our dreams!

Just for Today

What is it you want to do in life? What will bring you happiness and fulfillment? That's the long-term goal. Stash away any thoughts that it's impossible and find the small steps that can be used to reach that goal. Think of how exciting the journey will be – even if at times you know you'll feel scared or uncertain.

You Kind of Want to Try It

"When people tell you that you can't do something,
you kind of want to try it."
~ Margaret Chase Smith
Pathways to Recovery, p. 18

So many times people have told us in life that we can't do this or that. "You can't have a healthy relationship." "You can't keep a job." "You can't learn to play the piano." Whatever it was, we have usually proven them wrong. Why? Because we have within us a pride and a longing to live that no one's words can confine.

We can prove the myths about our experiences are incorrect. We can do whatever we set our minds to do. Don't try to stop us! We are a mighty force of people, sometimes straining at the bit. Other times, we're like live wires, touching everything we can and making our dreams come true.

Don't tell us we can't, because then we'll definitely try!

Just for Today
It's time to try something different again today! Make it something you've been told you can't do!

Truly Living Life

*"When we are motivated by goals that have deep meaning,
by dreams that need completion, by pure love that needs expressing,
then we truly live life."*
~ *Greg Anderson*
Pathways to Recovery, p. 10

Some of the greatest "doers" in the world have also been some of the greatest dreamers.

Elizabeth "Grandma" Layton struggled with bipolar illness and depression for more than 35 years, until she discovered drawing at age 68. Having lived through this, her artwork was fueled by the deep meaning she held for her subjects — those who were homeless, people with AIDS, older adults, individuals who were targets of racial discrimination. It also gave her the opportunity to give voice to these community issues.

Grandma Layton often described her passion for art, saying it saved her life. She had a goal with deep meaning and long-held dreams that needed completion. She shared her love through her work. As she moved toward a greater love of life through her creativity, her depression lifted and she enjoyed drawing until her death at age 83.

Grandma Layton — now that's a woman who learned, even late in life, the joy of truly living life.

Just for Today

Say to yourself, "I am creative." Make a list of the tiny things you could do today...then do them!

A New Person

"I've come to know that I can be a new person."
~ Telling Our Story of Recovery Workshop Participant
Pathways to Recovery, p. 376

Telling our stories awakens in us our "new person," bringing identity to ourselves once again.

Sometimes, after a battle with our symptoms, we must re-discover ourselves. In the process of reflection and sharing, of hearing others' stories, we discover we're not who we were before.

We change, we see things differently, maybe more clearly, and we leave behind things that don't work for us anymore. We grab the "new person" and our new, unique identity.

A diagnosis may render us motionless at first, but then there's a spark, a motion inside that even though we've struggled, we get up and re-form our identity. It's different and it's new, but it's us—in our pure form.

Just for Today

Ask someone to tell you a story. Listen, learn and see how you can make the story part of your own.

Experimenting with the Truth

"Our own life is the instrument
with which we experiment with the truth."
~ Thich Nhat Hanh
Pathways to Recovery, p. 7

Sometimes we let others define what the truth is for our lives. We may experience symptoms—such as depression or heart problems—and receive a diagnosis to help us understand those symptoms. Our experiences and diagnoses may lead us to believe we have limitations. We might feel limited in our ability to be in school, at work, to have relationships, to live independently or to have a family. We may start making decisions based on what we *can't* do, not on what we "can" or "could" do.

We may not see how big our lives really can be when we live on "limits" instead of "potentials." The truth of our solitary life is what we make it—and we can reach far and wide and tall to fulfill our dreams, no matter who we are, or what we've been through. We can do this when others set limits…because for every limit, there just has to be another possibility waiting to be discovered!

Just for Today

Don't limit yourself today! And don't let your own expectations
of yourself—or those of others—keep you from experimenting and
finding the possibilities life has to offer you!

Because I Want to Do It

"I want to do it because I want to do it!"
~ Amelia Earhart
Pathways to Recovery, p. 61

Where does motivation come from?

Amelia Earhart, the famous aviatrix, didn't let anyone tell her what she could or couldn't do.

Earhart was told repeatedly that she couldn't fulfill her dreams, but that never stopped her from trying, and she ended up being the first woman to fly solo across the Atlantic. She set several flying speed records. She never stopped doing what she wanted to do because of the expectations, or lack of support, from anyone else.

Doing what we want to do — simply because we want to do it — is the foundation of our recovery journey. Finding our own motivation, passion and commitment are essential to creating the life we want and to doing the things that we want to do!

Just for Today

Not sure what you want to do? Find some inspiration. Go to the library for a book or video of something you've always wanted to try.

Getting Ready

"Before everything else, getting ready is the secret of success."
~ Henry Ford
Pathways to Recovery, p. 118

Getting ready—the process of planning and preparing—is key to creating the life we really want. Without a plan, we can tread aimlessly through life, simply getting up in the morning and making it through the day, only to get up the next day and do the exact same thing. It can quickly become a life without meaning, without connection, without adventure.

Getting ready doesn't have to be overwhelming. Nor does planning for our life need to be complicated. When we decide on a goal, we need only to take one step at a time. We don't get to the other side of a river by taking one big jump. But with a firm plan, a little preparation, some encouragement and belief in ourselves, we can be successful.

Just for Today
The first step in getting ready is getting it out of your head! Begin a list of ideas you have and write them down. As you being to put your thoughts down, do you see where you can start to make a firm plan?

The Power to Change

"No one is in control of your happiness but you;
therefore, you have the power to change anything about yourself
or your life that you want to change."
~ Barbara deAngelis
Pathways to Recovery, p. 320

We can spend our lives being absorbed by all we've experienced, or we learn how to cope with our symptoms, find our wellness, and get up and do something positive with our lives. We can choose to be happy or unhappy. We have the power. No one else.

Sometimes when we just can't get things going, a change in our attitude is what gets us moving toward our goals, allowing us to use our true gifts. We *can* choose our attitudes. We must not let life pass us by because we choose to be miserable.

We can grab life in all its wonder. It's there for us to take.

Just for Today

Throughout today, think about the benefits of what you want, not the difficulties you might encounter.

The Most Interesting Game

"Rebellion against your handicaps gets you nowhere. Self-pity gets you nowhere. One must have the adventurous daring to accept oneself as a bundle of possibilities and undertake the most interesting game in the world — making the most of one's nest."
~ Harry Emerson Fosdick
Pathways to Recovery, p. 76

It's fascinating to watch birds in the spring. It's instinctive for many of them to gather twigs, leaves and a variety of other items to build a nest. Then they lay their eggs, sit on them, feed the hatchlings and then help them learn to fly so they can safely leave the nest. Finally, after all this, they take the next step toward maturity and independence.

Birds don't get told they can't build nests, lay eggs, raise a family and then migrate to a different climate when the weather gets colder. They just do what they do…and they do it well. Sure, things get in the way at times, like a spring rain that lasts for days, or a crouching cat that threatens to pounce on the nest. But nothing seems to stop the birds from taking charge of their nests — they stay focused and determined, even when the going gets rough.

We can also make the most of our "nests," building our lives with determination, joy and pride. Our lives hold so much possibility. We can promise to not let anyone get in our way why they say "you can't," because, even when we face difficulties, there are still so many things we *can* do. Life's surely an adventure waiting to be explored!

Just for Today
'Could' you do something or 'can' you do something? Which adventure will you choose today?

Staying In Shape

"Exercise is important. You have to stay in shape.
My grandmother, she started walking five miles a day when she was 60.
She's 97 today and we don't know where the hell she is."
~ Ellen DeGeneres
Pathways to Recovery, p. 358

Exercise is good for the mind, body and spirit. Exercise helps us work out the physical stress we carry. And, if we pick out something we enjoy as our regular exercise activity, we'll be more likely to do it.

Having been active as a child, one woman thought back on what she enjoyed doing when she was young. As a kid, she rode her bike every day and often went swimming. Thinking of these activities, she realized they'd helped her get away from the stress she had at home and school.

So she found a bicycle at a half-price store and enrolled at a local community center with a pool. She even began watching her eating habits.

In a few months, she'd lost 50 pounds and her health — both physically and mentally — had improved tremendously! She was able to take far less medication and her blood tests now have good results.

We don't need fancy equipment, we just have to move! The more we move, the more our brains function at a heightened level. We can relax then, having given the pleasure center of our brains a well-deserved boost!

Just for Today

Exercise and a healthy diet are essential in your wellness. What's one small change you can make today in your exercise or eating?

Those Who Hold Us Up

"Those whom we support hold us up in life."
~ Marie Eschenbach
Pathways to Recovery, p. 232

When we give to others, it's often the best way to feel better about our lives. When we share ourselves and our support for others, we feel better. We move out of our comfort zone, and we embrace the magic of giving.

Bono, lead singer of the band U2, once said that it's "one of life's great privileges that we get to help each other."

We *get* to help! It's not an expectation. It's not required. But it's something each of us *can* do. And in giving of ourselves—through our support, encouragement and love for others—we get back all we need to hold us up in life.

Just for Today

Find a way to help someone today...not because you have to but because you get to!

Different Forms of Strength

*"From the beginning of my illness through the journey of recovery
my different forms of strengths and abilities have played
a part in my remaining well and successful."*
~ Carrie Hunter
Pathways to Recovery, p. 129

It's almost as though *strength* is not a strong enough word when we think of the things we've gone through to get to where we are now.

It's strength! We are strong in many amazing ways!

But we don't always recognize when we're in trouble. We don't always know that our strengths are constantly right there for us to use, helping us get through the day.

Each and every day we must tell ourselves that we are strong and we have the ability to do only what we can do. No one else will do it for us. That's why we are who we are—and why we are here. Our strengths can keep us well and successful.

Just for Today
An important strength to nurture is the ability to ask for help when you need it. Try putting together a "fan club" — it's a list of all the people who you can call when you need a little support. Keep it handy and call on your fan club as needed!

Doing the Improbable

*"The world is divided into two classes, those who believe
the incredible, and those who do the improbable."*
~ Oscar Wilde
Pathways to Recovery, p. 7

We'll probably never fly to the moon, swim across an ocean, become president of a great country or discover the cure for cancer. But maybe we can find a way to live contentedly, knowing that what we do is enough.

Maybe we will do something everyone has told us we probably won't be able to do because of the challenges we've faced. Things we've been told we would never be able to do—like working full-time, writing a book, driving a car, living alone or waking up happy; these *are* possible.

Just watch us! We won't let anyone tell us what we can't do. Recovery is about claiming who we are and growing into roles in our lives beyond a diagnosis, beyond needing medical and psychiatric treatment, and beyond waking up stuck and afraid and uncertain about who we are and what we can do.

This journey of discovery is all about what we really want and *can* do—both incredible and as improbable as those may seem.

Just for Today

Many of your peers have become people doing the improbable. Talk with someone you respect who not only believes, but does. Ask them how they discovered the difference.

Lots of Steps to Take

*"My journey of recovery isn't over yet! I still have a lot of steps to take.
But I am looking forward to what challenges life has in store for me.
In the end, I have memories of people who have touched my life.
In turn, touching their lives."*
~ Janice Driscoll
Pathways to Recovery, p. 382

Recovery is not an end in itself. It's a process.

Recovery is not a place to stop. It's a place for beginnings.

Recovery is not the last step. It's the collection of many steps.

Recovery is not the only action. It's the action of beginning.

Discovery is what recovery is all about!

Recovery is all about discovery!

Just for Today
*Sometimes you can find discovery is not that far away or hard to
find. Take a few minutes today and clean out a closet or drawer!*

A Miracle Every Second

*"All change is a miracle to contemplate,
but it is a miracle happening every second."*
~ Henry David Thoreau
Pathways to Recovery, p. 332

We fight change. We avoid change. We wish it on others but not on ourselves. We push it away, content to live with whatever consequences happen from our current actions.

But in pushing change aside, we stop ourselves from doing new things, seeing new places or exploring new activities. We limit ourselves to the here and now. We stagnate. We're bored. We miss the challenges so necessary to our journey.

What a wondrous picture Thoreau paints for us! Change happens every second — and as we let change in, as we acknowledge the power it has, we find ourselves changed. We find the beauty and comfort around us. We find the miracles.

Just for Today

*A good way to recognize how change is happening every second
is to spend time watching the clouds. Look how they move, what
shapes they make and the different colors of the sky. Can you see the
miracle?*

Feel the Joy

"Why are we here?
We're here to feel the joy of life pulsing in us now."
~ Joyce Carol Oates
Pathways to Recovery, p. 324

We are here for this very moment, right now as we are, who we are, and what we're doing.

Yet we yearn to look ahead or back to the past.

To live now, we must look, observe, listen, touch and speak for the moment we're in. Let's pay attention to what we're doing at all times. One thing at a time, fully participating in each moment. Those moments will bring us more joy, peace and serenity if we are experiencing them as though we're savoring our greatest meal.

Just for Today

Do something today that you liked to do when you were a kid. Run through sprinklers, hang from some monkey bars, make a mess with finger paints or clay. Feel the joy!

September

"By all these lovely tokens,
September days are here."

~ Helen Hunt Jackson

Sharing Our Happiness

*"No medicine is more valuable, none more efficacious, none better suited
to the cure of all our temporal ills than a friend to whom we may turn
for consolation in time of trouble, and with whom
we may share our happiness in time of joy."*
~ Saint Ailred of Rievaulx
Pathways to Recovery, p. 233

The road to recovery often means reaching out for support.
We're told we need to change and grow, attend this group
or that therapy, take a prescription and work on altering
our lifestyles in a variety of ways. We start focusing on our
problems, unable to see the positive things about our lives.

The journey of recovery shouldn't be a burden, filled only with hearing
about the things we need to change. Sure, there are things we struggle
with—but it's not all dark and dreary! We can face our recovery with
enthusiasm!

One way to do this is by connecting with peers who are able to share
our journey. Through our peers, we grow friendships as we find
people who understand, support and nurture us.

Friends can't do our own recovery work for us, but they can support
our journey, giving us someone to share the down times with—as well
as the celebrations and joys!

Just for Today

*Play a game with a friend who lives out of town...you play in your
home, they play in theirs. It could be Monopoly, checkers or a crossword
puzzle. Share your happiness!*

Where I Intended to Be

"I may not have gone where I intended to go,
but I think I have ended up where I intended to be."
~ Douglas Adams
Pathways to Recovery, p. 96

Life travels like a circle. We go around to come around and we always come out in a different place from where we began.

In this circle of discovery, it's not what we've *thought* would happen, but what *does* happen that we find rewarding. Maybe our dreams haven't come true. But were they the dreams we intended? Are we where we need to be at any given time, learning what we need to learn and gaining strength we never had?

Life's circle goes round and round, changing constantly. Yet the journey taken step by step can take us to where we intended to be.

Just for Today

The circle of discovery can be pretty overwhelming. If you should find yourself feeling this way, try breaking your large tasks down into smaller commitments. When you can do this, you'll find your goals will be easier to achieve.

Be the Change

"You must be the change you wish to see in the world."
~ Gandhi
Pathways to Recovery, p. 19

No more sitting around, waiting for other people to change the world! We can do it today! When we live our lives in the way we'd like to see the world change, *we* begin to change. And then, we can become a living example of how the world could be.

But how do we get there? Sincere change requires not only good intentions, but also action. We can't expect others to change if we're not willing to do it ourselves. We can't wait for others to take risks without being willing to take them ourselves.

While it's pretty easy to find our comfort zone and stay there, in reality, staying there keeps us stuck. We must be willing to begin with ourselves. We must be willing to start making positive and life-affirming changes.

And what happens then? The change we seek will be the change we want.

Just for Today

As you seek change in your life, don't over do it. Make changes gradually and with purpose. You'll find it to be a whole lot less stressful!

Making a Difference

"It's easy to make a buck. It's tougher to make a difference."
~ Tom Brokaw
Pathways to Recovery, p. 159

There are those of us who love money — and there are those of us who love people and causes. Sometimes the two overlap, but those with the causes often make more than a buck. They are the ones who make a difference.

Peer support workers, advocates, volunteers and understanding service providers are truly making a difference in the lives of individuals across the globe. They don't do it for the money. They do it mostly to help others.

Helping others makes our own health better and our immune systems stronger. And that's worth more than a buck. It's worth its weight in gold.

Just for Today

Pay attention to your money. Spend part, save part and give part of it away.

Just Be Grateful

"You cannot be grateful and bitter. You cannot be grateful and unhappy. You cannot be grateful and without hope. You cannot be grateful and unloving. So just be grateful."
~ Unknown
Pathways to Recovery, p. 353

As we sit and think of all we can be grateful for, it's hard to believe we could ever be bitter or unhappy or without hope or love. All too often, our thoughts turn to the negative as we quickly become cynical, complaining about every little thing that doesn't go our way.

When a friend decided to move to the mountains, another friend asked him about the beauty of the place in which he was about to make his home. "What happens when you go to some place spectacular?," she said. "Don't you get tired of it? Don't you just look at everything the same? Don't you forget what it is that made you happy and grateful to move?"

"No," the friend replied. "You just start to see the details."

Just for Today

As you go through the day, notice the details around you...a quiet sunrise, laughter from the kids next door, the unique smells of the city. Notice each and every thing that comes you way...may you just be grateful for the details!

A Glimmer of Hope

*"For the longest time, [life] was a complicated matter,
but finally the day came when a glimmer of hope peeked through
and I started to begin to have hope and believe in myself."*
~ *Chris Shore*
Pathways to Recovery, p. 31

Hope is within us and we must find it. Hope is like a small spark waiting to be lit, a seed waiting to be watered, a child waiting to be born.

In all of us, there is hope for something — be it for life, love, health or happiness. We would not be here today without it.

However, tapping into one's hope is not always an easy thing.

We must rummage through all of the negative impulses we have, tear down the doors of our minds and reach out to that living spark within us. There is hope! Inside of each of us there's a responsive spark waiting to be lit, ready to shine it through!

Just for Today

Finding and keeping your hope can be hard work! Try reading or sharing uplifting stories, quotes, poems or parables with yourself and others.

Credit for a Job Well Done

"Every evening when my day is over, I reflect on what I have
accomplished throughout the day and give myself credit
for a job well done."
~ Julie Bayes
Pathways to Recovery, p. 294

At the end of the day, we all want to feel that we have accomplished something.

However, there are those days — sometimes weeks or longer — where we simply can't see the progress. If we have a 'to do' list, we've probably haven't marked anything off of it. Maybe we get to the end of the day and can't remember what it was we hoped to accomplish — thanks to stress and interruptions and unanticipated changes. Maybe our goals seem further away, unachievable, even though we keep trying. What do we do?

We can give ourselves credit for a 'job well done.' We can be willing to be our own cheerleader and find it within ourselves to see that to 'just be me' is an accomplishment.

Reward those small achievements. Celebrate the daily push forward with understanding. Keep trying. Keep moving. The journey toward the goal is worth making. The journey — after all is said and done — is the ultimate reward!

Just for Today
Why not pat yourself on the back today? Give yourself credit for your own job well done!

No One Can Make You

"No one can make you feel inferior without your consent."
~ Eleanor Roosevelt
Pathways to Recovery, p. 297

Ever said, "You make me feel so…?"

One of the hardest lessons we have to learn is that no one else is responsible for how we feel, especially how we feel about ourselves. Some of us play horrible tapes in our heads. Those tapes tend to make us suspicious of people. We think they want to make us feel inferior, that they want to hold us back.

But when the day is done, no one can make us feel any particular way unless we let them. Our feelings are our own. We are the ones making ourselves feel inferior through our own thoughts.

Let us take responsibility for our own feelings, allowing us to be free to become who alone we can be.

Just for Today
Taking responsibility for yourself means listening to yourself, too! Today, let go of the blame and excuses.

What We Make of Our Lives

"We have no choice of what color we're born or who our
parents are or whether we're rich or poor. What we do have
is some choice over what we make of our lives once we're here."
~ Mildred Taylor
Pathways to Recovery, p. 3

Most of us find ourselves, at some point, thinking, "if only things were different." We might wish we'd been born into a different family. Some of us wish we'd been wealthy and wonder what it would've been like to have a lot of money. Sometimes we might think, "If only I didn't have all these problems—then everything would be okay."

Truly successful people make something wonderful of their lives because, at some level, they choose to do so—not because they were or weren't born a certain way or place or into a certain family—but because deep inside, they know they've been wonderfully made, just the way they are.

Success is not defined in how much money we make, what sort of job we hold, what neighborhood we live in or how beautiful others might think we are. True success is when we say "thank you" to our soul and realize what a gift it is to be alive.

Just for Today

Don't be afraid to put your personal touch on life! Listen to the music you like, not what's popular. Decorate your home the way you like it. Wear clothes that make you feel good about yourself, not to fit the current fashion trend.

Catching the Right Wind

*"You must know for which harbor you are headed
if you are to catch the right winds to take you there."*
~ Seneca
Pathways to Recovery, p. 284

We play so many roles to so many people and in so many places that
sometimes we lose sight of who and where we really are.

Knowing what is expected of us in our daily lives is good, but if we're
not mapping our own course, we're not finding our unique purpose,
our passion or our place.

We need to "catch the right winds" in our lives. Those around us
will benefit—as will we—from knowing our own course, and not just
doing what is expected of us by other people. We can find the right
harbor.

Just for Today

*When you start out on a new path, stick with it. The longer you walk
the new road, it automatically loses its newness. Familiarize yourself
with each new step you'll need to take. Make sure you feel confident
before you move on to something else.*

Giving Radiance to Everything

"There is one thing which gives radiance to everything.
It is the idea of something around the corner."
~ G.K. Chesterton
Pathways to Recovery, p. 127

When we wake up each morning, we never know what's around the corner for that day. But we get up anyway, with the determination to make it through each hour, each minute, as best we can.

Hope springs from expectation—from the joyful radiance we can bring to our lives each and every day. Yes, it takes time and effort, planning, searching and probably even a little luck.

But we are the ones who can bring our lives that radiance. We are the ones who can have the expectation of something better, something spectacular, something special that's not that far away or out of reach.

Look for it! Strive for it! We can make our lives what we want them to be! The radiance is just around the corner!

Just for Today

Wake up believing something wonderful is going to happen to you today. Then go to bed thanking yourself for the things that did happen.

Beginning to Be Free

"The past is over and done and has no power over me. I can begin to be free in this moment. Today's thoughts create my future. I am in charge. I now take my own power back. I am safe and I am free."
~ Louise L. Hay
Pathways to Recovery, p. 363

Affirmations like this one by Louise Hay can certainly lift us up mentally, spiritually and physically. Changing our negative thoughts into positive ones is life-altering. Plus, it's amazing to see it happen!

As we begin to challenge the negative thoughts—and to replace them with more positive, supportive ones—we can watch our lives change. We start to think differently. We begin to see things in a different way, without complaining or placing blame. We move toward feeling better about ourselves and all that surrounds us.

Working to change our thoughts—letting go of the negative past— will change our future, giving us the courage to reclaim our power, to be in charge of our lives. We can begin to feel safe and free.

Just for Today
Constantly listening to the negative things in life only feeds your own negativity. Go through the entire day without listening to the news, reading the paper or checking out the current events on the internet. Do you really miss them?

Taking Ourselves Too Seriously

"Drop the idea that you are Atlas carrying the world on your shoulders.
The world would go on even without you.
Don't take yourself so seriously."
~ Norman Vincent Peale
Pathways to Recovery, p. 315

Sometimes on our recovery journey, we find ourselves trying to be everything to everyone. We feel like we've lost time—years and years of time that we can never get back.

It makes us sad because we've missed so much. It causes us to worry about the "coulda-shoulda-woulda's," even though we know we're not to blame. It can force us to take on more than we can reasonably do, just to catch up.

And when we've taken on all that we can, it's pretty easy to think that we're the only ones who can fix things or make things better. But we don't have to take on all of this!

The world will go on without us—as it always has and always will. What will be remembered are the times when we relaxed and just enjoyed the moment—holding the hand of a child, making the best catch, laughing at ourselves or running an errand for an older neighbor.

As we lighten up, we light up!

Just for Today
Call a few friends for a party. Have them bring their favorite 'comfort food' to share with everyone. Might be an odd meal, but it will be fun!

Friends are Relatives

"Friends are relatives you make for yourself."
~ Eustache Deschamps
Pathways to Recovery, p. 236

Friendships are very special relationships. Some of them last a lifetime, while others are fleeting. Friends leave a lasting impression in our lives. We share things with friends we don't with others...common interests, our deepest secrets, our saddest moments, our biggest joys.

Friends are the people we can turn to...like when we need help moving or we need to talk to someone in the middle of the night. Friends are people who will just show up when we need them the most.

Our friends want us to be happy. They want us to succeed. They want to share the good times with us—and they're also willing to be there when life gets rough. Friends are loyal—they keep our secrets confidential, they're trustworthy, supportive and positive towards us. We relax around friends because they let us be ourselves.

Friends motivate us on our journeys, and as they share with us, we find new ways of living and new opportunities to find joy, success, and purpose in our lives.

Just for Today

Choose someone you know well and pretend you've just met. See if you find anything new about them!

A Good Challenge

"College, postgraduate work…were times for utilizing my [strengths of] intelligence and being responsible. The challenge was a good one in my life because I was developing many skills. This makes me hopeful to stay on the path of a successful and pleasurable life."
~ Anonymous
Pathways to Recovery, p. 137

There was a woman who slept all day and did as little as she could to get by in life. She was fearful of living, of going out and becoming something, someone. She was told that she wouldn't ever be able to do anything more than be a "client" of mental health services. It was her job to survive in and out of the hospital. And to her, that job was daunting.

One day the woman awoke to find a gift beside her bed. Unsure of who left the gift for her, she opened it to find a rock inside. It wasn't a fancy rock, just a rock from the road, but around it was a piece of paper that said, "You are what you make of yourself." A tiny rock — and the words it bore — changed her life.

It's sometimes hard to see that we have control of our lives, but when we take on this responsibility, we can open ourselves to many wondrous things! A rock from the path can become a symbol of inspiration. Life can become what we want it to be — successful and pleasurable.

Just for Today

Has someone given you a gift like the stone? Why not pass a similar gift along to someone you see today? Share your inspiration with a person who needs it!

A Vision for Tomorrow

"[Gratitude] turns what we have into enough, and more.
It turns denial into acceptance, chaos into order, confusion to clarity…
Gratitude makes sense of our past,
brings peace for today and creates a vision for tomorrow."
~ Melody Beattie
Pathways to Recovery, p. 349

It's pretty common for us to see the bad in things. Finding the negative is ingrained in most of us and can keep us angry, cynical and without hope.

But when we begin to practice gratitude, our lives start to change. We begin to see the good things that happen and look at our struggles in a different way. When we practice gratitude, we begin to focus on the positive parts of our lives and look away from the negatives.

When we begin to be thankful, we start to feel better — more balanced, less stressed and certainly more full of possibility and hope. We look for solutions instead of blaming the past. Practicing gratitude allows us to better focus on our goals, opening up our creativity.

Gratitude pushes us not to dwell on the past, but to enjoy each moment we're given. And that's a tool that can help us into the future, no matter what happens to us.

If we can be grateful, we can get through just about anything!

Just for Today

It's not always easy to feel grateful. This morning, find an object to keep with you throughout the day. Let it remind you to be thankful. It could be a piece of jewelry, a favorite shirt or a hat. Each time you see your object, stop for a moment and say thanks.

Stilling Muddy Water

"If you take muddy water and still it, it gradually becomes clear.
If you bring something to rest in order to move it,
it gradually comes alive."
~ Lao-Tzu
Pathways to Recovery, p. 318

We must seek the quiet and stillness inside our minds, bodies and spirits to rejuvenate us, motivate us, feed us and bring us to life.

When seeking mental wellness, we sometimes must still our bodies, minds and spirits before taking action. We must respond from calm instead of a hasty reaction.

When we're working on something and can't seem to bring it all together, we must be quiet, reflecting to find a solution.

Our solutions are not born from chaos. Our solutions are born within the stillness that comes after the chaos.

Just for Today

A couple of the best times of the day to rest are during the sunrise and sunset. Plan to spend some time today watching the sun come up or go down.

What Buys Happiness

"Money, it turned out, was exactly like sex. You thought of nothing
else if you didn't have it and thought of other things if you did."
~ James Baldwin
Pathways to Recovery, p. 141

What is it that makes us feel happy? If that thing is taken away from us, would we still be able to find joy?

Many of us have experienced significant losses...of loved ones, careers, housing, pieces of our health and more. Losses have affected our ability to find joy. Losses have made it hard to find comfort, fulfillment or meaning in life.

Then at some point, we find the courage and healing to move out of despair. We start rediscovering what brings us joy. This takes faith and determination. It takes inner motivation and confidence that life can be full again.

To truly seek recovery, many discover that joy comes from being present in the here and now—in this very moment—and not trying to over think one's life. Opportunities have a way of presenting themselves when we live in the moment, knowing that what we have is enough for now. Living in the moment helps us to be grateful for what we have, and gives us a sense that—for now—we can stop seeking what we don't have, and start taking advantage of what we do.

Just for Today

Remember, you don't have to spend money to have fun! Go for a walk,
read, cook, write or watch a movie. Find your happiness today!

The Human Spirit

"No pessimist ever discovered the secrets of stars, or sailed to an uncharted land, or opened a new heaven to the human spirit."
~ Helen Keller
Pathways to Recovery, p. 294

Optimism is the key to the door of a successful life. If we allow it, this positive attitude can consume us and take over our lives in a way that only optimism can—by driving us onward and upward.

Finding things to be hopeful about is sometimes difficult. We've told ourselves too often that we don't deserve this or that. We tell ourselves that we can't enjoy something, that we can't laugh or that we're not worthy. Worse, as long as we stay in this mind-set, we'll go nowhere, do nothing and just exist.

To succeed, we must believe not only in ourselves, but also in the universal truth that we are what we think. Our thoughts have control over our actions, and those thoughts, if turned positive, can help us achieve great fulfillment. The sky's the limit!

Just for Today
Understand that your future doesn't have to be like your past. Believe in yourself, your coping skills and all that you've learned.

The Rat Race

*"The trouble with being in the rat race
is that even if you win, you're still a rat."*
~ Lily Tomlin
Pathways to Recovery, p. 314

One of the greatest problems we face is the feeling that we've lost valuable time. Maybe our symptoms began when we were just getting out on our own, ready to take on the world. Or maybe our lives were interrupted when we found ourselves overwhelmed by stress. Perhaps we feel like we never even had a life to begin with — it might seem as though we've always been struggling.

Once we find ourselves working toward our recovery, it makes sense that we try to make up for the time we've lost. We join this board or that committee. We jump into a full-time job without preparing for the stress. We take on more family and community commitments. We agree to more tasks and responsibilities just to compensate for what we've missed. And then we wonder why our world comes crashing down on us again.

There's nothing wrong with trying to make up for lost time. But what we need to remember is passion and balance. Passion to remind us to work toward goals fit for our life. And balance to make sure we're paying attention to the whole of our life, not just doing for the sake of doing.

Just for Today
Don't forget that you have to give yourself time; things will eventually happen if you give them time!

At Peace

"I'm at peace, and with that peace, I have strength."
~ Colleen Keagy
Pathways to Recovery, p. 89

When John Lennon begged over forty years ago to "give peace a chance," there was a major war, riots on campuses and civil rights issues coming to a head. Lennon saw peace as the answer to all of those situations.

Today, we seek inner peace. We believe we're at our strongest when we're at peace.

So why do we spend so much time worrying, being anxious, dreading something, or any number of other emotions or behaviors that keep us in chronic turmoil?

In peace, we find our inner strengths. In peace, we find beauty and solace. In peace, we can find our answers.

Just for Today

Spend some time alone today. Solitude can bring you the greatest peace and solace. Give it a chance!

Standing on Our Own Feet

"I shall always be able to stand on my own two feet
even when they are planted on the hardest soil of the harshest reality."
~ Etty Hillesum
Pathways to Recovery, p. 285

Are we working on goals we've set for our lives — or are we listening to the goals others have set for us?

Some of us struggle to recover because we have difficulty drawing boundaries between who we are and who others want us to be. We can work at recovery for years, yet relapse over and over again because we haven't been listening to our inner selves, that part of us that knows who we are and what's best for us. We struggle because we get dependent on others to lead our journeys for us.

When we get into the driver's seat of recovery, we find we're faced with a lot of responsibility. That can be scary and overwhelming, but we're resourceful and capable. Knowing how to recover doesn't come all at once. It also doesn't come when we try to be who we're not, or when we sit in the back seat of our lives, giving our power to others.

We can look to others for guidance and support — people like our peers who also walk a recovery journey — but ultimately, recovery is about standing on our own two feet, firmly planting them in the reality of our own lives, even when that's the hardest thing we've ever had to do.

Just for Today
Stop caring and worrying about what people think of you; it can put you in a bad habit of trying to please everyone. Ultimately, you won't please yourself.

What is Already There

*"Creativity often consists of merely turning up
what is already there. Did you know that right and left shoes
were only thought up only a little more than a century ago?"*
~ Bernice Fitz-Gibbon
Pathways to Recovery, p. 340

Why is it we fear creativity so much?

We deny our own creativity, choosing to see it in others but not in ourselves. We fight the urge to be creative, telling ourselves that it's silly or we don't have time. We narrowly define it in a way that eliminates all the possibilities we have to be creative.

Our lives become so much richer when we can express our creativity in ways that feel most comfortable to us. Yes, it *can* be art or drama or music. But it can also be in the way we think and the attitude we choose to have about life. It could be in our ability to build things or in the way we lead a meeting. Creativity can be engaged almost anywhere we live and breathe!

To let out our creativity, we can't deny its existence. We can't give it up to others or refuse to let it out. We simply need to risk digging a little deeper into ourselves to find our own creativity, knowing that the gifts we have to share with others can make change happen.

Just for Today

Today, answer this statement: "I have always wondered about..." You never know when your creativity can be engaged and change the way you look at your life!

What Do We Live For?

*"What do we live for,
if not to make life less difficult for each other?"*
~ George Elliot
Pathways to Recovery, p. 201

With the struggles and challenges of life can come a new sense of our spiritual selves. The hardships of life often take us within, where we find our connections with the world on a deeper level. This higher level is where we find meaning for our lives, as well as a sense of belonging.

With this spirituality, we begin to look at the world differently, often changing how we act or react with all that we come in contact. We are more gentle and compassionate with other people. We realize our world doesn't include just us, but also those around us who also may be struggling with life. We find new purpose and meaning and act accordingly. We realize we're not here just to satisfy our own needs, but also to give to others when they are most in need.

Journeying outside of ourselves is one of the most important aspects of healing. It's also what helps us make things less difficult for others.

Just for Today
It's so easy sometimes to make things difficult for others So today, why not find the waiter at your favorite restaurant or cafe and apologize to them for giving them a hard time! If it wasn't you, then apologize for others who have!

Don't Miss the Scenery

"Slow down and enjoy life.
It's not only the scenery you miss by going too fast — you also miss
the sense of where you are going and why."
~ Eddie Cantor
Pathways to Recovery, p. 168

There's more to life than we can possibly see or experience. But if we're orderly and mindful, we can enjoy the moments that are rare, precious and all our own.

Leisure and recreational activities help us enjoy all our moments more. When we're active, we get the blood flowing to our brains and bodies, healing us. And when we get going, we feel better.

But we can't move *too* fast! Sometimes we'll find ourselves moving way too much. It may feel beautiful at first, but we usually can't keep up this pace for long. We miss the scenery of everyday life. We miss the details and the small joys because we're moving too fast.

Recovery doesn't mean we have to go back and fix everything. Nothing about recovery requires us to do certain things or attempt to be different. Our journey will always be ours if we slow down long enough to figure out where we're going — and why. It simply keeps us on track and helps bring us both meaning and enjoyment.

Just for Today
Try to do less for one day. Slow down; don't feel like you need to get everything done today. Only do those things which have to be done. Give yourself time between activities or appointments so your pace for the day will be slower.

You Never Know

"You never know when you're making a memory."
~ Rickie Lee Jones
Pathways to Recovery, p. 250

A special song, the feel of a hand-sewn quilt, the smell of our favorite meal, the view from the front-row seats at our home team's game, the beauty of a glistening lake. Each of these things are seemingly small memories, but they can evoke strong emotions in us.

A spirit-breaking word, the loss of a dear friend or pet, changes in our community and our world, the tragedy of lives set back by the force of nature's winds or rains. These things also bring forth strong emotions.

It's easy and quite normal for us to hold on to the difficult memories. However, each thing we do during our day also gives us an opportunity to make new, bright memories.

You'll never know until you try it.

Just for Today
Have you ever made a "Memory Box?" It's simple. Focus on positive memories. Look for pictures, mementos or objects that represent these good things. Place them in a special box. When you're feeling down, pull out your box; maybe you'll even find a way to make new, bright memories from the old ones!

What's Your Religion?

"When I do good, I feel good. When I do bad, I feel bad.
That's my religion."
~ Abraham Lincoln
Pathways to Recovery, p. 192

Just like Lincoln, we can reflect on how we feel. When we feel good, we look good. If we feel bad, we generally look bad, to ourselves and others. It's the truth that what we do, whether good or bad, right or wrong, affects how we feel.

It's important to be able to look at ourselves in the mirror and be at peace with who we are, or we aren't truly living. A mirror is a splendid thing if we use it. Looking at ourselves and deciding we are worthy is necessary.

That reflection can guide us on our journey. It can tell us when we have done something not so good, or when we've done well. It's a tool to be used—a way of believing—we can count on.

Just for Today

What's your 'religion'? What is it that helps guide you on your journey? Pick up an inspirational book you've been wanting to read or spend some time in prayer or meditation.

A Blessing We Give to Another

"Gratitude is a blessing we give to one another."
~ Robert Reynolds
Pathways to Recovery, p. 348

Our blessings are always there, but most days we just don't take the time to notice them. They often show themselves in the little things—a friend shares a kind word, a co-worker offers to help when we're overwhelmed, we find a shoulder to cry on, we welcome the homemade meal from a neighbor.

When we stop to find the things we're grateful for, we open up a whole new world for ourselves. But we never know when we might open up a new world for someone else. It's one thing to recognize the things we're thankful for but it's another to actually *express* our gratitude.

Shared a kind word with someone lately who was feeling down? How long ago was it when we stopped to help a co-worker finish that last, tedious task? Are we sharing ourselves with others in need? Made a good meal lately but didn't think to share it?

Recognizing—and then sharing—our gratitude is one of the greatest gifts we can give to someone. And a grateful spirit always attracts more blessings.

Just for Today

Look for a stranger today and give them a compliment! The gift you give may just make you feel as though you've gotten one, too!

Life Is Good

"Happiness is to be found along the way, not at the end of the road, for then the journey is over and it is too late. Today, this hour, this minute is the day, the hour, the minute for each of us to sense the fact that life is good, with all of its trials and troubles, and perhaps more interesting because of them."
~ Robert D. Updegraff
Pathways to Recovery, p. 260

Yes, we've all gone through the trials and tribulations of life and we're better for it, even though sometimes we may not feel as though we are.

It's about seizing each moment, breathing in the positive thoughts and moving forward by making goals that we really want to achieve. Take the risks that are necessary to move forward, find our special talents and make our mark on the world. We have purpose, and some of us have learned our purpose through the tragedies we've lived through. And perhaps, just perhaps...we find our lives more interesting because of them.

Just for Today

Seize the moment of the day. Watch a bird or butterfly around you and see how they enjoy their moments!

A Miracle Every Second

*"A person's work is nothing but a long journey to recovery,
through the detours of art, the two or three simple and great
images which first gained access to their hearts."*
~ Albert Camus
Pathways to Recovery, p. 385

Each of us has a story to tell about the journey we've traveled.

The journey has, no doubt, had its ups and downs...and twists and
turns. But along the way, there've been times when we've felt loved
and given love. There've been times when we've felt at peace. There've
been times when we laughed and felt joy. There've been times when
we've felt sadness and grief. There've been times when we've been
scared and uncertain. There've been times when we've been well and
times when we have not.

When we discover what touches our hearts and moves our emotions
the most, we discover the deepest part of who we are. Let's push aside
thoughts and images that trigger unwanted emotions.

Let only that which brings joy to our heart and peace to our soul join
us for the journey.

Just for Today
*Do you ever find yourself settling for less than what you want or
deserve? Why? Try to surround yourself with only joy today!*

October

*"All things on earth
point home in old October."*

~ *Thomas Wolfe*

Having a Life

"What does recovery mean to me? An inner healing. Accepting the 'whole of me.' Having a life – your own – with its dreams, goals and consequences – with or without symptoms...
Living the kind of life that is of value to me.*"*
~ Cherie Bledsoe
Pathways to Recovery, p. 6

Recovery is all about *getting a life!*

Not the life that someone else wants for us, nor what may have been taken from us when we were first diagnosed. It's not a life that's just passing by, barely scraping through to the next day. No!

Recovery is all about the discovery, adventure and personal vision of what we want our life to be. Recovery helps us heal from the past, accepting the whole of what has happened to us – with self-forgiveness, compassion and respect for the journey. Recovery lets us define our own life, dream our own dreams and accept the consequences when things don't work out exactly as we planned.

Recovery is getting a life – our life – defined, created and lived by us.

Just for Today

Schedule at least an hour each week to go on an adventure. Maybe it's dancing or hiking or learning how to play an instrument. You decide!

Insight from the Journey

"Let the insight that the journey brought you
pervade your day to day experience."
~ Anonymous
Pathways to Recovery, p. 166

Each day that we wake up is our opportunity to learn—from others, from our experiences, from ourselves. While we can't get rid of the things that have happened to us, we can grow from them. We can't change them. We can't make the outcome any different, nor should we judge how we reacted to them. Instead, we learn.

Each day we wake up gives us the chance to start anew, to rewrite our story, to search for the things that bring us happiness, joy and peace. We have learned much from our journeys. We are different people because of the road we have trod.

It's our life and it's our journey. It's up to us to keep our past in perspective, remembering it—and all of its learning experiences—as both challenge and motivation to move forward each day.

Just for Today

Say this to yourself throughout the day: "My past does not represent who I am. It represents what has happened to me. My experiences don't make me any better or worse, they just make up who I am."

The Greater Part of Happiness

"I have learned from experience that the greater part of our happiness or misery depends on our dispositions and not on our circumstances."
~ Martha Washington
Pathways to Recovery, p. 295

It's amazing that two people can look at the same situation and get two opposite viewpoints about the experience. Some of us are "glass half-empty" people and some of us are "glass half-full" people.

If our glasses are half-empty, we look at our stressors with disdain, often getting stuck in our misery. We see a negative end to our challenges. We get lost in our problems.

If our glasses are half-full, we look at the positive aspects of each situation we encounter and plan for the best outcome. We problem solve better with a happier, more hopeful viewpoint.

We change our attitude and guess what? We change our life.

Just for Today

Find someone who has the attitude you'd like to have. Follow their lead and learn from their example.

Polishing Gems

"A gem cannot be polished without friction,
nor people perfected without trials."
~ Chinese Proverb
Pathways to Recovery, p. 283

How do we handle our mental health history?

Some of us are embarrassed by our experiences and we try to hide that part of our past. It's as if we don't want anyone to know what happened. Others feel the need to acknowledge that piece of our lives. We can talk about it with others, accepting this part of ourselves with greater ease.

Having a psychiatric history is different for each of us. Some of us have faced a lot of stigma. Some of us experienced terrifying situations. Some of us can't remember life without the symptoms, while others remember losing so much when the symptoms began.

In some cultures, people with certain mental health symptoms are seen as healers, shamans or mystics. They show us we don't have to be ashamed or embarrassed of who we are. The rough spots along the journey are opportunities for growth and for deepening our sense of personal pride, self-awareness and self-acceptance. As our stories develop, we find we have more and more to share with others. We can find new opportunities for using our resiliency and strength as we claim all the pieces of who we are.

As the proverb says, without friction, a gem can't be polished. We are diamonds in the making!

Just for Today
Identify yourself today as a survivor, not a victim. Your trials have perfected you into a beautiful, polished gem!

Don't Step On My Cake

"If you're going to dance on the table, don't step on my cake."
~ Unknown
Pathways to Recovery, p. 205

Each of us must celebrate the successes we have along our journey. However, we don't want to be hasty in celebrating our personal success at the expense of someone else. Remember, none of us arrive without the aid of others.

There are many opportunities to celebrate, but sometimes in our enthusiasm at what we've accomplished, we can overshadow those who have helped us along the way. Recovery happens with a lot of support. Remember those people.

No one can be an island. We get to where we're going in life by the assistance we get from others along the way, no matter what it is that we're trying to accomplish.

So, dance on the table—with great gusto. Just don't step on the cake!

Just for Today

Dancing and cake seem to represent a party. Dress up today! Even though there might not be a party, you'll be surprised at how good you feel...and others will too! Enjoy the compliments!

Images of Probabilities

*"The moment of enlightenment is when a person's dreams
of possibilities become images of probabilities."*
~ Vic Braden
Pathways to Recovery, p. 107

There are few things that feel quite as good as seeing a long-held dream become a reality. That dream doesn't have to be something huge for us to feel good about achieving it. We just have to put ourselves in that place of imagining possibilities.

Let's say we have a dream of becoming a teacher. Perhaps we loved school and there was a particular instructor who made us believe in learning—and we'd like to pass that on to others. We may believe that we could be a good teacher. We may have even taken steps to becoming a teacher. But each of these are dreams of possibilities. While we might think we'd be a good teacher, we can't see it.

Then one day, we wake up and our dream has shifted. We can see ourselves teaching. We see ourselves standing at the front of the room and walking the aisles of the classroom, gently urging our students on. We see ourselves planning lessons and creating new activities. Our dream has shifted.

Now, we look past just the possibilities—and we see probabilities. Our hearts fill with passion and we are enlightened. We know we can do this. What's more, we will do this!

Just for Today

Sometimes the best way to make things happen for yourself is to say no. Make sure you know what your priorities are today!

Leaving Better and Happier

"Let no one come to you without leaving better and happier."
~ Mother Teresa
Pathways to Recovery, p. 162

No matter how hard we try to stay hidden behind our masks, others still see us. So why not present something positive that they'll remember, something good to take away?

Even if it's just a smile, a touch or a kind word, it's more than some people get in a day. We can't worry about our imperfections—no one will remember them. It's our spirit, our willingness to give a little, that they will keep. It's these qualities, by which they will be encouraged. And as we share these, others will leave us feeling better and happier.

Just for Today

You probably don't need all the things that you have. Why not donate something today...you could leave someone better and happier!

Something Important

"Everybody is talented, original, and has something important to say."
~ Brenda Jeland
Pathways to Recovery, p. 383

Isn't it amazing that no two finger prints are the same? Of the millions and billions of people on this earth, not one person has ever been found to share the same finger print as another! So it is with each and every part of who we are.

Although our lives have gone in different ways than we planned, we've learned so much from those experiences. We've developed talents and skills that have helped us in our recovery.

Even though we share many things with others, we are original — with new thoughts, new ideas and new dreams that can carry us far.

We may have had our voices squelched in the past, but it's still important for us to speak up, to stand up for ourselves and to help others do the same.

We all leave our mark on this world — we leave our unique fingerprint — and nothing can ever change that fact.

Just for Today

Want to be unique? Next time you buy something, ask yourself if you need the item or if you simply want it. If you're getting it just to fit in, you probably don't need it!

Almost Through the Tunnel

"Accepting responsibility for my choices...being resilient and tenacious...having faith and hope...all were strengths that I used to keep me on the road of recovery. I am so grateful to be in the place I am...There is not only 'light at the end of the tunnel.' I am almost through the tunnel. Recovery is a wonderful process."
~ Donna Story
Pathways to Recovery, p. 129

Responsibilities, resilience, tenacity, hope ...all of these things help get us through the hardships of life. But there is something else. There is also gratitude for the journey.

We *can* be grateful for our life experiences. They've made us unique and incredibly strong human beings. While we may have had to bear more than seems fair in a lifetime, we can come out on the other side, out of the "tunnel" to brighter days.

Gratitude is a skill we can learn. It helps us feel content instead of thinking we surely deserve something more. Gratitude is what we give to ourselves no matter what our troubles.

We can accept our circumstances in life and we can be grateful for them. Why? Because they give us another chance to grow from all that we have been through and endured.

Just for Today

Do you see recovery as a wonderful process? As you walk through your day, notice the things that bring you joy or happiness. Are the things you're doing moving you forward or are there things that would be better left behind? Which will you keep?

Courageous Risks

"Courageous risks are life-giving, they help you grow, make you brave
and better than you think you are."
~ Joan Curcio
Pathways to Recovery, p. 38

"No, no! I don't want to take that risk! I don't want to step out of my comfort zone! I can't do it! I simply can't do it!"

Ever said something like that? Most of us probably have at some point in our lives. Taking risks—being courageous enough to try new and unknown things—is scary. But not taking risks is just as frightening. Not taking risks leaves us stuck and safe and right where we are.

Jumping out and taking risks—safe, educated ones—will help us become more of the person we've always wanted to be. Our courage and action will take us forward. They will let us say, "Yes, yes! I want to take that risk! I want to step out of my comfort zone! I want to do it! I simply have to do it!"

Just for Today
Try taking a risk as part of a group; it might make it more enjoyable!
You might even learn something from someone that you can use later.

Needing Joy

"People need joy quite as much as clothing…some need it far more."
~ Margaret Collier Graham
Pathways to Recovery, p. 254

We know that we need joy to have a happier, more content, peaceful and productive life. And part of that joy comes from the people who support us on our journey in life.

We must nurture our relationships with people, not only to receive joy, but also to give it away. Giving joy to others can make us feel happier.

Giving joy to others needn't be difficult. Such was a woman who was questioning whether she was a good mother. She mentioned her concerns one day to her neighbor. Having raised children of her own, the neighbor knew that the woman was bringing up her son quite well.

A couple of days later, the neighbor called her friend and left a voice message, praising her again for being a good parent. The neighbor wanted her to celebrate the joy of being a good and loving mother.

After listening to the message, the woman was reminded that she *was* a good mother. Hearing that from another, more seasoned mom made her feel good and gave her more confidence in her role as a parent.

We all need joy in our lives—just don't forget to be someone who spreads the joy with others!

Just for Today
Don't hide from others. They need to see you smiling…so smile like you mean it! Give away your joy!

Don't Compromise

"Don't compromise yourself. You're all you've got."
~ Janis Joplin
Pathways to Recovery, p. 285

The voices of negativity can be overwhelming. They tell us we aren't good enough. They tell us we aren't popular, attractive, smart, outgoing or accomplished enough…to do the things our souls are begging us to do. Negativity can leave us walking with our heads down, afraid to grasp the things about us that are perfect and inspiring.

In time, negativity can lead us to give up before we even attempt to use and share our gifts. Take, for instance, Thomas Edison. It's said that Edison was a creative soul who struggled to invent the light bulb. He failed at least 1,000 times before getting it right.

It's absolutely amazing that Edison didn't despair with all his invention attempts that didn't turn out quite right. There's no doubt people around him told him he was a failure. Aren't we glad he didn't give in to the negative voices and give up?

Edison is a great model for us. He kept looking ahead, trying again and again with his great imagination, wondering and wandering and experimenting with the exciting world of electricity. He saw what he could do, not what he couldn't do *and* in spite of any negativity that might have come his way. He had a special gift and he stayed focused on that, building confidence as he went. He didn't compromise himself. He gave it all he had.

Just for Today

Are you giving all you've got? If you need help, think about asking for support from a coach, mentor or someone you trust. People who have gained knowledge or skills are often pleased to be asked to share their expertise. Ask them today!

Tears and Sweat

"Both tears and sweat are salty; but they render different results.
Tears will get you sympathy, sweat will get you change."
~ Jesse Jackson
Pathways to Recovery, p. 12

We have always recovered—even when told not to expect it to happen. We are often given little or no help to recover, and we can face multiple barriers to recovery.

We may have denied our experiences and taken on one or more labels as if they define us. Yet we are resilient people! It's at this time that we must shake ourselves out of the comfort of tears and desperation and step onto our journey of recovery.

Recovery is change, and we know it takes work. When we're involved in it, we get things done, though, we move forward along our paths and find hope. We accept the change as good.

Just for Today

Sweat equals hard work. But have you ever thought about what time of the day you're able to work more efficiently? Are you a morning or an afternoon person? Try to get as much done during your peak time as possible, especially planning those activities or appointments where you need to be at your best.

Dorothy's Dream

"There's no place like home...
There's no place like home."
~ Dorothy from The Wizard of Oz
Pathways to Recovery, p. 131

Home.

What's it like? Does it reflect who we are or is it just a place where we end up each day? Do we take pride in the things we have? Are we pleased to have others visit our home, knowing it's a place of comfort and welcome? Does laughter fill its spaces?

Our home doesn't need to be elaborate or even need to be all that clean. For some people, it might not even be a place. Instead, it's where we can be happy, have our spirits lifted — where we can be ourselves, even on the worst of days. It's where we feel comfortable, where we're respected and where we can truly say and feel, "I'm home." There's no place like it!

Just for Today

Your home is more than just a place. It's where you feel comfortable and where you can rest at the end of the day. Find a space in your home where you can go specifically to relax. Maybe even make it a "clean sheet night!"

Begin in the Imagination

"All acts performed in the world begin in the imagination."
~ Barbara Grizzuti Harrison
Pathways to Recovery, p. 113

If we start with a vision of what we want in mind, we'll eventually get to where we're going — or at least somewhere that turns out to be much better. But first, we must have a vision, a goal, something we can look forward to accomplishing.

It's true that nothing ever comes to those who wait. We must get out of our comfort zones and begin to imagine, write down our goals and build a path for the things we want.

Our visions may be for the next day or the next month. Sometimes our visions go further into the future to six months, a year, or longer. But it's in the imagining — creating a vision of what we want and when — that makes it possible to realize our dreams.

Just for Today

Getting a new view can spark your imagination. Try being a tourist in your own community!

Light in the Strangest of Places

"Once in a while you can get shown the light
in the strangest of places if you look at it right."
~ Jerry Garcia
Pathways to Recovery, p. 325

Sometimes we learn the most in life from the people, places or things that seem the most different from us.

We might learn how to better break down stigma from a person who has lots of tattoos.

We could decide what we really believe in after having a heated discussion with someone who has radically different ideas.

While the role of a parent is to teach a child, there's always time for parents to learn from their children.

There are lots of opportunities for us to learn about ourselves from others. We are — all of us — on this globe to teach and we are all here to learn. If we but let the light shine through, even just a little bit, there's no telling what we might find.

Stepping out to those "strangest of places" might not be so bad after all!

Just for Today

Is there someone you know who appears to be very different than you? Why not strike up a conversation with them? Prepare some questions ahead of time if you need to. See if you can find the things you have in common!

Giving as Much

*"Many times a day I realize how much my own outer and inner life
is built upon the labors of my fellow men, both living and dead,
and how earnestly I must exert myself in order to give in
return as much as I have received."*
~ Albert Einstein
Pathways to Recovery, p. 242

It's easy for us to see strengths in other people. It seems as though everyone else has something going for them, but not us. Those other people succeed at their goals. They seem to be born with unique skills. They have fun and they live in the moment. But what about us?

It's not so easy to see strengths within ourselves. Instead, we struggle to see our own talents, goals and dreams. It could be that we never learned to look within at all the wonderful possibilities each of us holds or to ask ourselves what it was we wanted.

We are our dreams, our musings, our hopes and desires. We each have strengths, though often we don't even realize such truth.

Once we recognize in ourselves the many things that make us beautiful and unique individuals, we can open our minds to what every human being has—potential. Unleashing that potential is our gift to ourselves; it becomes our gift to the world.

Just for Today

*Create five cards with positive messages on them. Leave them for
someone else to discover...at the grocery store, library, bank or bus
stop. Give a gift to the world!*

Seeing Our Reflection

"When someone looks into the mirror they more than likely just see their reflection...rarely do they look any deeper...When I look deeper, it surprises me that I am here and functioning. As I look even deeper, I see a person who somehow has...not only survived, but lived..."
~ Stormie Woodward
Pathways to Recovery, p. 39

"Mirror, mirror, on the wall, who's the fairest of them all?" was, of course, the famous line uttered by the evil queen in the Disney movie *Snow White*. Her reflection was all the queen saw. But Snow White looked much deeper.

When we look into the mirror, we see our reflection. It's our choice, and up to us, to look deeper. To see someone who has many strengths. To look past just the outward reflection to see how our life experiences have made us stronger. To see a person who is smart and capable and powerful.

When we look, will we see someone who has not only survived, but lived to the fullest? Will we see there is more to us than who we see in the mirror?

Just for Today

To see your true self, it doesn't hurt to surround yourself with images that reflect your strengths and courage. Pictures of friends and family, pictures of restful vacations or creative self-portraits can allow you to see yourself!

A Thousand Windows

*"Here is someone at once so like you that you have come home,
and yet so different he opens a thousand windows on the universe."*
~ Michael Drury
Pathways to Recovery, p. 234

It's true that some people come into our lives and stay but a short time. It's also true that we have some people in our lives that we'd like to send home—for good!

But what about the person you meet, the one you know in an instant is someone who understands you, who shares the same values, and someone who immediately feels as though you've known them forever? These people are rare and if we're lucky, we'll find one or two of them in our lifetime.

Some people refer to these individuals as soul mates. Perhaps that's true. While you have met someone who is so much like you that it feels as though they are you, these true friends—these soul mates—are also the ones who can challenge us the most. They are the ones who push us to be better, to seek higher goals, to know ourselves better. They are always there. Why? Simply because they are so much like us.

But it's not the qualities that make us alike which matter. These individuals bring us home and then—without even trying too hard—they send us out again, encouraged, supported and ready to fling a thousand windows open to a grand new world!

Just for Today
Stay in touch with your friends...don't wait for them to contact you. A good friendship requires your time and effort, some fun and support during both good and bad times!

A Unique Being

*"At bottom every man knows well enough he is a unique being,
only once on this earth; and by no extraordinary chance will
such a marvelously picturesque piece of diversity in unity as he is,
ever be put together a second time."*
~ *Friedrich Nietzsche*
Pathways to Recovery, p. 387

When's the last time we felt a sense of awe and excitement as we realized there is no one else like us? Have we realized we have a magnificent story to share—one that nobody else can tell?

When's the last time we believed that the story we tell is ours—our life, our journey, our past, present and future?

It takes time to tell our stories, but telling them is a powerful way to see exactly where we've come from, where we're at and where we're headed. Telling our stories is a powerful way to see who we are, and to gain a better understanding of the unique people we've become. Sharing our stories gives us a chance to honor and celebrate who we have become...through the easy times and the struggles.

Today we can look inside to see ourselves for who we are. We can start to create—a little at a time—the special story of our lives, even if we never share them with anyone. Taking time to honor our lives this way is time well spent.

Just for Today
Try to tell your story. Come up with a theme or a focus. What is the main thing you want others to know about your life experience?

Let's Play Darts

"Everyone needs recognition for his accomplishments, but few people make the need known quite as clearly as the little boy who said to his father; 'Let's play darts. I'll throw and you say 'Wonderful!''"
~ *Unknown*

We all want to be recognized for our accomplishments, regardless of whether they're big or small. Having someone notice that we're making progress or that we've done something well gives us confidence and helps us keep moving forward.

But how many of us take the time — like the little boy playing darts — to ask for what we need? To show others what we've done and to be proud of what we've accomplished. We don't have to do it in a boastful way, but simply, sharing our joy with those around us. Because when we share our successes, we can stand back and welcome the praise from others, "Wonderful!"

We can also stand back and say "Wonderful!" to ourselves.

Just for Today

When you set goals, don't forget to build in rewards for yourself. Learn to say "Wonderful!" to yourself!

Something Complete and Great

"That is happiness;
to be dissolved into something complete and great."
~ Willa Cather
Pathways to Recovery, p. 254

There's lots of talk about being a part of something greater than ourselves. Some people find happiness in spiritual ways. Others look to nature for strength. But we also need a connection to others for us to be truly happy and complete.

Being a part of other people's lives and nurturing our relationships creates a oneness and wholeness with friends and family—and also within ourselves. Being "dissolved" within our support circle helps us become who we're truly meant to be. Our relationships help define us and give us purpose in life. They complete us. We live in greater fulfillment when we are genuinely connected to others.

We can find joy in our relationships and treasure those who support us. We must cherish them—knowing they are complete and great—

Just for Today

Do something selfless for one of your support people today. Help them out when they're in need. Don't do it for yourself; do it only with your thoughts for them!

When I Get This Feeling

"When I get this feeling, I need sexual healing..."
~ Marvin Gaye
Pathways to Recovery, p. 180

Sexual healing? How can we talk about this and mental health in the same breath? Do they really ever go hand in hand? Yes, they do!

Each one of us, no matter our histories, is a sexual person in some way or another. We may be sexual in all different kinds of ways, but just because we have mental health issues doesn't mean our need for intimacy and sexuality can't be a very important part of who we are.

Whether it be through relationships or self-pleasure, there are many activities and ways of imagining that can bring us pleasure. Not limiting ourselves to the traditional ways of satisfying ourselves is very important for each one of us. Seeking safe sexual pleasure — that can also be healing — can be a part of our lives.

Just for Today

Take time today to talk with someone new...just so you know that you can! You never know...

The Reward for a Good Deed

"The reward for a good deed is to have done it."
~ Anonymous
Pathways to Recovery, p. 161

Good deeds can require hard work. But mostly, good deeds require simple *heart* work.

Heart work doesn't always bring recognition or even get seen by others. But heart work always brings us great rewards.

We experience joy—deep and lasting joy—when we share our gifts. We feel happy, sometimes even giddy, when we give to others. Sharing ourselves is the greatest gift and one we all need to experience.

There've been times when we felt like we were on the other side of the giving—our lives turned into ones of receiving. But recovery naturally moves us past the role of receiver and into the glory of giving. We need to give our *heart* work.

Heart work helps us feel complete. It shows others that we really care. Heart work is always good...and sharing this caring brings us the greatest rewards. For what more could we ask?

Just for Today
Go the extra mile today! Do more than you're required or expected to do!

Slow Down

"The trail is the thing, not the end of the trail.
Travel too fast and you miss all you are traveling for."
~ Louis L'Amour
Pathways to Recovery, p. iii

The path to recovery is just that—a path. Along that road there are many wonderful things to see, to explore. But it's how we interpret what we see that determines what we get out of life.

Instead of rushing out in the morning, we can take a moment to smell the air and experience the seasons of life around us. Paying attention to all that is around us helps us see we are part of a greater whole.

Mindfulness is the capacity to pay attention—non-judgmentally—to the present moment. Mindfulness is about living in the moment, experiencing one's emotions and senses fully, yet with a fresh, new perspective.

Only when we slow down and really take in life does the path not seem so desolate. We have control over how we experience life. When we decide to take positive, life-affirming action, our trail begins to change for the better.

Just for Today
Take your time throughout the day. Slow down at everything you do. Take a look around as you move this way, noticing all the things around you. Take in everything you can, truly experiencing all that is on your life path.

What Nobody Can Take Away

"Nobody can take away your future.
Nobody can take away something you don't have yet."
~ Dorothy B. Hughes
Pathways to Recovery, p. 50

As we walk our recovery journeys, it's easy to look back and think of all the things that have been taken away from us. Relationships, jobs, innocence and freedom.

Illness, difficult experiences or loss can loom at us with great urgency. We've often been held back by something or someone—maybe even our own fear.

By looking at our life as beginning each and every minute of every day, it's possible to imagine different situations and new ways of living. If we start from exactly where we are at this moment, we see that nothing is holding us back. We may have an illness or feel painful loss, but this doesn't mean we don't have a future. It only means that our futures can look different, taking on new colors, shapes. And remember, no one can take our futures away from us.

Just for Today
Maybe you need to start over with a clean slate. Begin today to build your future...the one you want...with a whole new outlook and a solid foundation!

A Better Person to Do the Job

"I'm still discovering things about myself, and it will take a lifetime to do it. And I can't think of a better person to do the job than me!"
~ Linda Endicott
Pathways to Recovery, p. 89

Linda's right. If we take the time and do the exploring, we'll discover all sorts of things about ourselves!

There may be things we've forgotten or things we did as a child that would once again bring us joy and laughter. There might be information we learned in school that give us the skills we need to move in a new direction. Maybe a dear grandparent shared their gentle wisdom and advice, or a trusted friend gave us tools to learn more about our culture and its healing practices.

There are all sorts of strengths that each of us possess—skills, talents, abilities, knowledge and community or cultural resources. Sometimes it takes very little to call on those strengths to accomplish a task or goal. Other times, it can be a struggle to recognize the our strengths. But they are there! No one is without them.

Discovering our strengths gives us a better understanding of who we are and what we have become. And indeed, there is no better person for handling the job!

Just for Today

Need help identifying your strengths? Ask your friends to make lists of what they can see you doing well. They may know things about you that you haven't yet recognized!

Loved by Thousands

"Suddenly, all my ancestors are behind me. 'Be still,' they say.
'Watch and listen. You are the result of the love of thousands.'"
~ Linda Hogan
Pathways to Recovery, p. 354

We don't walk alone on our journey. Our ancestors have walked before us. Our friends and family walk beside us.

Our future lies before us. The wind gently pushes at our back, pressing us into the present, inviting us into the future.

The seasons lead the way as winter's chill becomes spring's wind... which becomes summer's flowers...which become the golden leaves that decorate autumn's trail. The sun rises above us and gently sleeps below.

We are not walking alone on our journey. We are loved by thousands... by people we know well, by strangers who encourage us with a smile, by those who walked this earth before us, and by those yet to come.

We are not alone. Are we watching and listening?

Just for Today

Approach the day knowing that what you do is important and your strengths are vital to the world we live in. Do one thing for yourself to reward yourself for identifying your strengths!

Achieve the Impossible

"Only she who attempts the absurd achieves the impossible."
~ Sharon Schuster
Pathways to Recovery, p. 362

Achieve the impossible? What about the obstacles? We all have them. And they are all in the way!

Encountering obstacles in our lives can create stress. Our symptoms can show up when we encounter stress…anxiety, depression, trouble concentrating, difficulty focusing.

In recovery, we realize some of the old ways we dealt with obstacles are probably not healthy for us now. Things like avoidance, turning to substances, giving our decision-making power over to someone else. Recovery requires being creative about what we'll do to overcome life's obstacles.

In time—and with practice—we realize we do have the ability inside to find workable, healthy solutions to move through any obstacles. They have less power over us than they used to. And as we discover this, we feel empowered and super-charged, realizing that we *can* make it through the tough times in life and *still* be on the pathway of recovery! We can achieve the impossible when we overcome our

Just for Today

Having a hard time finding solutions to your challenges? Relax. In most cases, solving a problem doesn't need to be stressful; it just may need more time. Sometimes if you can simply wait, the solution to any challenge may simply go away or be solved on its own!

I Just Know More

*"I can actually say that in the past I did the best
that I could, with what I knew.
Now I still do the best I can with what I know. I just know more."*
~ Vicki Darring
Pathways to Recovery, p. 261

If we really think about it, we've done our best. We've done what we've known to do. Often that's what has come naturally, or what we've learned in the past.

Sometimes, however, those old lessons get replaced with new ways of coping and living, and we do things better.

In recovery, we learn from past mistakes, finding fresh, new insights. We take that insight and use it to do better in the future. If we continually put ourselves down because of our pasts, then we have no room for learning.

It's time to open the doors to healing and walk a new path. This is the way to become the person we really want to be...because now, we really do know more.

Just for Today

It's natural to worry that the past will repeat itself. But as you move through your recovery, it's also natural to learn new things that can be helpful to your wellness. Coping skills, alternative treatments, activities you know that make you feel good are all skills that you have gained. So do the best with what you know...just remember...you know more now!

Discover the Buried Treasure

"Once I became aware of my inner power, I became the captain
of my ship so to speak, and I needed to plot a new course to
discover the buried treasure...me!"
~ Joan Lunden
Pathways to Recovery, p. 68

It's true. Once we can tap into our inner power, we can do just about anything we want.

But how do we find our inner power?

It starts with the desire to do so, to listen to our own inner voice as it tells us there is more than what we have now.

It helps to identify our fears or whatever it is that's holding us back. It takes a positive attitude and some heart-felt determination. A positive attitude is essential. It also takes a little creativity and patience.

But once we listen to that voice—and believe that anything is possible—we can plot a new course and discover new treasure in life!

Just for Today
Make sure your inner power is actually yours, not someone else's!
Focus on listening to yourself and what you want.

November

*"Fallen leaves lying on the grass
in November sun bring
more happiness than the daffodils."*

~ Cyril Connolly

Change and Dreams

"If you will it, it is no dream."
~ Theodore Herzl
Pathways to Recovery, p. 360

Never stop changing
With your heart open wide
To the variety in life
Then you can truly ride.

Through the storms and the
Rain there will a rainbow be
And the sun will shine
Once again on you and me.

Recreate yourself at each
And every turn
To continue life's journey
In commitment, to yearn.

Never stop being yourself
But let yourself see
That change in your life
Can create the you to be.

Just for Today

Change can be a powerful experience in your life yet it can also be hard to make happen. If you're looking at a specific change, consider making it part of your daily routine. Find the time and schedule it in!

Personal Change and Healing

"For the first time, I was changing because I wanted to.
I was drawing on my own inner strengths.
I had failed before because I was living for someone else....
this time I'm doing it for me, and because of that I will not fail."
~ Julie Bayes
Pathways to Recovery, p. 298

Many of us have been hurt by stigma and injustice. We've been told things that aren't true about our illness or diagnosis. We've been treated like we didn't deserve certain things. We've even had our rights taken away.

When we work through the pain of being hurt, we heal from the inside out. Healing can take a long time, sometimes in steps so small we don't recognize healing is happening at all.

At some point we realize how far we've come on the journey of healing. We begin to feel less pain about the things that have hurt us. We welcome change — in fact, we may crave it. We start reaching out to others — trusting them, making friends and working to advocate for others in need.

As we change, we heal. We learn to love, forgive and respect ourselves. We also do the same for others. We see there's still work to do, but we no longer retreat and feel incapable of taking action.

Instead, we continue taking little steps, one at a time, until we are marching with our heads held high, knowing our journeys have — and do — make a difference, not just for ourselves but for others.

Just for Today

Learn about the healing process. When you have to go through painful experiences, there are always things to learn. Don't feel sorry for yourself; recognize your own pain and find your own meaning.

Double Your Money

*"The safest way to double your money
is to fold it over once and put it in your pocket."*
~ Frank Hubbard
Pathways to Recovery, p. 145

Saving money for some of us is like trying to walk a floor filled with rubber balls. Our feet get wobbly and we can't find the floor. Instead, we look for other ways to make our money grow, like gambling or playing the lottery. And those rolling balls under our feet just keep growing in number. Soon walking becomes almost impossible.

Let's face it. The odds of winning the lottery or coming out ahead with any form of gambling are against us. If we put our money away to let it gain interest, or save it for another day, we'd find those rubber balls are less dangerous.

Walking on an unstable surface won't help us get ahead. We need to work for what we get—and then walking isn't as difficult. We can find our feet on solid ground with our money in our pocket.

Just for Today
Money is not you and you are not money yet your self-esteem is often connected to your financial worth. Identify what other things are important!

Like Everyone Else

*"Just as everybody else, we need to be in charge of our lives,
think and speak for ourselves."*
~ Adolf Ratzka
Pathways to Recovery, p. 16

We can be in charge of our lives. What a wonderful thought!

Yes, it's true we've had many past experiences we'd just as soon forget. We can give our power up to the past, letting it hold us back, keeping us from the future. Or we can realize that our past is just that—our past. It doesn't need to define who we are. And it doesn't mean we shouldn't be able to live our own lives, believe what we want or speak our own voice.

Today gives us a wonderful new perspective. As we take control of our life—the whole of our life—we can leave the past behind and create the future we want... just as everybody else.

Just for Today
Write down all the experiences you've had that you'd like to leave in the past. Then find a container and put the lists – along with any objects that represent these negative times – in the container. Find a place to bury the container...along with those negative remembrances!

Be Aware of Living

"Be aware of wonder, live a balanced life.
Learn some and think some and draw some
and sing and dance and play and work every day some."
~ Robert Fulghum
Pathways to Recovery, p. 319

Life becomes demanding and chaotic very easily. We all play many roles in our social, career and family lives. Each area demands great time and strength on our part, and often the time we spend on all of our roles isn't balanced, so decisions collide with one another — often to our disadvantage.

During all of the demands on us, we must make time for ourselves as well. If we don't take time to see the wonder in our own lives, to play and work in a balanced manner, we definitely risk hitting the wall with our health — mentally or physically.

It's absolutely okay to balance our lives in a manner that rejuvenates us, instead of draining us. It's absolutely okay to think some and draw some and sing and dance and play and work every day.

Just for Today
Make a fun kit today. Put things in it that always make you smile or laugh. When you're ready to sing and dance and play, you'll have something you can grab quickly!

Laughter by Definition

"Laughter is by definition healthy."
~ Doris Lessing
Pathways to Recovery, p. 365

Humor has been shown to be good for our health. And people who laugh always seem a little happier.

Watching a funny TV show or listening to someone tell jokes is a great way to get lost in the moment. It helps us forget our troubles…and even laugh at some of them. Laughter helps relax us, and when we laugh, we find that others often laugh along with us.

Whenever we think about what's good for our health—getting enough exercise, eating right, getting the right amount of sleep, using affirmations—we'll be sure to add laughter to the list!

Just for Today
Send a fun cartoon or note to a person who could use a good laugh. But be sure to read it yourself first! It'll make you feel good!

One Step Changes Everything

"This one step, choosing a goal and sticking to it, changes everything."
~ Scott Reed
Pathways to Recovery, p. 114

Many of us struggle with setting goals and sticking to them.

Sometimes that's because we've set unrealistic goals, or we don't plan the small steps that lead us to accomplish our larger goals. Sometimes it's from not having a clear vision of what we want. It's then that we're more likely to let other people in our lives set goals for us. Maybe we've been told so many times that we can't reach our goals that we've simply given up making any. There are several things that can help us as we set goals for our future.

We need to get curious—curious about who we are, what we want, what our true purpose is and what's available in our community.

We'll need to allow ourselves to have the freedom to see these options to help define where we want to be.

Our goals should approach life as though it were ours alone, and with openness to opportunities to build a life worth living. As we strive to succeed—stepping forward by using our strengths and the positive pieces of our lives—we will reach our goals!

Just for Today

Develop a habit of being curious! Ask questions if you don't know the answer to something. Explore the internet or your local library for topics that you might find interesting.

Simple Acts

"One of the most important results you can bring into the world
is the you that you really want to be."
~ Robert Fritz
Pathways to Recovery, p. 97

How do we find out who we really want to be? Is it even possible?

It is if we stop depending on others to care for us or make decisions
for us. It is if we stop fearing change and let ourselves take risks. It is
if we recognize the good inside of us and work to bring that out into
the open, letting everyone around us see who we really are.

Each of us has tremendous strengths within ourselves. We all have
talents that the world needs us to share.

Don't think of these as things that are huge or complicated. Simple
acts given freely, purely...these are often our greatest gifts.

 ## Just for Today
Contribute to your favorite cause. Most organizations are
grateful for even small donations. If you can't afford a
donation, consider giving your time to support the cause.

Create Something

"If you would create something, you must be something."
~ Goethe
Pathways to Recovery, p. 339

No matter what it is we're creative at, it's necessary to the art of being human for us to be a creator of something.

Some people see the force of creativity in everything around them. Every idea, word, memory or action we have, think, say or do is an act of creativity! When we have a feeling and act on it in a real way, we are using our own unique creative process.

There are no rules in creativity. We just need to find our own ability within us and use it. We must create to be healthy, to be happy and to know who we are.

Just for Today

If you're breathing, you're creative! But it's also important to nurture your creativity. Grab a calendar for the upcoming year and randomly choose six days and mark those. When you get to that day, pick a creative activity to enjoy!

Hope Is Crucial

"Hope is crucial to recovery,
for our despair disables us more than our disease ever could."
~ Esso Leete
Pathways to Recovery, p. 33

Hope is something that sometimes seems so far away. Yet, it's in living life through its ups and downs that we can—and do—discover hope.

Hope is something we hold onto when life sends challenges our way.

Hope is something we show others when we stay on the pathway in life, working towards goals—big and small—even when we feel like giving up.

Hope is something we see in others we admire—people who have worked through the hard times in their lives, people who we consider successful. We see hope in those who show kindness and goodness to others and make us know that life is worth living, even when it gets really, really tough.

Hope doesn't make all the bad things go away, but it helps put life in balance so we can see the light ahead, and not just the darkness around us.

Just for Today

Anticipate and plan for times when you might feel a lack of hope. Make a list or create a hope box with ideas for activities that you know will help you feel better. Don't give in to those hopeless feelings!

There Is Power

*"It takes a lot of courage to release the familiar and seemingly secure,
to embrace the new. But there is no real security in what is
no longer meaningful. There is more security in the adventurous
and exciting, for in movement there is life and
in change there is power."*
~ Alan Cohen
Pathways to Recovery, p. 341

Come out, come out!

Those who hide behind doors—doors many years old—often choose to stay inside. To stay there is to say *no* to life, to say "I don't care" to change and to say "phooey" to the inevitable.

Come out to see the day for what it really is—something only we can pass through. We must travel along our own road to see what waits at the top of the hill, peeking over the top at an astounding tomorrow.

Come out to face the power each of us holds—the power to become, to move from behind the doors that no longer need to hide us, but instead encourage new changes. Come out, come out to the adventure

Just for Today

Do you ever find yourself worrying? Write down all the things that you're worrying about. When finished, rate each worry on a scale of one to ten (with ten being the absolute worst thing that could happen). How will you let this information help you?

New Opportunities

"New opportunities await and abound. Never stagnate and settle."
~ Katherine Negermajian
Pathways to Recovery, p. 9

The path to recovery is just that—a path. Along that road there are many wonderful things to see, to explore. But, what we see is not necessarily all we get. It's how we interpret what we see that determines what we can get out of life.

Instead of rushing out in the morning, we need to take a moment to smell the air, listen to the sounds of life around us. We need to be mindful.

Mindfulness is the capacity to pay attention—without judgment—to the present moment. It's about living in the moment, experiencing one's emotions and senses fully, yet with perspective.

Only when we slow down and really take in life does the path not seem so desolate. We have control over how we experience life. It's in deciding to take control that our lives begin to change for the better.

Just for Today

Make a contract with yourself to look for the opportunities you want in your life. Include things such as a schedule to follow, the expectations you have for yourself, who you will need to ask for help or support and how you will celebrate your accomplishments.

Reaching the Mind

"Only those who are able to relax can create,
and then ideas reach the mind like lightening."
~ Cicero
Pathways to Recovery, p. 313

All of us have to take a break now and then. Many of us find ourselves vulnerable to stress, with a low tolerance to deal with the many stressors we face every day.

Therefore, taking time out to relax will help inspire us when we're busy. Planning vacations—even for a day or a weekend—can be a great way to get away from the stress in life and relax. We can do some of our favorite things around the house, explore our community or find a new place to discover—any activity that helps us to relax.

And once we find that relaxing place, our minds can settle down just enough to let the lightening strike!

Just for Today

What's your favorite way to relax? Take 15 minutes of your day to practice relaxing. See if you can start including a few minutes each day into your routine activities.

What We Make of Our Lives

"I feel recovery changes people by giving them a language – an understanding in which everyone can relate. I think most people are recovering or have recovered from something in their life – perhaps a disaster, a death, divorce or a financial or job loss. Most importantly, the message of recovery challenges [us] not to define [ourselves] exclusively within a framework of an illness."
~ Cherie Bledsoe
Pathways to Recovery, p. 15

Loss is something that happens to everyone. When we lose something important, it takes time to work through our grief. It takes time to find something new in life that brightens our souls and soothes our hearts. Loss is painful, but it's also part of the human experience.

We can feel very alone when we experience the symptoms of loss. Depression can set in and we feel its cloud surrounding everything we do. We might have trouble sleeping, eating or going to work or school.

But in time, depression can get better if we seek support and take time to tend to our inner needs. In time, our losses feel a little less intense, even though we'll always feel a sense of sadness and longing for how things used to be. Sadness no longer defines us, and we learn to move on in order to find joy again. It's this message of recovery that helps us find a balance between tending to symptoms and working not to let them define us.

Just for Today

Many people who experience depression find that getting plenty of sunlight is helpful. Get outside today and enjoy the sun!

Saddling Up Anyway

"Courage is being scared to death...and saddling up anyway."
~ John Wayne
Pathways to Recovery, p. 39

Finding our courage can be difficult and slow. We often wallow in muddy waters, where our footprints have been covered over, hands hung taut at our sides, waiting to see what comes next.

Nevertheless, finding courage is the only way we've gotten to where we are today. It's also the way we will become better tomorrow. As we take another step, we'll gather the strength to find our way.

It's only in movement that we can keep going; only with movement can we stay alive. It's knowing our fears, and taking a chance anyway.

Just for Today

Listen to your instincts! If you think a situation is going to be harmful to your health or well being, listen to those instincts and distance yourself from the situation.

An Extraordinary Gift

"The mind can also be an erogenous zone."
~ Racquel Welch
Pathways to Recovery, p. 187

As human beings, we are amazingly sexual. The experiences we've had don't need to take that away from us. Being able to express our sexuality can be a critical part of who we are. How we choose to experience our sexuality is not limited by relationships, only by our minds.

Discovering what turns us on, allowing ourselves to experience feelings without judging, and getting to know ourselves as sexual beings is an extraordinary gift we can give ourselves. We can explore our sexuality in different ways. The mind is the first and most important place to begin.

Just for Today

When you realize negative thinking breeds negative thinking —
especially when you're interested in intimacy with another — you can
start to accept yourself for all you are. Others will notice it too! Why
not compliment yourself all day?

As We Are

"We don't see things as they are, we see them as we are."
~ Anais Nin
Pathways to Recovery, p. 296

Sometimes we do damage to our relationships because we tell ourselves nothing but negative messages instead of hearing the positive things our supporters are trying to tell us.

Those nasty little comments in our heads, no matter where they come from or when they were planted, continue to plague us—and we are our worst enemy.

Sadly, when our loved ones express affection or appreciation to us, we meet them with a wall of "no you don'ts," or "you won't for long's." Because of what we think of ourselves, we reject the fact that people love us and want us to feel it.

We can get stuck in a pattern of self-stigma and self-loathing, refusing to see things as they are, clinging to our negative thoughts instead. How much better it is to accept who we are—and to see ourselves as the good and special people we are—just as we are!

Just for Today

Spend some time today thinking about what you like about yourself. It doesn't matter if someone else doesn't like your hair or they don't like the movies you watch. As long as you are happy with the choices you make—as long as you can accept yourself for who you are—what others think is not so important.

True Friendship

"True friendship is self-love at second hand."
~ William Hazlett
Pathways to Recovery, p. 243

To accept ourselves and love ourselves is like opening a door to others. Only through that door can friendship begin, grow and evolve. If that door is closed because of our own self-stigma, our own self-loathing or our own lack of self-esteem, then others can't touch us. Only in revealing ourselves, and accepting ourselves, can we invite true friendship into our lives.

How long have we looked for friends who will accept us for who we are? How long have we not accepted ourselves for who we are? It's all connected. One without the other can't take wing to soar as friendship can.

We can be open to friendship when we love ourselves. In that love, we respond positively as others reach out to us. We are able to let them accept us for who we are.

Just for Today

To love yourself, treat yourself today the way that you would like others to treat you!

Waiting to Back Up

"Having the world's best idea will do you no good unless you act on it. People who want milk shouldn't sit on a stool in the middle of a field in hopes that a cow will back up to them."
~ Curtis Grant
Pathways to Recovery, p. 268

In order to accomplish anything we must get organized in our lives. We need goals to achieve the things we want in life. We can't just wait for the cow to back up!

How do we set goals? By making a list of what we have in our hearts.

We don't have to limit our dreams because of our past. We simply get our thoughts together, write them down, and share our goals with those who can help us. We can put words to our intentions in order to get what we want for ourselves.

Sometimes taking the proverbial 'baby steps' is all we have to do to begin. Even though our dreams may be big, we still start by taking small steps, realizing our accomplishments along the way, growing as we move forward. As we take these initial steps, we'll begin to see and experience our own individual greatness.

If we walk the stool out to the cow, the milk comes a whole lot easier!

Just for Today

Keep in mind that the goals you set may affect those you love; be sure to include your supporters in your planning. You might be surprised at how much they're willing to help you!

The Vision to Go Forward

"Where there is no vision, people perish."
~ Ralph Waldo Emerson
Pathways to Recovery, p. 105

There's no use trying to go back. The past is over. We're not going to get the chance to change the old stuff or make the outcome any different.

But we can start today with a new vision for our life. Slowly. One step at a time. Right where we are. We can begin by setting goals with tasks that can be achieved.

We can start to make small changes in our thinking, allowing ourselves to believe we can have the life we've always wanted — living *with* an illness or trauma, not controlled by it. Today. With vision.

Just for Today

Using "what if" statements only add to your fear of taking action. Try to identify the possible consequences then let yourself know you can handle it. Plan alternatives, too, because things don't always work out the way you plan.

Decide What You Want

*"The indispensable first step to getting the things
you want out of life is this: decide what you want."*
~ *Ben Stein*
Pathways to Recovery, p. 288

It's often difficult to "go for the gold" in our lives, because we don't know for sure what we want and need. We also may feel burdened by the expectations of other people in our lives to perform a certain way. We often do what's expected of us by others, instead of directing our lives in our own way.

We must be the ones who figure out what we need and what we truly want, balancing that with what other people need from us.

We're the conductor of our journey in life. We're the ones who must set our own goals. We're the ones who must know what it is we want.

Just for Today

Don't get caught feeling guilty, worrying whether you should have done this or that! Guilt is an empty emotion that only wastes time and keeps you from living and making things better for tomorrow.

As Good a Compass as Any

*"The needle of our conscience is
as good a compass as any."*
~ *Ruth Wolff*
Pathways to Recovery, p. 66

When we come to the point of discovering where our past experiences and our recovery meet, we find within ourselves either the need to stay or the will to go on. It's a conscious decision which road we'll take.

Being diagnosed with an illness can be the most difficult thing we will ever face. Going beyond that diagnosis is difficult. However, making a conscious choice to not define ourselves by our diagnosis and claim who we really are is part of healing.

Only when we turn that corner will life make any sense to us. If we listen to our hearts and let them guide us, we can move on to become the wonderful people we are meant to be.

Just for Today
You are more than just an illness or diagnosis! So don't label yourself as sick or disabled or less than others. Say, "I am a person who..." Not accepting yourself for who you are delays healing. Staying stuck is not an option! Follow your own way!

Between Good and Great

"Everybody has their ups and downs
so I decided to have mine between good and great."
~ Daine Hoogterp
Pathways to Recovery, p. 363

We all have our good days and our bad days. Our lives have often been a roller coaster of emotions. At one time, this was all we could expect.

Now, however, we're gaining new techniques to deal with the ups and downs. We know that instead of yielding to a negative thought, we can replace it with a more positive one.

We are ultimately in charge of how we react to our surroundings, our thoughts and our emotions. We have a power inside of us that's so strong we can tell the negative thoughts that they aren't real. We can give ourselves more positive, self-affirming thoughts, such as "I can do this." Following this plan leaves us with emotions and reactions that are somewhere "between good and great." What a thought!

Just for Today

A lot of people start having "the dreads" somewhere around Sunday afternoon...starting to fret over the week to come. If this is you, make your Sunday evenings special, treating yourself to whatever it is that makes you feel good...perhaps even great! What a fabulous new perspective to start each week!

See the Other Whole

"Blessed is he who has found his work; let him ask no other blessedness."
~ Thomas Carlyle
Pathways to Recovery, p. 152

Finding our work is one of the most important things we can ever do.

While many of us have received a lot of mixed messages about our abilities to work, as we learn more about recovery, we know that work can be an important part of our journey.

In most cultures and societies, our main identity is wrapped up in what we do. Go to any party and the first question you're asked by another guest is "What do you do?" If we haven't figured out what our work is, it's a pretty hard question to answer.

There are lots of ways to find our work. Some of us look to our heart and our values. Some of us have a passion for certain skill or we've got a great role model who has helped us see what we'd like to do. Still others find themselves motivated by an increased income or desire to follow a family trade. We can even find our work by volunteering or through pursuing education.

So, regardless of whatever illness or symptoms we experience, we can all work. And we can all feel blessed because of that work.

Just for Today

Take your strengths in your hand today! Find one place where you can put your unique gifts and talents to work.

Take Your Life

"Take your life in your own hands and what happens?
A terrible thing: no one to blame."
~ Erica Jong
Pathways to Recovery, p. 287

It's pretty easy to place blame in our lives. We blame the system. We blame our families. We blame our landlords, our providers and our neighbors. Lots of time, we also blame ourselves.

A huge piece of recovery is the acceptance of self-responsibility. Coming to realize that we *do* have control over our own life is freeing, powerful and provides us with a tremendous sense of pride. We can take back our lives. We can make informed decisions. We can trust our own judgment and make our own choices. We no longer need to rely on others for the whole of our life. Taking things in our own hands means we can challenge ourselves to be better and reach for higher goals.

But it also means we can no longer place blame on others for our circumstances. Taking back our lives means we can't make excuses or follow the easy path anymore. It means we purposefully seek to learn new ways of coping and staying well.

Taking back our lives changes our path and gives us greater direction. Taking back our lives is recovery at its best. Enjoy it!

Just for Today

Ever have trouble making decisions? Do your best to look at both sides of the situation but don't delay deciding for fear that you don't have enough information or you're not sure if you'll be right. If all else fails, try going with your gut feeling. The more you trust yourself, the easier it will be to know what is right for you!

Healing Yourself

"If you just set people in motion, they'll heal themselves."
~ Gabrielle Roth
Pathways to Recovery, p. 66

So much of the time, a psychiatric diagnosis or trauma can stop people in their tracks. Stops the dreams and stops the goals and stops the happiness. We stop because someone with more power or authority tells us what to do. We stop because we feel as though we've been sitting at a red light all our lives, waiting for the green light to signal go! We stop our education or our desire for a family and children. We even give up on a job or career that brings us fulfillment.

 Recovery calls us to find the movement. Get up off that couch, get out of that chair and move! We are the only ones who should be telling ourselves what to do. We can reach into our past and reclaim our goals! We can find the activities that bring us joy and the work that gives us passion.

We can find healing for ourselves. Once we realize we can set ourselves in motion, watch out! There's no telling how far we'll go!

Just for Today

To keep your mind busy, keep your body moving...a little bit every day. Start slowly and don't take on too much at one time. When you set yourself in motion...emotionally and physically...you'll feel better!

If You Ask Me Why

*"If you ask me why I came into this world,
I will tell you that I came to LIVE OUT LOUD!"*
~Emile Zola
Pathways to Recovery, p. 344

Finding our creative and playful spirit is an important part of our recovery. We often look at ourselves and don't see anything creative about us. That spirit may have been squashed, or never really discovered.

In each of us is a creative streak that sometimes just needs to be recognized. So many things we do and are can be creative, such as the ability to laugh, or cook or find the positive in others.

Being able to survive has been very creative for each of us — and we've each accomplished it our own way.

As we take the time to be adventurous, we'll probably find it easier to "LIVE OUT LOUD!"

Just for Today
If you could do or be or feel anything this week, what would it be? Go ahead and live out loud!

Seeing Things Invisible

"Vision is the art of seeing things invisible."
~*Jonathan Swift*
Pathways to Recovery, p. 106

An artist has the vision of a beautiful painting before she creates it.

A builder has vision of how he would like to construct a home. Without this vision, the house would surely crumble.

A writer has the vision of a story, long before the details are decided about each of the characters or the plot.

Each of us has the ability within us to look to the invisible—that which we cannot see right now—and turn those visions into reality. Our beliefs and values will guide us. Our vision will be ours and only ours. Our vision will help us see what it is we really want.

Just like the artist, the builder and the writer, once we can see the invisible things, our vision can then become our greatest reality.

Just for Today
Have a spouse, roommate or child? Stop what you're doing today and just listen to them. Give them your undivided attention!

The Price that Life Extracts

"Courage is the price that life exacts for granting peace."
~ Amelia Earhart
Pathways to Recovery, p. 40

Risk-taking is what keeps life interesting. It's in our courage to take risks that we truly live life. If we hide and isolate ourselves, we're being fearful and not living life to the fullest.

Taking small risks helps us build up to the bigger risks. And remember, we cannot succeed without first failing. Risk-taking means we may fail at something before we master it. Failure is just an experiment for success. Keep going.

Just for Today
Fill in the blank..."If I don't do _____, what will I miss? How will I feel if I don't do this thing?" Stay focused and keep taking risks; courage will come and you'll be glad you didn't give in!

Getting Rolled in the Dirt

"Do not be too timid and squeamish about your actions...
What if you fail and get fairly rolled in the dirt once or twice?
Up again: you shall never be so afraid to stumble."
~ Ralph Waldo Emerson
Pathways to Recovery, p. 245

Imagine the world we would have had if there'd been nobody willing to take a fall...

There'd be no electricity or Tootsie Roll Pops.
There'd be no cameras to record our favorite events.
We'd sit on logs instead of soft cushions.
We'd eat with our fingers and there wouldn't be soup.

There'd be no ping pong or cool ceiling fans.
There wouldn't be books or taffy or toasters.
We'd never know what soccer was and we'd never fly in a plane.
We'd walk everywhere—which wouldn't be far—and wonder why the moon was so much bigger than the stars.

So next time it seems really easy to say no, fearful of the tumble, remember...It's only through stumbling—and getting back up—that our ideas become our reality.

Just for Today
Are you willing to take a fall? What would the world not have if you hadn't stumbled? Find one thing to do today where you throw away your timidity and welcome the dirt!

December

*"I heard a bird sing
in the dark of December,
A magical thing
and sweet to remember."*

~ Oliver Herford

We Carry it Within Us

"We all carry it within us: supreme strengths, the fullness of wisdom, unquenchable joy. It is never thwarted, and cannot be destroyed."
~ Huston Smith
Pathways to Recovery, p. 96

There was a woman who thought she had no strengths, who found little joy in life and believed that she was a bother to everyone.

Then one day, a friend's child came into her life. Spending time with that child, she soon realized that she did have joy, that she was actually good with children. She found the dark clouds that had followed her around for so long were beginning to fade away.

But her discoveries didn't end there. Having the courage to watch her friend's child led to other courageous acts. She began reading about child development. Eventually she took a class at her local junior college. One thing led to another until the day she started her first job working in a day care center. She is enjoying her life more than she ever expected because she had the strength, wisdom and courage to keep going.

Just for Today

Too often, we give ourselves up to others without taking the time to figure out who we are and what we feel. Challenge yourself to look inside for your own wisdom! Write down your thoughts and feelings. Look for a pattern that can help you make life changes.

Finding Ourselves

"To find yourself, think for yourself."
~ Socrates
Pathways to Recovery, p. 142

It's a dangerous thing to let others think for us. When we give up the responsibility for ourselves, it becomes increasingly hard to make decisions and finally, we just give up. We let that other person choose for us because we're lost and we've forgotten what it was we really wanted.

When we give up thinking for ourselves, we lose our power. Our road gets rocky because we haven't set our own firm foundation. And as sincere as others may be, they simply can't *always* have our best interests at heart. That's not their job—it's *our* responsibility!

When we think for ourselves, we take back our power. We become stronger and wiser. We gain courage. We begin to make goals and achieve them. We learn and grow.

And in the end...we find ourselves.

Just for Today

Disagree with someone today! You have much to learn from those with whom you don't see eye-to-eye. A good discussion with someone you disagree with can help you better think and understand yourself!

A Trigger for Transformation

"Every intention is a trigger for transformation."
~ Deepak Chopra
Pathways to Recovery, p. 27

All of us must take the events in our lives and see how they transform us on our journey of recovery and possibility.

Looking toward the future with hope and courage is where we start. We must look at the chances and decisions we make in our lives to have peace and transformation in our health, our relationships and our endeavors, whatever they may be.

When we look at life with hope, we see the greatness in ourselves. When we take risks to make our lives better in the face of adversity, we show the courage to continue our hope for fulfilling lives. They go hand-in-hand.

Just for Today

Keep track of everything you do today. Is there something you need to intentionally start or stop that would lead to a personal transformation?

Small Stones

"The man who moved a mountain
was the one who began by carrying away small stones."
~ Chinese Proverb
Pathways to Recovery, p. 307

Changing a habit takes weeks of effort. If there's something we want to stop doing, it isn't possible to make the change instantly. We have to make a commitment to change, and then work towards it a moment at a time, a day at a time, a month at a time.

If there's something we want to start doing to improve our health—such as taking vitamins or exercising daily—it will take time. But as we continue trying to change, our behavior will become a good habit.

Like the Chinese proverb says, the man who moved a mountain did it by carrying away small stones…one at a time. If he'd tried to move the whole mountain at once he probably would've sat down and given up. We can look at recovery that way—encouraging ourselves and each other to take one step at a time toward reaching our greater goals of wellness.

Just for Today
Start to see yourself in a new, positive habit. Post pictures and positive affirmations. Let yourself know you can do this! Set realistic goals and if you falter, start over the next day. Don't beat yourself up!

Really Listening

"Listening, not imitation, may be the sincerest form of flattery."
~ Dr. Joyce Brothers
Pathways to Recovery, p. 244

To be a true friend, one must find the ability to listen actively, to find the meaning in what we hear and to practice listening well. Listening is not something we do by nature. It's learned through nurturing and having an open attitude to what others have to say.

Distractions—like thoughts, other activities, outside input or conflict within ourselves—can cause us to not listen well. Only when we really commit to the individual who is talking to us do we really hear what is being said, verbally and non-verbally. Being a good listener is one of the greatest gifts we can give to someone else...it's also a great gift to give to ourselves.

Just for Today

Ask yourself if you are doing your best to listen to others. Or are you trying to get them to listen to you instead? Truly listen to all that is said to you today...you'll love the gift!

Whatever You Call It

"Call it a clan, call it a network, call it a tribe, call it a family.
Whatever you call it, whoever you are, you need one."
~ Jane Howard
Pathways to Recovery, p. 219

None of us live in isolation. In fact, it's pretty hard to do, even if we try.

Positive relationships are so important in our recovery journey. We need others to make our lives rich and rewarding. We need people who will support us, encourage us and challenge us to be better. We need connections to those who believe in us, to people who trust us and are there for us whenever we need them.

It doesn't matter if these people are our family members or not. The old adage that "we can choose our friends, but not our family" certainly holds true. Finding—and then nurturing—the people with whom we feel comfortable and safe is what's important...because we need them.

Just for Today

So many people look down as they walk. See if you can change that up... smile at everyone you see today. Remember to smile at your own clan, too!

What We Believe

"We are what we believe we are."
~ B. N. Cardozo
Pathways to Recovery, p. 85

If we continue to look at our illness or diagnosis as all we are, then that's all we'll ever be.

If we believe we can be well, we will find our wellness.

If we believe we're courageous, we will be courageous.

If we believe we're worthy, we will do worthwhile things.

If we believe we can succeed, we'll look at failure as a tool for learning what will lead to eventual success.

If we believe in ourselves, we can do anything we set our minds to do.

Just for Today

Speak up with your opinions at work, school or home. When you break out of the role of letting others squash your ideas, you will build confidence in your own voice and judgment!

Reaching Goals

"Hope works in these ways: it looks for the good in people instead of harping on the worst; it discovers what can be done instead of grumbling about what cannot; it regards problems, large or small, as opportunities; it pushes ahead when it would be easy to quit; it 'lights the candle' instead of 'cursing the darkness.'"
~ Anonymous
Pathways to Recovery, p. 32

Where's our hope? Sometimes it surely feels harder and harder to find on our own. We hear how we'll never get better and we're told what we can't do. "It's easier to give up," we say. And the light? "Ha! That's not something I'll ever see."

No doubt, most of us can relate to a lot of these comments. But if we believe these things — and we often do — we'll never find our lives moving in a positive direction. We'll just be stuck.

Recovery isn't for the weak of will. It takes a lot of moving, learning and trying again. So we might as well look for the best in things. We can stop grumbling and blaming. Problems? Let's think of those as learning experiences, nothing more. Let's keep going, even when we want to quit.

But most of all, let's light our darkness with a new, bright, glorious candle of hope!

Just for Today
Let others see the good in you today! Wherever you are, take fifteen minutes and open the door for everyone!

Breaking Free

*"It is time to let go of the judging voices and to let yourself feel the joy
and humor that was silenced within you but wants to break free."*
~ Gay Hendricks
Pathways to Recovery, p. 292

If we could just break away from the things that have kept us from
realizing our highest potentials, what would it look like?

To get there, we can first make a list of what it is we want to be doing
in life. We'll try not to let any limitations enter in. We'll just make the
list and dream as high and as far as we want!

Then we can make a second list. This list would be all the reasons,
excuses, and realities that get in our way. It's a good idea to make this
list without passing judgment; just let it be what it is.

Then we can make a third list. This list would be ways we're resourceful
and strong. Now is the time to start saying "no
way" to the limits, reasons and excuses. Sure,
some things are stressful and may trigger us.
Sure, there is stigma. And sure, there are some
things we can do, and some things for which
others are better suited.

But really, there are way more things we can do
than ones we can't. And once we break free of the limits imposed on
us, we really start living with joy and a passion where nothing can
stop us!

Just for Today

*Make your own 3-part list today using the instructions above. Feel
your joy and let your humor help you break free!*

The Greatest Prize

*"There is nothing on this earth more to be prized
than a true friendship."*
~ St. Thomas Aquinas
Pathways to Recovery, p. 234

Ah, the glory of a true friendship!

Our friends—our *true* friends—are the people we want to have in our lives. They may come quickly and stay forever or they may have to wiggle their way into our lives, slowly and deliberately. But a true friend—they're always be there, regardless of what we do or say or become.

Our true friends may not agree with us, but they challenge us to think.

Our true friends may not understand us, but they respect us enough to let us be who we are.

Our true friends may not live nearby, but they inhabit our hearts.

Our true friends stand by us. They comfort us and make us laugh. They hold our hands and they hold our hope when it seems impossible for us to hold our own.

True friendship…what a glorious prize!

Just for Today
Respect differences of opinion…these happen in any good relationships! Differences are also what make friendships exciting. Be sure to be objective and open-minded!

A Light Heart

"A light heart lives long!"
~ William Shakespeare
Pathways to Recovery, p. 306

Just what is a 'light heart?'

A light heart is one that is open and not weighed down heavily by stress, or pain or burdens. A light heart is ready for anything; it's patient and accepting and genuine.

A person with a light heart isn't free from worry, nor are they immune to anxiety, fear or sorrow.

But a person with a light heart is able to understand their own sorrow, learning and growing from all their experiences. A person with a light heart is ready — at all times — to let the joy in, to let the peace surround the chaos. They're able to accept life's changes with understanding, knowing that things will be better...things *always* get better.

A person with a light heart lives long...not always in years, but definitely in the amount of joy and happiness they allow into their lives.

Just for Today

Talk to your friends about any regrets you may have. The burden of your feelings can often be lessened by sharing them with a trusting person.

One Outrageous Thing

"My goal is to say or do at least one outrageous thing every week."
~ *Maggie Kuhn*
Pathways to Recovery, p. 342

Who wants to "fit in" with everyone else? Well, most of us do. We work to make friends, and not to feel left out or different. We worry about the way we look, the way we act and the way we talk. We put a lot of energy into trying to be "normal"…which can take energy away from just being who we are.

How can we let go of the fears and anxieties we have about who we are? What can we do to lessen our inhibitions, to just accept ourselves for the wonderful, beautiful, talented people we are?

We begin by telling ourselves that we are okay—just the way we are. Of course, there may be some things we're working towards, but focusing on all the negatives pulls us away from the opportunities we have to embrace the good things about ourselves, those things that have helped us survive—and thrive—in spite of the difficult times.

Just for Today

Be silly today! Blow bubbles. Make a funny face or laugh for no reason. Wear a hat or skip through the park. Be outrageous!

We Have What We Seek

"We have what we seek. It is there all the time, and if we give it time, it will make itself known to us."
~ Thomas Merton
Pathways to Recovery, p. 78

Finding strength from within is often second-hand in nature. But realizing those strengths does not come as easily.

Each of us knows of things we've done or have gone through that, when looking back, we realize, "Wow! I withstood that," or "I can't believe that happened to me and I made it." It's in these moments that we know what we're made of—a strong will and an imaginative sense of survival.

These are strengths we must not discount or push away. They are ours, and we should celebrate them each and every time they come to mind. Once we learn to do that, we see that we are as strong as the next person. We have nothing to fear, because we are strong.

Just for Today

It takes patience to wait...for just about anything! Try to become aware of the things that cause your impatience. What recovery tools do you have that can help you when you feel like this?

The Museum of Our Soul

"That which we elect to surround ourselves with becomes
the museum of our soul and the archive of our experiences."
~ Thomas Jefferson
Pathways to Recovery, p. 132

What's in our museum? What is it we surround ourselves with?

Are we hanging around people who don't nourish us? Are we working at a job because someone said it was all we could do? Are we holding on to the past, thinking it will somehow change?

Are we moving forward on our own dreams or have we let someone else's expectations of us lead the way?

Are we surrounding ourselves with people who support us and challenge us to be better? Are we looking at ways to use our passion to earn a living? Are we surrounding ourselves with learning and education and positive action? Are we setting our own goals and reaching them because that's what we want to do?

Surrounding ourselves with good things, positive people and meaningful activities lets us see the beauty of all that is in our personal museum. It lets us see the richness of our experiences. It lets us be who we want to be.

Just for Today
Surround your environment with beauty, too! Fix up something you've had for a long time. Make it look new or beautiful!

Getting the Test First

"Experience is a hard teacher because she gives the test first, the lesson afterward."
~ *Vernon Law*
Pathways to Recovery, p. 137

Yes indeed! We've had the test!

We've had losses so we can appreciate what we have.

We've failed but we've learned how to change.

We've been hurt so we could understand how to love.

We've walked a path we didn't create for ourselves. But we've found out how to make the road our own.

And pain. Yes, we've had enough of that! But in the pain, we've learned how to truly live.

Experience is a hard teacher and the tests we've had are some of the most difficult. But then again, the lessons we learn are tools for growth. They pave the way for our journey and give us the courage, strength and understanding to find our way.

Just for Today

Take comfort in the simple things in life. Each day you can face change or hurt or loss. Find the moments that give you strength and comfort; hold on to those as you find your own way!

Stand Up

"Fall seven times, stand up eight."
~ Japanese Proverb
Pathways to Recovery, p. 282

Many of us wish we could return to a time in our lives before we began to experience symptoms. Some of us take off on our recovery journey and try to head "back to the past." Many of us had careers, goals, relationships and roles that were taken from us as our mental health challenges claimed more and more of our lives. Some of us can't remember life without symptoms, but still, the past is familiar and we somehow think recovery is supposed to be about going back to the way it used to be.

Recovery is about discovery! It's about changing and exploring and finding new opportunities for living. As we journey the road of recovery, we're going to find we're not the people we used to be. We have changed. Other people have changed. Time has gone by and the opportunities we once had are no longer there.

We don't have to forget our pasts. Even though we've changed, we still carry certain qualities and skills that we can use in new ways. We continue to be resourceful, and find new opportunities to use our interests and talents. We don't have to give up the past entirely; we just find new ways to reclaim who we are as we stand up—again—to discover what lies ahead.

Just for Today

Allow yourself to be taken care of and nurtured today. Be kind to yourself and you can then turn that kindness toward others.

Things that Money Can't Buy

*"It's good to have money and the things that money can buy,
but it's good too, to check up once in a while and make sure
you haven't lost the things that money can't buy."*
~ *George Lucas Lorimer*
Pathways to Recovery, p. 141

Sometimes we get so focused on trying to make, win or get money that we lose sight of the things which mean the most in life. Our relationships are worth more than gold. They're what help us get from day to day.

What we do have—love, friendship, the ability to do something well—we must strap to our backs and keep close in our minds. It's not what we can buy that will get us to where we're going. It's what we already have.

Just for Today
Gifts don't have to be bought. How about giving one of your favorite books to a friend or the library with a note to the next reader telling them what you liked about the book?

A Passport to the Future

*"Education is our passport to the future,
for tomorrow belongs to the people who prepare for it today."*
~ Malcolm X
Pathways to Recovery, p. 136

An education lasts a lifetime and helps us get to where we're going in life's path. It's definitely one gift we can give ourselves that no one can ever take from us.

Today it's next to impossible to find a j o b without some level of education. Defining education is something else. How many years have we learned how to cope with life day-to-day? How much of an education have we been supplied by deciding to live? Education comes in many forms—and many of us have PhDs in living, surviving and making life worthwhile.

It's never too late to start an educational program that could lead to something new or different, getting us more prepared for life's journey. Education is often our passport to new dreams—and a new life.

Just for Today
Check out some local schools and see what kind of educational experiences are available to you. It's never too late for education!

The Frame of Our Destiny

"We are not permitted to choose the frame of our destiny.
But what we put into it is ours."
~ Dag Hammarskjöld
Pathways to Recovery, p. 352

Ever heard any of these messages? "Go to this doctor's appointment." "Take this medicine." "Try this new therapy." "Just get a job, and then you'll be okay." "You can get rid of this if you just try hard enough."

We've all heard one or more of these messages during our journey. But this could be a path designed by someone else.

Each of us has had expectations set for us—some too high, some too low. But we must remember we are the ones who live our life and we are the ones who get to create what it looks like. We get to develop our own goals and we get to learn from our mistakes. We get to decide what goes into our body and what treatments are most helpful. We are the ones who know we don't pull ourselves up by our bootstraps, but that we must work hard and dig deep for our resilience.

We may not choose our frame, but the picture we create of our lives—that's truly ours!

Just for Today
Striving for perfection in yourself is a good thing, but it's not everything! You'll live a healthier life without so much stress or the unrealistic demands you place on yourself. Do your best; sometimes it will be perfect and sometimes it will just be enough!

A Different Kind of Artist

*"The artist is not a different kind of person,
but every person is a different kind of artist."*
~ Eric Gill
Pathways to Recovery, p. 339

There's a stereotypical image that comes to mind when we hear the word "artist." Artists are often thought of as eccentric. We think of them as wearing funky clothes and having trend-making hairstyles. We think of them as social activists who often go outside social norms, making paintings, movies, dances and poetry that speak to issues such as social justice or peace.

Each of us is an artist in our own way. We don't have to wear funky clothes or break social rules to be an artist. We're artists because we're able to see new ways to live.

We're artists as we set recovery goals and work to break out of habits that no longer work for us. When we're problem solving and finding new approaches to living, we're being artists with a vision. When we turn to more positive thoughts and activities — ones that bring us to a more peaceful and happy state of being — we're being artists. And, as we "paint" the pathway to recovery, the opportunities to be creative are limitless!

Just for Today

What kind of artist are you? Can you think of one activity you can do today that will help you identify how limitless your creativity can be? Try to see creativity in a whole new way!

It is Most Important

"Whatever you do may seem insignificant,
but it is most important that you do it."
~ Mahatma Gandhi
Pathways to Recovery, p. 120

Sometimes our eyes see and our hearts feel drawn to those who have less than us, those who struggle with life and living. We know there are those whom we can't touch, even though we would take their burdens away if possible. It's daunting and frustrating to be where we are and not be able to do something.

It's precisely at these times when we must realize what we do as individuals is what makes the world go 'round. We have to look hard and deep to discover we do what we can with what we have.

The fact that we care is the first step to helping others. What we do with the care we have in our hearts remains up to us. But whatever we choose to do, "it is most important that we do it."

Just for Today
Surround yourself with beautiful things...fresh flowers, books you love, objects that remind you of good times. Having these special things is significant and most important!

Finding Adventure

"Life is either a daring adventure or nothing."
~ Helen Keller
Pathways to Recovery, p. 306

Life is all about getting out and experiencing everything we can. It's about doing things and living in a way that keeps us moving forward, learning and growing and creating.

But at the same time, most of us crave security. We think security will bring us happiness. We're sure we need to know what and when things will happen in order for us to be ready, to be prepared.

But security doesn't really exist. The harder we try for security, the harder it eludes us, keeping us from becoming who we'd really like to be.

Life is about change. Life is about finding adventure in everything we do. And adventure—true adventure—is full of learning and growing and healing. It's a stepping stone to happiness and the path to contentment.

So isn't it better to go ahead and seek adventure—even though we don't know what will happen or where we'll end up—than to stay right where we are, getting nothing?

Just for Today
Work on simplifying your life and cutting out things that complicate or add stress to your life. Doing this can help you find the time to set out on your daring adventure!

Going After Dreams

*"[In my recovery] progress did not come easy, by any means.
Often it was a matter of reminding myself that three steps forward
and two steps back, is still progress. Other times, it has been
necessary to try to conceive of the fact that three steps forward
and five steps back, is still progress...
Relapse is a part of recovery. It is not a failure."*
~ Donna Orrin
Pathways to Recovery, p. 302

Ever hear the old proverb, "Anything worth having doesn't come easy?" That sounds like the slogan for recovery!

It's pretty hard to feel good about relapse, especially when we have a few bad days and begin to worry that we're heading down another dark, endless tunnel. It's difficult to think about relapse without feeling a tinge of self-pity. It looms over us, ready to pounce at a moment's notice.

But we really don't have to give in to relapse so quickly. Think of all the ways we've learned to help ourselves. Look for the people who've become our supporters. Remember these things and try to reframe the experience of relapse in such a way that it doesn't seem so overwhelming. The former person might give in, but not us!

Let's give ourselves credit for what we've been through but not hold on to our past. We may have a relapse, but we aren't a failure.

Just for Today
*Many problems are brought on by our thoughts. Don't stay alone
with those thoughts so they take you over. Going out with others can
help you clear your mind! Enjoy yourself!*

I'm Not Where I Was

"It's been 15 years of staying with my recovery and not giving in. I can announce with pride 'I'm not where I want to be yet, I'm not where I am going, but thank God I'm not where I was.'"
~ Cindy
Pathways to Recovery, p. 97

Sometimes we can get really stuck, feeling miserable about our lives. Regrets about the past fill our thoughts and cloud our hopes for the future. The list of things we wish we hadn't done gets so long that it seems like we think of nothing else.

When we're feeling stuck, we may be bored and feel like nothing ever changes. It might seem like we're making the same mistakes over and over again. We get discouraged when we lose sight of our goals.

Remember, recovery is a process. Sure, many of us fall off track. But the time it takes to get back on course will happen quicker each time as we choose to hold onto hope and focus on the positive things about our recovery journey. When we look at where we are at today and compare it to where we were the first day of our recovery, we'll see the progress we've made. Let's take pride in that and let go of regrets. Let's use our energy for the good things still to come!

Just for Today

There will always be someone that will have more than you or who is further along in their journey. You don't have to feel bad about it because what you have is what you've achieved! That person may appear to have more but they lack what you have!

A Moment of Joy

"Celebration is the recognition of a moment of joy."
~ Peter Megargee Brown
Pathways to Recovery, p. 100

We have so much to celebrate. But are we really taking advantage of one of life's greatest activities?

We usually reserve our celebration for big events—a birthday, a wedding or a holiday—in order to roll out the red carpet, blow up the balloons and have a great big party. But is that really enough?

No! Our lives should be all about celebration—each and every day! But how do we do that?

We can wake up each morning grateful for all we have. We can make sure we recognize the little moments that pass, turning seemingly ordinary experiences into extraordinary ones. We can look at the small details in life without giving up on the grand events. Celebration requires us to find the magic that exists all around us and recognize the joy these things bring.

Celebrate each and every day. Celebrate each moment. Celebrate who we are and what we have become. Celebrate our passion and celebrate our choices. Celebrate our moments of joy!

Just for Today
Participate today in a random act of kindness. Spreading joy to others who don't know it's coming will make you smile as much as they will!

What We've Already Achieved

*"Don't be run so much by what you lack
as by what you have already achieved."
~ Marcus Aurelius
Pathways to Recovery, p. 142*

It's especially difficult to find something good in ourselves when we've experienced the pain of having someone tell us differently. How many times have we heard the phrase, "You failed." How many times have we said it to ourselves?

In order to feel better about ourselves, we need to look at our past and our present and do an inventory—an honest inventory—of what we've done, or can do, that gives us a feeling of satisfaction.

We need to think back to what we did last year, tuning out those old messages that no longer work, always remembering the things we did right. A smile shared, a kind word, a finished book, a job well done—these are all accomplishments. And there are many more achievements, if we just look.

Just for Today

If you only look at the big moments in life as your achievements—graduating from school or a class, finding a partner, moving to a nice home—you will miss out on all the other achievements you've made. Start a list today of the things you've done right in life. What an achievement!

Who You Think You Are

*"It's not who you are that holds you back,
it's who you think you're not."*
~ Unknown
Pathways to Recovery, p. 293

Who am I but what I see?
    I am more
        More than the thoughts which control me
    I am more than the things I think I am capable of
        I am that which I am in my dreams
I am the possibilities that awaken me and drive me to be
 more.

Who am I but what I see?
    I expect that things will work out
        More than I thought I did
    I expect to thrive in my own individual way
        I expect the most that life can give
            I expect the best that waits for me
                that I have worked so hard for.

Who am I but what I see?
    I will be that which is possible
        More than others thought of me
    I will be the drive in my own life
I will trust in those things that tell me I'm whole
    I will be that which I want to be.

Just for Today

Realize there may be people in this world who may not want to accept you. No worries! It's their loss and your gain. Push those thoughts aside and focus on those people who do want you in their lives!

Permanent Hope

*"Hope is the feeling you have
that the feeling you have isn't permanent."*
~ Jean Kerr
Pathways to Recovery, p. 6

What is hope and how do we define it?

Do we define it as an inner feeling? How about defining it as a sense of knowing things are going to be okay, even if we don't feel so great about things right now? Maybe it's a sense of knowing we have some control over our future.

Hope is so much more than just words. Hope is something to hold on to. It's something that gives us courage and inner strength. Hope helps us know that today will get better and that what happened in the past will be healed. Hope is something special inside all of us — that spark of life that shines inside. It's up to us not to let anything blow it out.

Just for Today

Practice social optimism! Be hopeful for others and you become an encourager of others. Soon, it will become easy to do when you meet someone who is needing their hope recharged!

Who We Want to Be

"I am proud of who I am and my recovery. I use courage and my strengths...You can become the person you want to be!"
~ Sandy Hyde
Pathways to Recovery, p. 87

Who do you want to be? It's not such an unusual question to ask ourselves. In fact, it's probably something we've asked ourselves many times throughout our lives.

Then how do we go about becoming the person we want to be?

We can start off by looking at what's important to us — our values, our relationships, our passions. Once we can identify these, it becomes easier to figure out what it is we want.

We can look to others who may hold similar values or experiences. We can talk with them about how they figured out these things. We can surround ourselves with people who will support us, challenge us and encourage us.

We can then put our beliefs into action by using our strengths and finding our courage. It will take will power and a commitment to change. It may take rearranging our lives or letting things go. But we can do it...we can become the person we want to be!

Just for Today
What is your mission statement in life? What is it you hope to accomplish? Take some time today to put your own mission together... it doesn't have to be long. Simply start by saying "My mission in life is..."

More Painful than the Risk

*"And the day came when the risk to remain tight in a bud
was more painful than the risk it took to blossom."*
~Anais Nin
Pathways to Recovery p. 35

At some point in time, we've all had that little voice inside us that
tells us to play it safe. "Don't rock the boat," it says. "Let it be
and stay right where you are." We let ourselves be held 'tight in
the bud.'

We hesitate, afraid to jump in. We don't ask so we don't get. We
worry about what other people might think or do. We don't take
responsibility for our own life, willing to let things go instead of
having the courage to succeed.

But when we don't take risks, we never get to see the wonder of
all that could be. We don't get to experience the joy of something
new. We don't touch the things we truly want.

If we don't take risks—safe, responsible risks—we risk staying
where we are. And is that *really* what we want? Isn't that more
painful than the risk?

Just for Today
*Evaluate your recent risk taking and ask yourself, "Was it worth it?"
Do you think you'll do it again? Don't let it be more painful!*

To Make an End

"What we call the beginning is often the end
and to make an end is to make a beginning..."
~ T.S. Eliot
Pathways to Recovery, p. 317

A new beginning often starts with the ending of something. If we want to make changes in our lives—in our relationships, our health, our activities or anything else—then we'll have to put an end to something.

Yet most of us will fight those endings. Or we'll get so excited about the "something new" that we fail to put any closure on the things we're needing to let go.

Either way, to make an end—or a beginning—means change. Change that moves us out of our comfort zone and becomes, well...probably uncomfortable, at least for awhile.

But change also brings us power and strength if we let it happen. We'll need to take that first awkward or uncertain step forward. And as we move, the end will indeed become the new beginning—a glorious new beginning.

Just for Today

Never quit and never give up! There will be times when you'll want to, but don't do it! Tell yourself that you can and you will! It's often during the times when you feel most like giving up that the answer will come to you. Don't ever quit!

It was an honor for each of us to be part of the team of writers for this book. Our passion — and ability to write about wellness comes so much more from our personal experience and friends, than from any formal education. With the support of each other, we might all struggle to fully discover the true colors that lie within us. Our journeys must be so much more about joy than struggling to overcome that which oppresses our bodies and minds and spirits.

Lori Davidson

Lori was one of the original authors of *Pathways to Recovery* and continues her work with the book. She uses her story to let others know there are lots of different kinds of recovery. It was in her mind that the book swirled around for so long.

Suzette Mack

Suzette has a long history of involvement in creative projects, including *Pathways to Recovery*. She is an artist, dancer, author and poet who you will often find outside reveling in whatever nature has for her that day...

Lesa Weller

Lesa is an artist and writer who uses her creativity and artistic talents to support her recovery journey. She is passionate about and advocates for mental wellness. She is also the only author of this book who always met her deadlines.

Julie Bayes

Julie was also one of the original authors of *Pathways to Recovery*. She is an writer and communication specialist, sharing her talents as an advocate and person in recovery throughout her life's healing journey. She now enjoys sushi with her partner!

Jan Kobe

Jan was the main illustrator for *Pathways to Recovery;* she graciously let us use her artwork again. Jan's creativity has been a major part of her life & she has created an arts program for her peers. She's also writing a children's book.

"Before I found Pathways, my mental illness defined me.
When I began the workbook, I realized my recovery defined me.
By the time I finished it, I realized I could define my own life."
~ Pathways to Recovery Reader

Pathways to Recovery: A Strengths Recovery Self-Help Workbook

This quote by a *Pathways to Recovery* reader points to the impact the workbook—and its accompanying group facilitator's guide—continue to have for individuals who experience symptoms associated with mental illness or trauma.

Pathways was listed as one of the top three national recovery education tools by the Center for Psychiatric Rehabilitation and it also received the Lilly Reintegration Award. It has also been widely used by the U.S. Veteran's Administration, several state Departments of Mental Health and a wide variety of peer-run organizations. Individual readers, family members, peer supporters and other mental health providers throughout the United States and internationally have used the workbook with great success.

Working in partnership with recovery educators, consumer co-authors and an advisory group of Kansas consumers to develop the materials, *Pathways to Recovery* translates the evidence-supported approach of the Strengths Model—which was developed in Kansas and has been used effectively for over twenty years worldwide—into a person-centered, self-help approach. *Pathways to Recovery* puts the process of setting goals and creating personal recovery plans into a self-guided format.

The workbook doesn't concentrate on psychiatric symptoms, treatments or disorders. Instead, it guides readers through a process of exploring their own recovery journey while creating a long-range vision for their lives. The workbook format gives individuals a chance to explore their current lives and set goals across ten life domains that include creating a home, learning, working, nurturing a social circle, intimacy and sexuality, wellness, leisure and spirituality.

Here are a few of the unique elements of *Pathways to Recovery*:

- Over 30 first-person recovery stories are included and lots of guidelines so readers can create and share their own stories.
- In addition to individual use—as a self-help guide or with a trusted provider—*Pathways* was designed to be adaptable for many different group settings. The workbook is currently used as a foundation for peer support training, in hospital groups, as a text for introductory mental health courses and within family advocacy groups.

Pathways to Recovery Group Facilitator's Guide

The current guide was designed to be easy to navigate and use, even for first-time group facilitators. Each session includes:

- An overview and goals for the topic
- Recommended readings, materials and handouts
- Specific tips for facilitators and notes to guide each session
- Detailed agendas with suggested activities

The guide gives group leaders all the information needed to facilitate a *Pathways to Recovery* group, including tips on how to adapt the sessions to meet specific needs. While some groups have taken over a year to cover all the material in the workbook, still others have found it possible to cover one chapter a week. In whatever way you decide to conduct your local group, the material found in this guide will be helpful to you.

Information

University of Kansas School of Social Welfare
Office of Mental Health Research & Training
www.pathwaystorecoverybooks.com

Order

Pathways to Recovery via:
www.createspace.com/3701314 or www.amazon.com
Pathways to Recovery Group Facilitator's Guide via:
www.createspace.com/3795173 or www.amazon.com